D0124117

U.S. SUPREME COURT 1962

Standing left to right: Justices Byron White, William J. Brennan, Jr., Potter Stewart, Arthur Goldberg

Seated left to right: Justices Tom Clark, Hugo L. Black, Chief Justice Earl Warren, William O. Douglas, John M. Harlan

the MAKING of JUSTICE

THE SUPREME COURT IN ACTION

JAMES E. CLAYTON

E. P. DUTTON & CO., INC.
New York   1964

114815

Published simultaneously in Canada by Clarke, Irwin &
Company Limited, Toronto and Vancouver

Library of Congress Catalog Card Number: 64–11079

FOREWORD

THE SUPREME COURT OF THE UNITED STATES HEADS WHAT HAS been called the "least dangerous branch" of the government. Certainly it is the smallest branch, in terms of manpower. It is inherently the weakest branch since it has no power to enforce its own determinations.

Through much of its history, the Supreme Court has not been well known or understood by the general public. This is natural enough, since its activity is necessarily technical. Much of its work is essentially "lawyers' stuff" and cast in language which is not familiar to the ordinary citizen.

Yet, over the years, it has often been apparent that the Supreme Court and the federal judicial system, despite their innate weakness, do in fact exercise great power to affect our governmental structure, and the lives and actions of our citizens. The Supreme Court and its decisions should not be left to lawyers alone. They are too important for that. They should be known and understood by a wide segment of our citizens. Yet there is a dilemma here. When lawyers write about the Supreme Court and its work, they naturally write in professional terms, and what they write is likely to be no more intelligible to the general public than the opinions of the Court itself. On the other hand, when nonlawyers write about the Supreme Court and its work, they often fail to understand what is really involved in the Court's decisions. In putting their writing in popular terms, they may miss the essence of what they are writing about.

Over much of the past, this dilemma has been generally resolved by leaving the Supreme Court severely alone, except for technical publications. Popular writing about the Supreme Court has often been of the "now it can be told" variety, on the one hand, or violent denunciation, on the other.

Only recently have there developed some writers who know how to write in nontechnical style, but who also have the knowledge and understanding of the business and procedure of the Court, so that they know with technical accuracy what they are writing about. One of these writers is James E. Clayton, of the staff of *The Washington Post*. He has been writing intelligible and understandable articles about the Supreme Court and its decisions for the past several years. Now he has devoted his talent to the production of this book which makes available to the general reader an understanding of the Supreme Court in action.

The method adopted by Mr. Clayton is to recount the work of an entire term of the Supreme Court, from October to the following June. Thus, one gets a sense of the real flavor of the Supreme Court's business—the cases involving widespread public interest, and the run-of-the-mill and technical cases as well. In the process the reader is given an explanation of the way cases come before the Supreme Court, of the way they are heard and considered there, of the sorts of issues which confront the Court, and of the intellectual processes by which decisions are reached. The justice rendered by the Supreme Court is justice according to law. Yet the Supreme Court Justices are men. Mr. Clayton skillfully shows the important role of the law, and also the influence of the men who participate in the decisions.

With his description of the work of the Court, he interweaves thumbnail sketches of each of the Justices. These are not "exposés"; nor are they what might be called "appreciations." They are vignettes of people, who appear as human beings and yet as men with great technical qualifications and an earnest desire to meet the vast responsibilities which rest on the shoulders of any Supreme Court Justice.

Through this book, the ordinary citizen can gain a better understanding of the Supreme Court, of its work, of the men who sit on it, and of the place and function of the Court in the American governmental system, than is available in any other work. It is important that our citizens have such an understanding. The Supreme Court is not above criticism. Nor does it ever claim infallibility. Yet it carries heavy burdens, and should not have to submit to thoughtless and irresponsible attack. Thoughtful criticism can come only with an understanding of the nature of the problems before the Court and of the methods by which the Court deals with these problems. For too long a time the Court has been a mystery to most sections of the public. This book will remove much of this mystery, and shed much light and understanding on the functioning of our great tribunal.

In essence, the distinction between civilization and savagery is the willingness to settle disputes by other means than force. We say that we are governed by the rule of law, which means that we accept decisions by impartial courts rather than by force of arms. If we are going to remain civilized, we must continue to accept the decisions of our courts, whether we agree with them or not. We are more likely to be willing to accept judicial decisions if we understand them, and the process by which they are brought about. This book can do much to add to this understanding.

ERWIN N. GRISWOLD
Dean of the Faculty of Law

Harvard University
Cambridge, Massachusetts

PREFACE

*To the people we come sooner or later; it is upon
their wisdom and self-restraint that the stability of
the most cunningly devised scheme of government
will in the last resort depend.*

James Bryce, 1886

IT IS IN THE HOPE THAT A BETTER UNDERSTANDING OF THE
Supreme Court will contribute to that "wisdom and self-
restraint" that this book is written.

For as long as I can remember, I have been fascinated by the
Supreme Court. My first recollection of it comes from the days
of FDR and the court-packing plan when I heard my father
talking with visitors to his law office in a small Midwestern town
about the "nine old men" in Washington. It has been my good
fortune in the last four years to spend most of my time watching
the Court in operation, reading its opinions, and talking about its
actions. No one can devote that much time to the Court without concurring in Mr. Justice Clark's remark that the Court is
seldom understood.

This book is an effort to help the non-lawyer gain a better
understanding of the Court's role in American government, of
its Justices, and of the problems they face. It is not, and does
not purport to be, a definitive work on any single phase of the
Court's activities or on all its work in a single term. Dozens of
its activities, as well as all its Justices and many of its opinions,
merit books of their own. Rather, this is an effort to provide a

quick insight into the goings-on at what John P. Frank has called the "Marble Palace" on Capitol Hill.

The debts of gratitude one owes upon writing a book of this kind are tremendous. None of the Justices has talked with me in terms of this book but many of them have helped me to a better understanding of the Court and of themselves. The same applies to officials of the Department of Justice and to many private practitioners of the law. Over the years, the law clerks and the Court's staff have been helpful within the limits their responsibilities place upon them. My special debts are to my family, who created and fostered my interest in the Court; to the professors at Princeton and Harvard under whom I studied the Court; and to *The Washington Post*, which has made my years at the Court possible. My friends, John and Beth Vanderstar, made many helpful suggestions. To Helen Faust and Marlene Kleine, I am grateful for late evenings and weekends spent typing the manuscript.

JAMES E. CLAYTON

Arlington, Virginia

CONTENTS

	Foreword	5
	Preface	9
1	A Court in Trouble	15
2	The Term Begins	28
3	The Term Ahead	56
4	The First Arguments	71
5	Goldberg's First Opinion	82
6	Ethics and Law	95
7	The First Sharp Disagreements	105
8	Justice and the State Courts	123
9	The Attorney General Comes to Court	141
10	The Midwinter Recess	156
11	The Law Is Never Still	163
12	Banks and the Law	178
13	Religion in the Schools	191
14	Two Young Justices	215
15	A Rare Day for the Court	221
16	Segregated Lunchrooms	237
17	A Fight over Water	250
18	The Final Monday	258
19	The Government Is Neutral	266
20	Freedom to Worship	281
21	The Last Decisions	285
22	The Term Is Over	292
	Notes	303
	Index	311

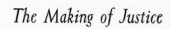

The Making of Justice

chapter 1
A COURT IN TROUBLE

As its new term began in the fall of 1962, the Supreme Court of the United States was a court in trouble. In many parts of the country, politicians were running for office by denouncing it. Hardly a day went by in Congress without a Representative or a Senator criticizing one or more of its decisions. Some lower court judges—both state and federal—regularly aired their distaste for it and its members. Civic groups in many cities met to discuss how they could protect the nation from it and its decisions. The John Birch Society was preaching that the Court was giving aid and comfort to the international Communist conspiracy. Other right-wing organizations agreed, and some Congressmen gave lip service to the idea. A few critics even said some of the Court's members were part of that conspiracy. Throughout the summer of 1962, these charges had been heard again and again across the nation. They were summed up on large billboards, particularly noticeable in California, Texas, and Louisiana, that carried the message: "Save America. Impeach Earl Warren!"

Two decisions announced by the Court late in the 1961–62 term had set off this new wave of criticism. The Justices had infuriated political and legislative leaders in many states by ruling that the way a state divided the seats in its legislature among its citizens was subject to review by the federal courts.[1] A few weeks later, the Court raised the ire of millions of Americans by holding unconstitutional a New York rule setting forth a prayer for public school students to recite each morning.[2]

The criticism of the Court for the reapportionment decision had come in muted tones. The Court's action had been widely interpreted as an effort on the part of the Justices to assure every voter fair representation in his state capital. Few of the politicians whose power was threatened by the decision chose to attack the principle of fair representation. Instead, they argued that the Court was usurping the power of the states by permitting federal courts to rule on questions always before left to the state legislatures or, in rare instances, state courts. The Supreme Court, in fact, had previously refused to enter what Justice Frankfurter called the "political thicket" of reapportionment. His argument was that any involvement of the judicial system in something as highly political as the boundaries of legislative districts would eventually destroy public confidence in the impartiality of the courts. In 1962 the Court rejected his view, perhaps because it had become clear that unless the courts acted, many states would never give voters who lived in cities equal representation with those who lived in rural areas. But when a majority of the Justices ruled that the courts could force changes in the apportionment of legislative seats, they were trampling on the feet of many powerful political figures. These were the rural politicians who had kept a strangle hold on the legislatures of many states by refusing to provide new representation for the expanding populations of urban and suburban areas. In Florida, for example, the "pork chop gang" had refused again and again to provide any substantial increase in the number of seats in the legislature for the Miami area as its population grew from less than 1 per cent to almost 19 per cent of the state's total. In Florida, and in dozens of other states, powerful forces began to smolder as a result of the reapportionment decision. This was, the cry rose, another effort by the Supreme Court to seize power, to centralize government, to destroy the states.

The spark that brought life to that and other criticism came on the day the Court announced its ruling in the prayer case. A wave of criticism, unprecedented in breadth or vehemence, swept the country. The wave came from every corner of the nation—from clergymen who regretted that public schools could no longer be used to teach religion, from individual citizens who wanted their children or the children of others exposed to religion in the schools, from politicians who either agreed with the other critics or saw a chance to make political capital by joining them.[3]

"They put the Negroes in the schools and now they've driven God out of them," boomed Representative George Grant of Alabama.

"The next thing you know," said old Judge Howard W. Smith, a Virginia patriarch who had long controlled the powerful Rules Committee of the House of Representatives, "they'll be telling us we can't open our daily House sessions with prayer."

"I know of nothing in my lifetime that could give more aid and comfort to Moscow than this bold, malicious, atheistic and sacrilegious twist by this unpredictable group of uncontrolled despots," said Representative Mendel Rivers of South Carolina. "The Court has now officially stated its disbelief in God Almighty."

"I should like to ask whether we would be far wrong in saying that in this decision the Supreme Court has held that God is unconstitutional and for that reason the public schools must be segregated against him," said Senator Sam J. Ervin of North Carolina.

These were Southern politicians talking. Their statements had to be discounted because of their persistent anger at the Court for its school desegregation decision in 1954. But politicians from other parts of the country chimed in with them this time. Representative Frank J. Becker of New York called the decision "the most tragic one in the history of the United States." Former

President Herbert Hoover demanded a constitutional amendment to stop what he called "a disintegration of a sacred American heritage." And Senator Robert C. Byrd of West Virginia said, "Is this not the first step on the road to promoting atheistic and agnostic beliefs? . . . Somebody is tampering with America's soul. I leave it to you who that somebody is."

Religious leaders leaped into what had become an orgy of criticism. Francis Cardinal Spellman, the ranking Roman Catholic prelate in the nation, said, "I am shocked and frightened that the Supreme Court has declared unconstitutional a simple and voluntary declaration of belief in God by public school children. The decision strikes at the very heart of the Godly tradition in which America's children have for so long been raised."

The *Pilot*, newspaper of the Boston Catholic hierarchy, said the decision was "stupid," "doctrinaire," and "unrealistic." It is a decision, the paper went on, "that spits in the face of our history, our traditions and our heritage as a religious people."

The Reverend Billy Graham, an evangelist ordained in the Southern Baptist Church, which had long fought for strict separation of church and state, said, "This [decision] is another step toward the secularization of the United States. Followed to its logical conclusion, we will have to take the chaplains out of the armed forces, prayers cannot be said in Congress, and the President cannot put his hand on the Bible when he takes the oath of office."

The case that precipitated this attack on the Court came from New York. The state Board of Regents, which is responsible for the conduct of the public schools, had composed a short prayer and sent it to all local school boards, telling them to use it if they wanted religious exercises in their schools. The prayer was as innocuous to religious sensitivities as any prayer could be, but it still offended a group of parents on Long Island. They promptly protested to the local school board. By requiring that the prayer be said each morning, they charged, the board was abridging their religious freedom and was establishing an official religion. Faced with this issue for the first time, the Supreme Court said the New York plan did put the state's stamp of approval on one form of religion. This was unconstitutional, the Court said, because the First Amendment requires government in the United States to be neutral in religious matters; government cannot prefer one brand of religion over another, even Christianity over Judaism or Buddhism. A state board cannot constitutionally compose an "official" prayer, the Court said, and local boards of education cannot constitutionally direct students to recite one.

Some political and religious leaders did defend the Court and this decision. President Kennedy called for support of the Constitution and recognition of the responsibility of the Supreme Court in interpreting it. He told the Court's harshest critics, "[We] have in this case a very easy remedy and that is to pray ourselves. . . ."

In a similar vein, Senator Kenneth B. Keating of New York said that what concerned him most was the wild denunciation of the Court and the Justices. Announcing first that he disagreed with the Court's decision, Keating said, "It does not serve any point of view in this controversy to heap abuse upon its members or undermine its status."

Jewish leaders, including those in Congress, supported the Court. Said Representative Emanuel Celler, chairman of the House Judiciary Committee, "All parties agreed that the prayer was religious in nature. This being so, it ran contrary to the First Amendment—which is well grounded in history and has served to save the United States from religious strife." A few Protestant spokesmen agreed with this view.

Sterling M. McMurrin, Commissioner of Education for the United States, said, "I believe it is no loss to religion but may be a gain in clarifying matters. Prayer that is essentially a ceremonial classroom function has not much religious value."

Most newspapers in the country also took the decision more

calmly than did either the clergymen or the politicians. The *Los Angeles Times*, however, blared: "At first one is outraged by this perverse decision, but then one is alarmed, for six Justices of the Supreme Court have been persuaded by a small group of guardhouse sophists to make a burlesque show of the world's first complete declaration of religious tolerance." But across the country, the respected *New York Times* said, " . . . nothing could be more divisive in this country than to mingle religion and government with the sensitive setting of the public schools." Similar views were expressed by the *Chicago Daily News*, the *Washington Post*, the *Milwaukee Journal*, and the *St. Louis Post-Dispatch*. The *Detroit News* was not excited about the decision. "If our religious faith is weakened by lack of public school prayer," the *News* said dryly, "it is already on the road to extinction." Dissents were entered by the *New York Journal-American* ("a misinterpretation of the Constitution"), the *New York News*, and the *Raleigh News and Observer* ("out of the realm of common sense").

Those few among the nation's lawyers and judges who said anything about the prayer case in the first days after it was rendered also denounced it. John C. Satterfield, segregationist president of the American Bar Association, said that if the prayer was unconstitutional, the words "In God We Trust" on coins were also unconstitutional. Millard Caldwell, a member of the Supreme Court of Florida, charged that the Justices were trying to "abolish God."

Much of this criticism was incredible. One had to read it again and again to believe it had actually been voiced. For a politician to say that the Court was out to abolish God or that its Justices did not believe in God was to engage in demagoguery of the worst kind. Justice Black, who had taught Sunday school for many years in the Baptist Church, had written and announced the Court's opinion. No one who heard him could have doubted his sincerity as he said the First Amendment was "an expression of principle on the part of the founders of our Constitution that religion is too personal, too sacred, too holy to permit its 'unhallowed perversion' by a civil magistrate." His voice trembled with emotion as he paused over "too personal—too sacred—too holy." Then he went on, "It is neither sacrilegious nor anti-religious to say that each separate government in this country should stay out of the business of writing or sanctioning official prayers and leave that purely religious function to the people themselves and to those the people choose to look to for religious guidance." To say, as some critics did, that the Court was striking all vestiges of religion from public life was to ignore a long foot-note in Black's opinion that obviously had been designed to head off just such criticism. The footnote said:

There is of course nothing in the decision reached here that is inconsistent with the fact that school children and others are officially encouraged to express love for our country by reciting historical documents such as the Declaration of Independence which contain references to the Deity or by singing officially espoused anthems which include the composer's professions of faith in a Supreme Being, or with the fact that there are many manifestations in our public life of belief in God. Such patriotic or ceremonial occasions bear no true resemblance to the unquestioned religious exercise that the State of New York has sponsored in this instance.[4]

It was clear that the public discord deeply disturbed the Justices. Black departed from his normal practice of not replying to critics and answered some of the letters that came to his chambers. Justice Clark, who supported Black's opinion, made a sharp break with custom by speaking in public about the decision. Justices rarely talk about cases off the bench but, in August, Clark told the Commonwealth Club in San Francisco that the news media had given the public an incomplete version of what the Court had decided. He said:

The prayer case came down on the last day of the term with some fifteen other cases. The result was that the announcement, in the words of a July 29 story in *The New York Times*, is often "misinterpreted by the communications media." The story quotes Richard Aldrich, a cousin of Governor Rockefeller, as saying with reference to the Prayer Case: "Most commentators suggested that the Court had outlawed religious observance in public schools when in fact the Court did nothing of the kind." Traditionally Monday is our decision day and sometimes we may announce over a dozen opinions in one day. The newspaper man is pushed to even get the result much less the reasoning back of each judgment. As a consequence the news media announcements as the *Times* story indicated were not complete, most of them merely reciting the content of this twenty-two-word prayer and the fact that the Court had held it unconstitutional for a teacher to have her pupils recite it.

Here was a state-written prayer circulated by a school district to state-employed teachers with instructions to have their pupils recite it in unison at the beginning of each school day in state-owned buildings. . . . The Fourteenth Amendment to the Constitution as interpreted by the Supreme Court for over a score of years incorporates the prohibitions of the First Amendment against the states—which means that both state and federal governments shall take no part respecting the establishment of religion or prohibiting the free exercise thereof. "No" means "No." This was all the Court decided. Questions of official recognition of a Divine Being or the validity of the inscription on silver coins or currency of "In God We Trust" or public acknowledgment of the fact that the United States is a religious nation—were not involved nor passed upon. As one commentator said, the trouble is that the Court—like the old complaint of the wife—is "never understood." [5]

As the summer wore on, the tone of the criticism changed. The avalanche of letters reaching the Justices began to include many from Americans who thought the Court was right. Assistant Attorney General Burke Marshall vigorously defended the

Court. He said the decision "reflected deep religious convictions. . . . The attacks on the Court are a product of a failure to understand what the Court was deciding, what issues were at stake and what reasons compelled its action." It was not hostility to religion that brought the decision. "It was the conviction, embodied in the First Amendment, that governments in this country should stay out of the business of writing or sanctioning official prayers, and should leave what the Court called 'that purely religious function' to the people and those to whom the people look for religious guidance."[6]

Perhaps the deluge of criticism should have been expected. By 1962 the nation was accustomed to hearing all its ills blamed on the Supreme Court. A few weeks before the prayer decision was announced, Senator James O. Eastland of Mississippi, Chairman of the Senate Judiciary Committee, had renewed his long-running attack on the Court for its decisions in the area of internal security. The Justices, Eastland said, had upheld "the positions advocated by the Communist Party" or its sympathizers in forty-six of seventy decisions, a .657 average. He named the Chief Justice and Justices Black, Douglas, Frankfurter, and Brennan as voting pro-Communist more often than other members of the Court. "The Court must be restrained," Eastland said. "Unless it is, it will not only snap and bite but will tear to pieces and devour constitutional government."[7]

Over the years, Eastland had made many speeches of this kind. His reasoning was that a Justice who voted in favor of a constitutional claim made by a Communist must be pro-Communist. It follows, of course, that a Justice would be pro-Democrat if he cast a vote in favor of a constitutional claim made by a Democrat. And in a case involving two defendants, one Democrat and one Republican, the Eastland logic would make a Justice pro-Democrat and pro-Republican at the same time. This speech by Eastland was part of a sustained assault on the Court that had been under way since 1954. The attack was three-pronged—

accusing the Court of being for integration, for communism, and against states' rights.

The attack by the segregationists was the most bitter. Since the 1930's no part of government, federal or state, had moved more determinedly against segregation or had done more to give Negroes equal rights than had the Court. In a way, the Court seemed to be making up for its past. In the latter part of the nineteenth century the Court had taken the impact out of Northern efforts to give Negroes equal rights. In landmark decisions the Court had ruled that separate facilities for the white and colored races on railroads were constitutional and had narrowed the reach of the Fourteenth Amendment by ruling that its bar against discrimination applied only to action taken by governmental bodies or officials.[8] These two decisions provided the legal justification for all the discriminatory practices that later arose. As the years passed, however, the Court steadily undermined both decisions. The concept of what was "state action" sufficient to fall within the Fourteenth Amendment's bar against discrimination was broadened. The separate-but-equal doctrine was rejected in some areas.

This process was gradual and aroused little resentment from those Americans to whom segregation was a major part of daily life until May 17, 1954. On that day the Court ruled that separate public schools were unconstitutional because such schools were inherently unequal, denied Negro children an equal opportunity to grow up as full-fledged Americans, and necessarily deprived them of the equal protection of the laws guaranteed by the Fourteenth Amendment. The storm brought over the Court by that decision was immense. The comment of Senator Strom Thurmond of South Carolina in 1956 represented the attitude of much of the South. "I do not and cannot have regard for the nine Justices who rendered a decision so clearly contrary to the Constitution," he said. Southern legislatures adopted resolutions calling for the impeachment of the Justices for "high crimes and misdemeanors." Across the South, the message of political leaders was that the Court's order requiring desegregation of the public schools was not law because it was in violation of the Constitution. Again and again the Southern leaders, particularly the lawyers, were warned that they were sowing a whirlwind, that the decision was the law of the land and would be enforced, that if it were not accepted the entire legal system would be in jeopardy.

The charges that the Court was pro-Communist grew out of an entirely different line of cases, although segregationists had tried repeatedly to link with communism all those who favored integration. The basic charge about the Court and communism was directly traceable to the late Senator Joseph McCarthy. The McCarthy era had awakened some naïve Americans to the dangers of international communism, but the resulting hysteria had brought severe impingements on the rights of individuals by congressional and state investigating committees and by security programs in state and federal governments. For ten years the Court stood staunchly in favor of individual rights despite the charge that by so doing it was endangering national security. It reversed the convictions of a group of second-string leaders of the Communist Party because the instructions given to the jury did not properly explain the line between illegal advocacy of overthrowing the government by force and violence and the constitutionally protected right freely to advocate ideas. It reversed the contempt-of-Congress convictions of several alleged Communists or Communist sympathizers on the ground that the investigating committees had deprived them of rights normally accorded witnesses. It struck down the Defense Department's Industrial Security Program on the ground that neither the President nor Congress had authorized it. It struck down the State Department's passport control regulations on the same ground. In the latter decisions the Court noted that if the programs had been authorized, difficult problems involving the constitutional rights of individuals would have been presented. In all these cases, Congress or the Executive Branch had claimed that the regulations or investigations were necessary to national security. The decisions of the Court, many Congressmen and some Executive Branch officials claimed, exalted individual rights at the expense of national security.

The third charge against the Court was that its decisions were destroying the states and centralizing governmental power in Washington. This was the charge made by state legislative leaders after the reapportionment decision. It was also the charge made against decisions holding that various state criminal procedures failed to meet federal constitutional requirements. At its heart, however, was the distaste of many Americans for the trend in government since the New Deal. They disapproved of many new undertakings of the federal government—regulation of wages, hours, and working conditions, health and welfare programs, aid to education. They wished that the Court would, as it had so often in the past, use its power to declare these Acts of Congress unconstitutional. But in recent years the Court has been reluctant to deny to Congress power to regulate economic activity. At the same time, however, it has been forcing the states to meet higher standards in criminal trials and to be more considerate of rights of individuals in other areas.

Throughout the 1950's criticism of the Court mounted in all three of these areas. The voices of the segregationists blended with those of the states' righters and the anti-Communists. Together, they almost drowned out the civil libertarians who saw the Court's decisions as an effort to retain for Americans their historic tradition of individual freedom. Added to this uproar in 1962 were the voices of the militantly godly.

Many of the Justices were deeply concerned about this criticism. They knew that, in the long run, the only real power of the Court depends on its standing with the American people. With the people's respect the Court can withstand any attack, as the most popular President of all, Franklin D. Roosevelt, learned when he attacked the Court in 1937. Without such respect, the Court is nothing. Possessing neither physical force nor taxing power, it relies on the President to enforce its orders and on Congress for all its funds and most of its jurisdiction. Whether the bitterness created by the prayer and reapportionment decisions, when added to that already existing, was enough to destroy the public's respect for the Court and open it to reprisals was a question that the Justices had to face as the new term began.

It would have been appropriate to repeat for them the toast offered in 1801 at a dinner honoring the Justices: "To the Judiciary of the United States—independent of party, independent of power, and independent of popularity."[9] A year or two in which the Court faced no cases of great political or emotional impact was needed to allow public resentment to abate and to give the Court time to recover its lost prestige. But 1962–63 did not promise to be such a year.

chapter 2

THE TERM BEGINS

WHEN DAWN BROKE OVER THE CAPITOL ON OCTOBER 1, 1962, THE lights still burned in the White House. President John F. Kennedy and his brother, Attorney General Robert F. Kennedy, with a few aides, had spent a long night there, pacing from room to room as they kept in touch with events in a small Southern town best known previously as the home of William Faulkner. Two men had died that night and scores more had been injured. A near-rebellion, brought about by one Negro's decision to exercise a right the Supreme Court said was his, had been suppressed only after 29,000 Regular Army troops had been dispatched to Oxford, Mississippi. The decision to send troops, to pit American soldiers against American civilians in a sleepy Southern town, had been a bitter one for the President to make. At the moment he turned to the Army the lives of 200 United States marshals and several high-ranking officials of the Justice Department, as well as that of the twenty-year-old Negro, James Meredith, were in danger. But more than lives had been at stake on the campus at the University of Mississippi that night. In those hours the prestige of the Supreme Court of the United States, the integrity of all courts, and the effectiveness of their decisions had been on trial. If one decision of the Supreme Court could not be enforced, if James Meredith could not be enrolled as a student at the state's major university, then all the Court's decisions were open to challenge by force. If Mississippians could successfully defy the Court's decision that segregation of public schools was unconstitutional, citizens of other states could defy other decisions; two of the fundamental precepts of American law would be gone: that nine men in the massive building on Capitol Hill interpreted the words of the Constitution, and that their interpretation was the supreme law of the land until they changed it or the Constitution was amended.

The whirlwind about which Southern leaders had long been warned had now devastated Oxford. The people of Mississippi, urged for years by their leaders to defy the Supreme Court and all federal courts, had failed to distinguish between their leaders' verbal defiance and defiance by arms and violence.[1]

As morning came to Washington the President heard that peace was being restored to Oxford. He went upstairs in the White House at 5:30 to sleep for a few hours. To the east a handful of guards patrolled the halls of the Supreme Court building. The words carved in marble high on its west façade—"Equal Justice Under Law"—seemed to take on a new luster.

Less than five hours later, a long, black limousine pulled into the basement of the building. From it stepped the President and the Attorney General, their faces still strained and tense. They shook hands with Perry Lippitt, the Marshal of the Court, and walked quickly to an elevator that whisked them to a deserted corridor next to the courtroom. As the Kennedys entered the high-ceilinged chamber, a gavel sounded, the lawyers and spectators rose, and Lippitt announced, "The President of the United States."

The President and his brother walked toward two chairs in front of the bench and to the right of its center. When they reached them, the gavel directed everyone to be seated. A restless air filled the quiet courtroom. Spectators strained to get a better look at the President, and whispered about his handling of the Mississippi situation. Behind the long mahogany bench, resting on a marble platform a foot or so above the courtroom floor, were nine large black swivel chairs, all of them empty.

Four minutes later, at precisely 10 o'clock, the red velvet draperies behind the bench parted with a flourish as Lippitt banged his gavel again and announced, "The Honorable, the Chief Justice and the Associate Justices of the Supreme Court of the United States." The audience, including the President, rose as eight Justices stepped briskly through three openings in the draperies. As they moved to the bench, page boys in knickers pulled back their chairs. Slowly and solemnly, Lippitt intoned the traditional words:

> Oyez! Oyez! Oyez! All persons having business before the Honorable, the Supreme Court of the United States of America, are invited to draw near and give their attention, for the Court is now sitting. God save the United States and this Honorable Court. Be seated please.

The Justices stood silently, surveying the courtroom, as Lippitt spoke. Some of them bowed their heads as he called upon God. In front of the center chair was the Chief Justice of the United States, Earl Warren, a white-haired, kindly-looking man who was hearing Lippitt's words at the beginning of a new term of Court for the tenth time. To his right was the senior Associate Justice, Hugo L. Black, whose lithe figure gave no indication that this would be his twenty-sixth year behind that bench. To their right were Tom C. Clark, the calm, soft-spoken Texan; William J. Brennan, Jr., the vigorous ex-trial judge from New Jersey; and Byron R. White, the former All-American football player from Colorado. To the left of the Chief Justice were William O. Douglas, the mountain climber from the West; John M. Harlan, the dignified ex-Wall Street lawyer; and Potter Stewart, the young and handsome Ohioan. A vacant chair was at Stewart's left. A ninth man, dressed in a long black robe like those of the eight Justices, waited patiently at a small table to the far right of the bench.

As the Justices and the audience, acting on Lippitt's words, took their seats, the Chief Justice looked up, smiled, and nodded at the President. Picking up a piece of paper from the bench, the Chief Justice read:

> With the concurrence of my colleagues, I announce with regret the retirement of Mr. Justice Frankfurter who has served this Court with distinction for the past twenty-four years.
>
> All of us, with the exception of Mr. Justice White, have had the pleasure of serving for years with him, and we exceedingly regret that the condition of his health compelled his retirement. We are reconciled to the situation, however, by the opinion of his doctor that if he is relieved of his arduous Court work he will still have years of usefulness to the profession to which he has been devoted for sixty years. We look forward to such a speedy and complete recovery because he has so much to give from his vast experience.
>
> As scholar, teacher, public servant, enlightened critic, and member of this Court for almost a quarter of a century, he has already made a contribution to our jurisprudence rarely equaled in the life of our Court. Through each of these facets of his long and notable career, he looms large in the history of our country and we, his colleagues, have been the most favored beneficiaries of his wisdom and his fellowship. These we may continue to enjoy because our association with him is not ended. It will continue unabated in another form.
>
> Our appreciation of that association and for his great service to the Court is amplified in a letter to him which, with his response and the exchange of letters between him and the President on the occasion of his retirement, will be spread upon the Minutes of the Court.

When he finished reading the announcement, the Chief Justice smiled at the audience again and said, "We are fortunate, however, that his successor was appointed to fill the vacancy before the opening of our 1962 Term." He explained that Arthur J. Goldberg had been nominated by the President to succeed Justice Frankfurter and that the nomination had been confirmed by the Senate. He said that Goldberg had taken the constitutional oath of office a few minutes earlier in a private ceremony with only the other Justices as witnesses. The Clerk of the Court, the Chief Justice continued, would now read Mr. Goldberg's commission and administer the judicial oath. After John F. Davis read the archaic words of the commission, Goldberg stood facing him and the audience with a hand on a Hebrew Bible. In a firm voice he said:

> I, Arthur J. Goldberg, do solemnly swear that I will administer justice without respect to persons, and do equal right to the poor and to the rich, and that I will faithfully and impartially discharge and perform all the duties incumbent upon me as Associate Justice of the Supreme Court of the United States according to the best of my abilities and understanding, agreeably to the Constitution and laws of the United States. So help me God."

As he spoke, there were tears in the eyes of Dorothy Goldberg, who sat with their two children in a reserved section on the far right of the courtroom.

When the oath was completed, the Marshal escorted Goldberg behind the raised platform to his seat at the far left end of the bench. Justice Stewart turned in his chair to shake hands with the new Justice as he sat down. President Kennedy suddenly stood up and Lippitt banged his gavel once again. The President stepped forward and hopped up on the marble ledge in front of the bench so that he, too, could shake Goldberg's hand. As he did, the Justices and the other spectators rose. That movement was the Court's only formal recognition that the President of the United States was in attendance. Nowhere else could he go and receive so little recognition. This particular morning, a few hours after the President had placed all his power and prestige behind the judicial system, that symbol of the gulf between the Executive and Judicial branches of American government loomed unusually large.

As the President left the courtroom and his footsteps echoed in the corridor, the spectators took their seats noisily. They quieted down when the Chief Justice said, "Admissions to the Bar." The admissions of forty-five lawyers were completed shortly after 10:30 and Lippitt announced, "This Court now stands adjourned until 10:00 A.M. on Monday, October 8."[2]

The newspapers that afternoon told of the swearing-in of a new Justice and the beginning of a new term of Court. It was a routine story, driven off the front pages by the events in Mississippi. But those close to the Court knew it was not the routine beginning of a new term nor the routine swearing-in of a new Justice. Something was different this time. Felix Frankfurter was gone.

Without Frankfurter the Court would never again be quite the same. No longer would an attorney appearing before it be in such danger of unnerving questions, embarrassing comments, and endless needling. No longer would the wide marble halls of that massive building resound to a whistled "Yankee Doodle" as the little white-haired Justice strode to his chambers. No longer would the young wives of law clerks be subjected to probing cross-examination when they stopped by to meet the Justice.

An era in the Court's history had ended on the day Felix Frankfurter stepped down, and everyone acquainted with the Court knew it. For more than twenty years his scholarly mind had enriched the Court. His debates with Justices who disagreed with him had enlivened the courtroom and crammed the pages of the Court's official reports with long and thoughtful discourses on the law and on American government. To his followers, Frankfurter was the exemplar of a Supreme Court Justice and the most important figure on the federal bench. To his critics, he was a liberal gone sour or a scholar so devoted to intellectual pursuits that he had lost touch with the practicalities of life.

The end of Frankfurter's long career came suddenly and unexpectedly in April, 1962. He was working in his chambers and suddenly slumped to his desk. A few hours later, the Justice was carried from the building, protesting loudly that his shoes were being left behind. But his protests had lost their spark. Four months and two more heart attacks later, Frankfurter made the decision that he would be unable to resume his duties. He told the Chief Justice, who told the President, and the President named Arthur Goldberg to succeed him.

As Goldberg left the courtroom that first Monday in October, he knew the dimensions of the man he was replacing. He had told his friends he was awed by the thought of filling a seat occupied in the last sixty years by only Frankfurter, Benjamin Nathan Cardozo, and Oliver Wendell Holmes. At a press conference the day after his appointment, Goldberg said of Frankfurter, "I cannot fill his place. I say this with all humility. I can only try . . . to carry on the traditions of the Court."[3]

Goldberg's nomination by President Kennedy to replace Frankfurter was criticized, just as the nomination of Frankfurter to succeed Cardozo had been criticized twenty-three years earlier. Both Goldberg and Kennedy's first appointee to the Court, Byron R. White, were close to the President. As members of the Kennedy Administration, both men were tagged as "New Frontiersmen" who were "liberal" and "aggressive." Arthur Krock, pundit of *The New York Times*, set the tone for much of the criticism:

> [The] direction [of the Court], now stabilized in so far as can be guessed from the record of the political philosophy of justice-designate Goldberg, is toward these national goals: (1) The supremacy of the Court in making public policy, which has included reversing its own precedents and amending the Constitution by interpretation instead of act of Congress or by the process prescribed in the national charter. (2) Expanding Federal Executive Government intervention in the activities of American life. (3) Increasing restraints on the investigatory procedures of Congress, newly discovered in the First Amendment. (4) Employment of the "equal rights" guarantee of the Fourteenth

Amendment to take jurisdiction over controversies the Court long excluded as "political." If both of Mr. Kennedy's Court appointees . . . obstruct these goals, the President is not the only citizen who will be greatly surprised.[4]

Krock, obviously, did not like either the trend of Supreme Court decisions or Kennedy's two appointments. His analysis of that trend, superficial as it was, reflected all the criticism that had been made of the Court throughout the late 1950's and early 1960's. Because the Court had refused to invalidate Acts of Congress and actions of the President as readily as it had done prior to 1937, the critics said it was expanding federal influence on everyday life, although it was Congress, not the Court, that was passing the laws and the President, not the Court, who was enforcing them. Because the Court had reversed old decisions in the area of race relations, the critics argued that it was amending the Constitution, although the Justices thought they were merely correcting earlier erroneous interpretations so as to revive the Constitution's true meaning. Because the Court had never before had occasion to consider the application of the First Amendment to congressional investigating committees, the critics said the Justices had recently "discovered" new restraints in the Amendment. Because the Court was now willing to help correct what almost everyone agreed were abuses by state legislatures of their power to apportion legislative seats, the critics said the Justices were intervening in "political" affairs.

Both *Time* and *U.S. News and World Report* agreed with much of Krock's criticism. The appointment of Goldberg, *Time* said, "would seem likely to make the Court lopsidedly liberal." By selecting Goldberg as well as White, the magazine went on, the President was "tipping the wobbly balance" that had existed on the Court between "liberals" and "conservatives." *U.S. News* said, "Signs are that, with Mr. Goldberg as a Justice, President Kennedy can count on a Court majority to uphold most of the policies he wants to follow."

Strangely enough, the *Chicago Tribune,* hardly a supporter of President Kennedy or of what is known as liberalism, entered a dissent. "Those who think that Mr. Goldberg will be a radical judge because he represented great trade unions as a lawyer may be fooled as others were fooled when Justice Frankfurter was appointed to the Court," the *Tribune* said.

The *Tribune* was remembering a lesson that many other commentators had forgotten. It was a lesson in the fundamental difference between a good politician and a good judge. A politician is free to vote and to conduct the public business as he sees fit, checked only by the wishes of his constituents. A judge, though he lacks the threat of future elections as a check on his votes, is limited by other factors. Frankfurter was the prime example of the difficulty and foolishness of trying to predict how a new Justice will vote. His appointment to the Court in 1939 was criticized because he was a "left-wing radical" who was certain to be too "liberal" for the Court's and the country's good. When he retired, the 1962 counterparts of his 1939 critics were sorry to see him go because they regarded him as the "conservative" on the Court. This was a change neither in Frankfurter nor in the critics. It was, instead, a manifestation of what Frankfurter believed his duty as a Justice to be. He once wrote:

> To assume that a lawyer who becomes a judge takes on the bench merely his views on social or economic questions leaves out of account his rooted notions regarding the scope and limits of a judge's authority. The outlook of a lawyer fit to be a Justice regarding the role of a judge cuts across all his personal preferences for this or that social arrangement.[5]

Frankfurter believed the scope of his duty was sharply limited. His fundamental task was to determine whether the Constitution was being violated. In making that determination, he must defer to the judgment of the legislature if he had any doubt. Frankfurter once described this view of a Justice's duty:

Judicial power . . . must be on guard against encroaching beyond its proper bounds, and not the less so since the only restraint upon it is self-restraint. When the power of Congress to pass a statute is challenged, the function of this Court is to determine whether legislative action lies clearly outside the constitutional grant of power. . . .

Rigorous observance of the difference between limits of power and wise exercise of power—between questions of authority and questions of prudence—requires the most alert appreciation of this decisive but subtle relationship of two concepts that too easily coalesce. No less does it require a disciplined will to adhere to the difference. It is not easy to stand aloof and allow want of wisdom to prevail, to disregard one's own strongly held view of what is wise. . . . But it is not the business of this Court to pronounce policy. It must observe a fastidious regard for limitations on its own power, and this precludes the Court's giving effect to its own notions of what is wise or politic. That self-restraint is of the essence in the observance of the judicial oath, for the Constitution has not authorized the judges to sit in judgment on the wisdom of what Congress and the Executive Branch do.[6]

Probably no member of the Supreme Court, past or present, ever disagreed with those words about self-restraint. Where many Justices, currently Black in particular, disagreed was in their application. Perhaps more than any other Justice, Frankfurter had been hesitant to say that an Act passed by Congress or by a state legislature was unconstitutional. His attitude of extreme deference to the judgments made by legislatures was partially explained by his belief that the Supreme Court could destroy itself by opposing too many projects that had the support of a majority of the people. Part of his deference also came from his belief that on the people and the legislatures, more than on the courts, rested the basic responsibility of preserving free government. In a letter to Justice Harlan F. Stone explaining an opinion he had prepared, Frankfurter once wrote that his intention "was to use this opinion as a vehicle for preaching the true democratic faith of not relying on the Court for the impossible task of assuring a vigorous, mature, self-protecting and tolerant democracy by bringing the responsibility for a combination of firmness and toleration directly home where it belongs—to the people and their representatives themselves."[7]

With this philosophy as a starting point, it was easy for Frankfurter to vote in the late 1930's and early 1940's to uphold the constitutionality of economic regulations passed by New Deal Congresses. His critics at that time said he was voting as they expected, as any New Deal liberal would. Because Frankfurter would have been a vigorous advocate of many of the New Deal programs if he had been in Congress, they assumed he would advocate them inside the Supreme Court. That simplistic view misconceived Frankfurter's philosophy just as it would the philosophy of almost every Supreme Court Justice. The Court, the Justices have said again and again, does not pass on the wisdom or desirability of statutes, but on whether Congress or the state legislatures have power to enact them. This was borne out by Frankfurter in 1943, when it became clear that his deference to legislative action carried over from laws of which he approved to those of which he deeply disapproved. In that year Frankfurter dissented when the Court invalidated West Virginia school board regulations requiring all public school pupils to salute the American flag. Students who were Jehovah's Witnesses protested that their religion forbade worship of any graven image, which they considered the flag to be. A majority of the Justices agreed that the West Virginia law unconstitutionally abridged the religious freedom of those children. The Court's opinion, by Justice Robert H. Jackson, was an eloquent expression of the basic constitutional guarantee of freedom of religion. Jackson wrote:

> The case is made difficult not because the principles of its decision are obscure but because the flag involved is our own. Nevertheless, we apply the limitations of the Consti-

tution with no fear that freedom to be intellectually and spiritually diverse or even contrary will disintegrate the social organization. To believe that patriotism will not flourish if patriotic ceremonies are voluntary and spontaneous instead of a compulsory routine is to make an unflattering estimate of the appeal of our institutions to free minds. We can have intellectual individualism and the rich cultural diversities that we owe to exceptional minds only at the price of occasional eccentricity and abnormal attitudes. When they are so harmless to others or to the State as those we deal with here, the price is not too great. But freedom to differ is not limited to things that do not matter much. That would be a mere shadow of freedom. The test of its substance is the right to differ as to things that touch the heart of the existing order.

If there is any fixed star in our constitutional constellation, it is that no official, high or petty, can prescribe what shall be orthodox in politics, nationalism, religion, or other matters of opinion or force citizens to confess by word or act their faith therein. If there are any circumstances which permit an exception, they do not now occur to us.[8]

Perhaps no position Frankfurter ever took caused him the pain his dissent in that case did. It began:

One who belongs to the most vilified and persecuted minority in history is not likely to be insensible to the freedoms guaranteed by our Constitution. Were my purely personal attitude relevant I should wholeheartedly associate myself with the general libertarian views in the Court's opinion, representing as they do the thought and action of a lifetime. But as judges we are neither Jew nor Gentile, neither Catholic nor agnostic. . . . As a member of this Court I am not justified in writing my private notions of policy into the Constitution, no matter how deeply I may cherish them or how mischievous I may deem their disregard.[9]

As the years went on, Frankfurter's philosophy of deference to the legislature was often confused by commentators on the Court with his opinion of the merits of the laws he voted to uphold. His votes to sustain the power of Congress in investigations and to uphold congressional acts cutting into the constitutional rights of Communists were called the votes of a "conservative." Although the votes may have supported the views of political conservatives in the country, it was misleading to say they were cast by one who agreed with those views. A relevant comment is attributed to the late Justice Oliver Wendell Holmes. Holmes is reported to have explained his vote to uphold as constitutional a law he thought particularly obnoxious, "Son, if they want to go to Hell, my job is to help them."

This philosophy is not all of the rich legacy Frankfurter has left for American law, but it is a major part. It is a philosophy that has been vigorously disputed by several Justices, led by Black and Douglas. They believe the Court has a duty to act whenever a constitutional issue comes before it, a duty it cannot escape by modest deference to the views of other branches of government. The Court, they believe, must be diligent in protecting the people's liberties from even the slightest encroachment and it has no choice but to give that protection, letting the criticism fall where it may. Black and Douglas are "judicial activists," so called in contrast with Frankfurter's concept of "judicial restraint." No issue is argued more sharply in legal journals than this one, but the commentators often make the dichotomy seem clearer than the Justices do themselves.

Another major disagreement within the Court in which Frankfurter led one faction concerned the proper interpretation of the Bill of Rights and the Fourteenth Amendment. Here, too, his views squarely collided with Black's, and they debated it often through the years. Frankfurter believed that the guarantees of the first eight amendments, which include the rights to free speech, assembly, and worship, and the protections against unreasonable searches, self-incrimination, and double jeopardy, must be somewhat flexible; Black does not. Frankfurter believed that only some of those guarantees were carried over by the

Fourteenth Amendment to protect individuals against the state as well as the federal government; Black disagrees. Before his retirement, Frankfurter's views usually prevailed. Though often by meager 5-to-4 majorities, the Court had rejected Black's view that the First Amendment guarantees, of free speech for instance, were "absolutes" that Congress could under no circumstance abridge. Instead, it adhered to Frankfurter's view that those guarantees are not absolute but may be limited in some unusual situations because, in the balance, the dangers of respecting them are greater than the dangers of limiting them. This was the basis on which the Court, over the dissents of Black and Douglas, upheld the constitutionality of the Smith Act's ban on *advocacy* of overthrowing the government by force. The majority had also rejected Black's view that the Due Process Clause of the Fourteenth Amendment "incorporated" all the guarantees of the Bill of Rights and restricted the states just as the Bill of Rights restricted the federal government. Instead, the Court had with Frankfurter accepted the more traditional view that the Fourteenth Amendment's Due Process Clause included only those guarantees that were, in Justice Cardozo's phrase, "the very essence of a scheme of ordered liberty."

Frankfurter's imprint on American law, however, reached far beyond the Supreme Court and its decisions. His followers are scattered throughout the court systems and the law schools of the nation. One tribute after another has been piled upon him. Perhaps of all these, the one that touched him most deeply was that paid by the Harvard Law School a few years before his retirement when it added his bust to the four already gracing its great library. The others were men whose influence on American law had been widely recognized—Holmes, Cardozo, Louis D. Brandeis, and Learned Hand. At the dedication ceremony, Frankfurter said, "That my name should ever be coupled with the names of those . . . would have seemed a strange emanation

THE MAKING OF JUSTICE
42

of a diseased brain fifty years ago and even tonight it sounds like fanciful talk."[10]

But Frankfurter was even more than a remarkable jurist. After his retirement, Dean Acheson, a former Secretary of State and one of his best friends, wrote of him:

> One could read everything that he has written—a formidable task from several points of view—and still have little more than an inkling, if that, of why this man has evoked in so many such passionate devotion and exercised for half a century so profound an influence. I can think of no one in our time remotely comparable to him, though it would not surprise me if in another time Dr. Franklin might have had something of the same personal influence.
>
> In the same way, the words, especially the written words, of another cannot convey the reality of Felix Frankfurter. There is no substitute for the apprehension of the senses. One needs to see, to hear—particularly to hear his laugh, his general noisiness—to realize what an obstreperous person this man is, to have one's arm numbed by his vise-like grip just above one's elbow, to feel the intensity of his nervous energy. Above all one needs years of experience to know the depth of his concern about people. He lives in personal relationships as a fish lives in water. This is no secluded scholar immured in library or laboratory, absorbed in intellectual problems, but a man immersed in people. At a moment's notice he will concentrate his mind and heart on their interests, their joys and their troubles.[11]

Frankfurter was born in Vienna in 1882, and moved with his family to the United States when he was twelve. He learned English in New York—coming home one night before he had quite mastered the language to remark that a man named "Laundry" must be very wealthy to own so many stores. But within a few years Frankfurter graduated near the top of his class at the College of the City of New York and was named by his dean as the "most outstanding student" in the 1906 class of the Harvard Law School. With the exception of a few months immediately after graduation, Frankfurter spent the rest of his life either working for the federal government or teaching at the Harvard Law School. His first contact with Franklin D. Roosevelt, who later appointed him to the Supreme Court, was during World War I when Roosevelt was an Assistant Secretary of the Navy and Frankfurter was Chairman of the War Labor Policies Board. During the 1930's Frankfurter became a power behind the New Deal, consulting frequently with FDR and sending a stream of bright young lawyers to Washington. They were known as the "Happy Hot Dogs," from the Latin meaning of his first name and the American version of his last. He had finally gone back to Washington after a telephone call one night while he was dressing for dinner under pressure from his wife to hurry. Years later, Frankfurter recalled that conversation:

"You know," the President said, "I told you I don't want to appoint you to the Supreme Court."

"Yes," Frankfurter said, "you told me that."

"I mean this. I mean this. I don't want to appoint you to the Supreme Court," the President said.

There he stood, recalled Frankfurter, in his BVD's, and the President was teasing him.

"But," the President finally said, "unless you give me an insurmountable objection I'm going to send your name in for the Court tomorrow at 12 o'clock."

"All I can say is that I wish my mother were alive," Frankfurter replied.[12]

The task of succeeding Frankfurter that had now fallen to Goldberg was enormous, but he started with many similarities in his background. When President Kennedy announced his selection of Goldberg for Frankfurter's old post, Ed Leahy of the *Chicago Daily News* wrote that Goldberg's success story was "almost too corny." The last of eleven children of an immigrant Russian Jew, Goldberg had pulled himself up from one of the poorest sections of Chicago. At age twelve he was a delivery boy in a shoe factory but, before he was twenty-one, he had graduated with highest honors from the Northwestern University Law School and had been admitted to the bar (which required a waiver of the minimum age requirement). He worked for several law firms in Chicago before his efforts in the 1936 campaign on behalf of President Roosevelt brought him in contact with Chicago's labor leaders. Within the next few years Goldberg became a dominant figure in American labor law. He played a major role in merging the two rival labor movements into the AFL-CIO and then in driving the Communist-led unions out of the new organization. He built such a reputation for calm, scholarly presentation of his positions that businessmen and their attorneys recognized him as a man to whom they could talk comfortably. By the time President Kennedy named him Secretary of Labor in 1961, Goldberg had a reputation for integrity that no one could challenge. As Secretary, Goldberg traveled around the country, making speeches here and mediating labor disputes there. He was about to fly to Chicago on August 28, 1962, when the President called him to the White House. Mr. Kennedy told him that Frankfurter was retiring and that he intended to appoint Goldberg to the Supreme Court sooner or later. The only question was whether this was the appropriate time. A few hours later, Kennedy spoke with Goldberg again, this time to ask who should be Secretary of Labor if Goldberg were named to the Court. The next day, after Goldberg arrived in Chicago to try to mediate a railway dispute, the President telephoned. The call came to Goldberg in a hotel room from which, as he learned of his appointment to the Court, he could look down on South Side Chicago where his father had once sold vegetables to hotels and restaurants from a pushcart.*

* In light of the tragic events of November 22, 1963, President Kennedy's decision to appoint Goldberg sooner rather than later certainly changed the life of Goldberg and, perhaps, the direction of American law. This was the last vacancy on the Supreme Court that Mr. Kennedy had an opportunity to fill before he was assassinated.

Why did the President select Arthur Goldberg, of all the lawyers in the country, to replace Frankfurter? No one knew for sure except John F. Kennedy, but he, like other Presidents, must have considered many factors. Some Presidents, notably Franklin Roosevelt, tended to select top figures in their administrations or their close advisors for Supreme Court seats. Some, most recently Dwight Eisenhower, preferred to appoint men who were serving on lower courts. A few, like Harry S. Truman, appointed their personal friends. But, even given a preference by the President for men with a particular type of background, there remain other factors. A man's ability as a lawyer, his political connections and associations, his reputation for integrity and judicial temperament, his place of residence, his philosophy of government, his past association with the President, and his religion may all go into the decision-making process.

Geography was once of major importance in Supreme Court appointments. In the early years of the Court it was imperative that the Justices come from various parts of the nation. For one thing, the interstate and intersectional rivalries of that time made it necessary that the Court be composed of men who could be thought to represent various sections of the nation. For another, the Supreme Court then had much less business, and the Justices "rode the circuit," sitting as trial judges in cities and towns around the country as well as on the Supreme Court. The physical problems of transportation made it desirable that they have homes somewhere in the circuits they traveled. The importance of geographic considerations is now far less, but it is still difficult to think of the Supreme Court lacking a Justice from the South or from the Far West or from New York.

To many Presidents, the first prerequisite of a potential Supreme Court Justice is allegiance to the President's political party. Only once has a Democratic President appointed a Republican to the Court. That President was Harry S. Truman and the Republican was Harold H. Burton, an old Senate colleague. Republican Presidents have placed Democrats on the Court on seven occasions, most recently when President Eisenhower selected Justice Brennan.[13]

Another political aspect of Supreme Court appointments comes from the fact that every appointee must be approved by a majority of the Senate. In the nineteenth century many nominees were rejected on strictly political grounds. President Cleveland's first two choices for a vacancy were turned down by the Senate in 1874. Since that time, however, only one man nominated for the Court has been rejected. He was Judge John J. Parker who was nominated by President Herbert Hoover in 1930. The liberal elements of both the Democratic and the Republican parties joined to defeat that nomination because they thought Parker was too conservative in his views, particularly on labor matters. Paradoxically, Parker went on to compile an outstanding record as a federal circuit judge, a record much more agreeable to the tastes of the Senate liberals than that of the man whom they subsequently confirmed for the Supreme Court seat, Owen J. Roberts.

While religion, integrity, and temperament have always been important in the selection of Supreme Court Justices, they are rarely discussed openly. In recent years there has been no instance in which the integrity of a Justice or of a nominee has been seriously questioned. While there have been complaints that some members of the Court lack that almost indefinable qualification known as judicial temperament, such criticism is often difficult to evaluate, because it usually comes from men whose political and philosophical views diametrically oppose those of the Justice whose temperament they consider "unjudicial." Until President Woodrow Wilson nominated Brandeis to the Court in 1916, a Jew had never been appointed. That appointment was vigorously opposed in the Senate, mainly because Brandeis had vehemently and often condemned the abuses of early twentieth-century capitalism. But overtones of anti-Semitism did creep into the debate and later into the Court itself. One of President Wilson's other appointees, James C. McReynolds, made no effort to hide his extreme dislike of Jews in general and Brandeis in particular. Since the appointment of Brandeis, however, the Court has always had at least one Jewish member.

Perhaps the most important factor in the mind of most Presidents is a prospective Justice's philosophical attitude toward government. That attitude can be misread, as Theodore Roosevelt learned to his regret. Roosevelt selected Justice Holmes in 1902 largely because he thought Holmes would vote the way Roosevelt would have voted if he were on the Court. But in one of the first major cases after he joined the Court, Holmes voted against the government in a trust-busting suit close to Roosevelt's heart. Holmes did so, Roosevelt said privately, because he had lost his nerve to oppose the nation's financial leaders. "I could carve out of a banana a Judge with more backbone than that," the President supposedly said. Of course, it may have taken more backbone to oppose Teddy Roosevelt than to oppose any number of financial leaders. In any event, history proved Roosevelt wrong, for during his twenty-nine years on the bench Holmes was one of the Court's sturdiest and most outspoken members.

Despite the difficulty of being sure how a new Justice will vote, a President at least likes to believe that his appointee thinks the way he does and is likely to vote the way he would. Surely President Jackson was satisfied with his selection of Roger B. Taney as Chief Justice, just as President Franklin D. Roosevelt must have been satisfied years later with the votes and opinions of Hugo Black. President Jefferson, on the other hand, complained bitterly about many votes cast by Justice William Johnson.

Despite the fact that a Justice is nobody's man but his own, the appointment of a particular Justice at a particular time can have a lasting impact upon the Court and upon the constitutional history of the nation. If John Marshall had not been appointed Chief Justice in 1801, the American system of government might be a quite different thing today. Marshall dominated the Court as it has never been dominated by any other man and contributed immeasurably to the development of the strong central government that he believed the new country must have. If his opponents had prevailed, the federal government might never have been acknowledged as having the powers it has now long exercised, and the states would have become far more important. To a much lesser degree, the course of American law in recent years might have been different if Warren and Brennan had not been among President Eisenhower's first three appointees. These two Justices formed, with Black and Douglas, the wing of the Court in favor of an active role in government. Without their votes in the mid-1950's, the outcome the Court reached in some of its most controversial decisions might have been different.

Presidents have been urged, particularly in recent years by some members of Congress, to appoint to the Court only men with experience on lower federal and state courts. Few Presidents have taken seriously this argument that men with prior judicial experience are best qualified to understand and cope with the problems a Supreme Court Justice faces. For that matter, the argument has rarely been considered valid except by the Court's chronic critics, because the task of a Justice is quite different from that of the lower court judges whose decisions he must review. The necessity that a Supreme Court Justice be more than just a lawyer or a judge or a politician was once stated by Learned Hand, the greatest jurist who never sat on the Supreme Court, with his characteristic fluency:

> I venture to believe that it is as important to a judge called upon to pass on a question of constitutional law, to have at least a bowing acquaintance with Acton and Maitland, with

Thucydides, Gibbon and Carlyle, with Homer, Dante, Shakespeare and Milton, with Machiavelli, Montaigne and Rabelais, with Plato, Bacon, Hume and Kant, as with the books which have been specifically written on the subject. For in such matters everything turns upon the spirit in which he approaches the questions before him. The words he must construe are empty vessels into which he can pour nearly anything he will. Men do not gather figs of thistles, nor supply institutions from judges whose outlook is limited by parish or class. They must be aware that there are before them more than verbal problems; more than final solutions cast in generalizations of universal applicability. They must be aware of the changing social tensions in every society which make it an organism; which demand new schemata of adaptation; which will disrupt it, if rigidly confined.[14]

It is the factor of which Hand spoke that makes the Supreme Court so different from any other court in the world. Its power to declare laws unconstitutional gives the Court a major part in the American political process. It can, and has, blocked Congress and the President in their attempts to solve social and economic problems. It can, and has, acted to compel solutions to some of those problems itself. Much of this power stems from necessity; the broad language in which the Constitution was written must be interpreted to meet the needs of a modern world. If the Constitution had not been written that way, it probably would not have survived the many changes that have taken place since 1789 and could not then have been predicted. A document written when transportation was by horseback and communication only by word of mouth, when an industry was two men working together and when a city was large if it had a thousand residents, can be applied successfully in the modern world only if its words are interpreted in the light of the principles that lie behind them and of the world that now exists. The Constitution says nothing about Congress having power to regulate railroads or stock markets or to make the interstate transportation of women for immoral purposes a crime or to set wage and hour standards, but the Supreme Court has found support for these powers in the constitutional grant of power "To regulate Commerce with foreign Nations, and among the several states, and with the Indian Tribes." To find that support, a Justice must be more than a judge and a lawyer. To be a great Justice, he must have the breadth of interest and understanding of a Renaissance man. He must understand the philosophy on which the American system of government was built. He must be able to relate that philosophy to the economic, political, and social needs of his day. Some Justices have done this well; others have not. But there seems to be no correlation between the prior judicial experience of Justices and the judgment history has made of their performances. Almost every student of the Court would include Holmes, Brandeis, Van Devanter, Hughes, Sutherland, Stone, Cardozo, and Jackson among the ten best Justices in the first half of the twentieth century. Of these, only Van Devanter, Cardozo, and Holmes had long experience as judges in lower courts. The others had little or none.

It was obvious that President Kennedy had thought about many of these factors long before he had the opportunity to select a new Justice. He talked about the Court to several visitors in 1961 and early 1962, and asked for suggestions of possible nominees. He received from his advisors a list of six names—Deputy Attorney General White, Secretary of Labor Goldberg, Professor Paul A. Freund of the Harvard Law School, Judge William Henry Hastie of the United States Court of Appeals for the Third Circuit, Judge Walter B. Schaefer of the Illinois Supreme Court, and Judge Roger J. Traynor of the California Supreme Court.[15] When the President received word of Whittaker's retirement in the spring of 1962, he sat with his advisors to study the list. Robert Kennedy, just back from a trip around the world during which he had been deeply impressed by the attention given to United States racial problems, immediately

brought up Hastie's name. A Negro, Hastie had been a federal
circuit court judge since 1949; before that he had been governor
of the Virgin Islands, dean of the Howard University Law
School, and a federal district judge in the Virgin Islands. He
was widely known in legal circles and generally regarded as the
most able Negro lawyer of his generation. The two questions
about Hastie which concerned the President and his brother
were whether he was qualified for the Supreme Court seat and
whether the President could afford politically to give his first
Supreme Court appointment to a Negro. Assistant Attorney
General Nicholas deBelleville Katzenbach made a careful study
of Hastie's record as a judge in order to answer questions about
his past decisions. At the same time, the President and his
brother talked with other White House advisors about the political problem. If the President should appoint Hastie, critics
would say it was a move to get the Negro vote. Regardless of
Hastie's qualifications, the President felt, this would put him in
a difficult position on the Court. He would be attacked constantly on the ground that he was there solely because of his
race and not because of his ability. Both the President and the
Attorney General decided that these difficulties might not exist
if the President should decide later in his term of office to
appoint a Negro. When it became clear that the problems of
putting Hastie on the Court were insurmountable, the President
and his brother turned to the other names on the list. The Attorney General consulted with Chief Justice Warren and other
members of the Court as well as with high administration officials. Freund, who inspired the same sort of enthusiasm at Harvard that Frankfurter had in his day, had the vigorous support
of several members of the White House staff but equally vigorous opposition from others. Schaefer and Traynor were known
to the Kennedys only by reputation. As the two brothers studied
the situation, they realized that they wanted the new Justice to
be one who looked at the problems he would face from the same

perspective as they did. Thinking back on the process months
later, the Attorney General tilted back in his chair and said:

> You wanted someone who generally agreed with you on
> what role government should play in American life, what
> role the individual in society should have. You didn't think
> about how he would vote in a reapportionment case or a
> criminal case. You wanted someone who, in the long run,
> you could believe would be doing what you thought was
> best. You wanted someone who agreed generally with
> your views of the country.

Both he and the President believed that White and Goldberg
met that test. They could not be as sure of the others on the list.

Late on the afternoon of March 30, 1962, the President announced his selection of White and the morning papers the
next day headlined the news that the Supreme Court would soon
have its first All-American football player. Known to most
Americans as "Whizzer," the All-American back who carried
the University of Colorado to an undefeated season in 1938,
Byron Raymond White played professional football before becoming a Rhodes Scholar at Oxford and later while he studied
law at Yale. He first met John F. Kennedy in Europe prior to
World War II. Their paths crossed again in the South Pacific
during the war when White wrote the report of the PT-boat
incident that made Kennedy a war hero. After the war, when
Kennedy was a freshman Congressman from Massachusetts,
White was in Washington working as a law clerk for Chief
Justice Fred M. Vinson, and the two young men saw each other
occasionally. While it seemed only natural for White in 1960 to
become, first, Kennedy's leading representative in Colorado
and, later, chairman of the Citizens for Kennedy Committee, his
aversion to Richard M. Nixon played as great a part in his
decision to support Kennedy actively as did his old friendship.
After the election White gave up a corporate law practice in
Denver and moved to Washington as the Number Two man in

the Department of Justice, bringing with him characteristics that Attorney General Kennedy had not yet demonstrated—skill both as a lawyer and as an administrator. As Deputy Attorney General, White quietly built up an impressive record in both areas, adding luster to it by his handling of the violence that broke out in Alabama in 1961. When mobs attacked a band of "Freedom Riders," federal marshals headed by White went to Montgomery to restore order. Order was restored quickly and no one who heard White giving directions to local police officials could forget the icy voice that demanded and got instant obedience.

Justice Charles E. Whittaker's retirement from the Court had been quite unexpected. In mid-March of 1962 he had entered Walter Reed Medical Center for a physical examination. The doctors concluded that he was exhausted, physically and mentally. They thought he had pushed his endurance so far during his five years on the Court that his life would be in danger if he resumed his duties. For Whittaker the diagnosis was bitter. Few men had risen so far. He had grown up on a small farm in Kansas and, as he later recalled, "I went to school in a little white school house on the corner of my father's farm through nine grades and then I went to high school in Troy, Kansas, and rode a pony to school through six miles of mud night and morning for about a year and a half. When my mother died, it broke my heart. She died on my birthday in 1917. I felt I couldn't go on and I quit high school."[16]

Whittaker never returned to high school and never entered college. He saved the money he earned by selling the skins of animals, mostly skunks, he trapped in the woods and in 1920 set out for Kansas City. There he worked as a clerk in a law firm by day and studied at the Kansas City Law School by night. Whittaker eventually became one of the Midwest's best trial lawyers and in 1954 was appointed a federal district judge by President Eisenhower. Two years later, he was promoted to the Eighth

Circuit Court of Appeals and a year later to the Supreme Court. During his short stay on the Court, Whittaker cast crucial votes in dozens of cases but had little opportunity to write major opinions, which are normally assigned to senior members of the Court. Off the bench, Whittaker had a delightful sense of humor but his attitude in the courtroom was serious, almost somber. He worked hard to keep pace with the intellectual brilliance of Frankfurter and the fully developed, powerful philosophy of Black, and by 1962 he had literally worked himself off the Court.

With its two new Justices, the Supreme Court was a very different body as the 1962–63 term began than it had been a year earlier. Whittaker had usually agreed with Frankfurter on the two basic philosophical issues that divided the Justices—judicial restraint versus activism, and the meaning of the Bill of Rights and the Fourteenth Amendment. Harlan regularly voted with them. Black and Douglas, of course, consistently opposed Frankfurter's position on those issues, and Warren and Brennan usually voted with them. Clark and Stewart voted more frequently with Frankfurter than with Black, so the Frankfurter group had been in the ascendancy. There had been, of course, some major exceptions. One was the reapportionment case in which Clark and Stewart abandoned judicial restraint, leaving Harlan and Frankfurter alone since Whittaker was ill. Another was a decision barring the use as evidence in state courts of material seized in violation of the Fourth Amendment; Clark joined Black, leaving Frankfurter, Harlan, and Whittaker in dissent. Stewart thought there was no Fourth Amendment violation so dissented without reaching the basic issue. It would be on issues of that kind that the votes of the two new Justices would be crucial, not in the areas of segregation and religion where there seemed to be a much clearer consensus among the other seven Justices. On judicial restraint and the meaning of the Bill of Rights, no one could predict with any certainty what the attitudes of the two new men would be. White had participated in a few decisions late in the preceding term but not enough to indicate his thinking about the basic problems. Goldberg had never spoken about them. But these were among the issues before the Court in this term. Reapportionment, states' rights, and congressional investigations, as well as racial discrimination and religious exercises in the schools, were on the calendar. The votes of the new Justices in these areas could change the course of American law. As usual, the public was more interested in other matters. There were riots in Mississippi, communism in Cuba, an election, and the World Series. But to the Court's students, and its critics, the new term was already of greater than usual interest.

chapter 3

THE TERM AHEAD

ANYONE UNFAMILIAR WITH THE SUPREME COURT IS LIKELY TO be stunned by the amount of work that confronts the Justices. More than 2,500 cases flow into that marble building on Capitol Hill each year. On each of these, each Justice must cast his vote at least once. For each of the 140 or so on which the Court agrees to hear arguments, each Justice must study hundreds of pages of briefs and records and arrive at his decision. After that, one Justice must write an opinion for the Court explaining why it decided the case as it did. Those who disagree with the result or the reasoning may write dissenting or concurring opinions. As White and Goldberg went to work in October, they must have felt the way Stewart had a few years earlier when he joined the Court after serving as a judge of the United States Court of Appeals for the Sixth Circuit. Not long after he joined the Court, he said:

> I used to think I worked hard there and I did. I worked harder there than I had to in private practice. But this Court takes more time. Arriving at the beginning of a term, as I did, makes it particularly difficult. The first cases were rearguments. Within two weeks, I received an 85-page document on one of the cases. I thought, I can't do this! A month later I discovered that the document was the result of a summer's work. Then I figured out a schedule that let me be fully prepared on all the certs before Friday and on all the cases before they were argued. But I hadn't given myself a minute to write opinions. It's a job that's never done.

As the Justices settled down to work after that first Monday in October, it was clear that the next nine months would be one of the busiest and most important terms in the Court's history. Before they had departed for summer vacations late in June, the Justices had placed ninety-one cases on the calendar for argument during the fall and winter. These involved subjects ranging from regulation of agriculture to the sovereignty of the United States government. A few cases were fairly easy; the Justices must settle disagreements among lower courts on minor points of procedure and it makes no great difference which way they are settled. Others presented the problem of interpreting, for the first time, what Congress meant when it passed a particular law. Still others raised fundamental questions about the meaning of certain phrases and clauses of the Constitution.

Of the ninety-one cases, the Court had already heard arguments in sixteen. These had been put back on the calendar late in the spring after Frankfurter fell ill and Whittaker retired. Although the other seven Justices had not indicated why they wanted to hear the cases argued again, it was clear that at least eight of the sixteen were unusually difficult. Perhaps the Justices felt these merited the attention of a full Court; perhaps they had been unable to reach anything close to a unanimous decision on them. The other eight cases involved rather mundane matters and had probably been held over because with two Justices missing the others could not finish all the work before the summer recess. While White wrote a few opinions in the spring, he could not participate in cases argued before he joined the Court.

The most unusual of these cases involved a dispute between several Western states over the water in the Colorado River. For years both California and Arizona had claimed the right to take most of that water and use it for agricultural, industrial, and residential purposes. When Arizona urged Congress in the late 1940's to build the Central Valley Reclamation project, congressional leaders said the question of which state was entitled to the water must be answered before the project could be considered. As a result, Arizona filed suit in 1952, asking the Supreme Court to decide how much water each state had the right to use. If Arizona won its case, its deserts would bloom and California, particularly the Los Angeles area, would have to turn elsewhere, perhaps to the sea, to obtain enough water to meet its growing needs. If California won, its water supply would be assured for years to come and Arizona's dreams of a great agricultural development near Phoenix would be ended.

The case had little in common with most of those the Supreme Court decides: there were no constitutional issues; the dispute had no broad impact on the law; and the problem seemed far more political than judicial. Yet the case came to the Supreme Court under the only jurisdiction it is guaranteed by the Constitution. The Constitution gives the Court "original" jurisdiction "in all Cases affecting Ambassadors, other public Ministers and Consuls, and those in which a State shall be Party." In such cases the Justices sit as a trial court from which there is no appeal. This may be the only jurisdiction the Court has that Congress cannot tamper with.[1] All other cases reach the Court under its "appellate" jurisdiction under which the Constitution empowers the Court to review certain types of lower court decisions as and when Congress provides. The present congressional authorization is to entertain "appeals" and "petitions for certiorari"—"petitions for cert" in the legal jargon. (The Latin word *certiorari* means, in a loose translation, "give us the certified record." As used by the Supreme Court it means "send the case to us.") Broadly speaking, appeals may be taken in cases where a statute, state or federal, has been challenged as repugnant to the United States Constitution, while certiorari may be requested in all federal court cases and in state court cases presenting questions of federal law. The Court is required to hear the appeals, though it may dismiss attempted appeals in which the constitutional question is insubstantial. Its grant or denial of petitions for certiorari is discretionary.

When Arizona invoked the Court's original jurisdiction in the water dispute, the Justices appointed George I. Haight of Chicago as a special master in the case. His tasks were to take evidence on the facts in dispute and to make recommendations to the Justices on both the facts and the law. Haight died in 1955 and was replaced by Simon H. Rifkind, a former federal judge then practicing law in New York City. During 1956, 1957, and 1958, Judge Rifkind (Judges, like Senators, use their titles for life.) conducted the trial in San Francisco where he heard 106 witnesses. He received the testimony of another 234 witnesses through written depositions. The trial record thus compiled was more than 26,000 pages long. In addition, the states filed more than 4,000 pages of legal briefs and other documents. There were about 6 million words before Rifkind, enough to fill sixty normal sized books, and his report, submitted to the Justices on January 16, 1961, ran more than 135,000 words. Although he ruled largely in favor of Arizona, Arizona as well as California objected to Rifkind's report. In addition, Nevada, Utah, New Mexico, and the United States government asked the Justices for permission to participate in the case because each felt it had a special interest in the outcome. The Justices devoted sixteen hours to the oral arguments in the fall of 1961. That amount of time—a full week, when the Court normally schedules only one or two hours of argument in each case and hears only fourteen weeks of argument a year—emphasized the importance of the case. Now it was back on the Court's calendar, this time for six hours of further argument in November.

Two other cases brought over from the spring of 1962 carried direct challenges to the constitutionality of laws passed by Congress. Two federal courts, one in California and one in the District of Columbia, had held unconstitutional the parts of two laws that automatically revoked the citizenship of anyone who, in order to evade the draft, remained outside the country during a national emergency. The Department of Justice had promptly appealed the decisions. One of these cases involved Francisco Mendoza-Martinez, a native Californian who fled to Mexico during World War II. He returned to the United States after the war and served a year and a day in a federal prison for draft-dodging. Four years after his sentence was completed, the government tried to deport him as a non-citizen. In the other case, Dr. Joseph Henry Cort had gone to England in 1951 and failed to return to be drafted. When he applied for a renewal of his passport the State Department denied it on the ground that he was no longer a citizen. Both men argued successfully in the lower courts that the Constitution did not permit their citizenship to be revoked because of draft-dodging. The federal government contended that it did.

Two other cases brought the Court back to an area in which its decisions during the 1950's had brought it great criticism. One involved Edward Yellin, who had been convicted of contempt of Congress for refusing to answer questions put to him by the House Un-American Activities Committee. The other involved William Presser, an Ohio union boss convicted of obstructing justice by refusing to produce documents demanded by a Senate committee investigating labor-management misdeeds. The votes of the two new Justices in these cases would be watched carefully from across the street in the Capitol. In the past, four Justices—Warren, Black, Douglas, and Brennan—had frequently spoken out against the sweeping investigations of the Un-American Activities Committee and the Senate Internal Security subcommittee. They had made clear their view that the Constitution prohibited a congressional investigating committee from probing into the political beliefs and associations of any American citizen, even one suspected of being a Communist. In cases upholding convictions for contempt of Congress, these four Justices had consistently dissented. In many cases they had been able to pick up a fifth vote to reverse the convictions, but those reversals were on narrow, procedural grounds. The fight inside the Court over these cases had been bitter. Black and Harlan had exchanged some of their harshest comments on this issue, the one on which Arthur Krock charged the Court with "finding" new restrictions in the Constitution. If either of the two new Justices voted with Warren and Black in these two cases, it would have a far-reaching effect on the balance between individual liberties and efforts to assure national security.

In another pair of holdover cases the Justices were confronted with difficult legal questions raised by the activities in the South of the National Association for the Advancement of Colored People and similar groups. In an effort to restrict such activities, Virginia had tightened its laws governing the relationships between lawyers and their clients. The NAACP said the laws would put it out of business in that state. In the other case Episcopal Bishop Theodore R. Gibson of Miami had been convicted of contempt of a Florida investigating committee for refusing to produce a list of all the NAACP members in the state. The committee said it needed to know who belonged to the NAACP to learn whether it was being infiltrated by Communists. Bishop Gibson said the committee really wanted to give the list to others who would harass NAACP members.

But these cases were only a small amount of the work that faced the Justices in that first week of October. During the summer recess, about 800 appeals and petitions for cert had accumulated on the docket. Within the first week, the Justices must decide what to do with a good many of these and, in doing so, would choose most of the issues that would be before them in the next few months. Most of the Justices had spent some of the summer recess working in their chambers on the cases they knew would come before them in October. By doing so, they gained a considerable head start on Goldberg. He had moved into his chambers soon after the Senate confirmed him, however, and had become acquainted with the members of his staff and unofficially looked over some of the material he would be handling in the months ahead.

It did not take Goldberg long to survey those chambers and meet that staff. As Secretary of Labor he had headed a department with thousands of employees, occupying a huge building, with enough staff aides to do any research or other work he wanted done. At the Court he had a suite of three rooms and a staff of four: his long-time secretary, Mrs. Jeanne Trexler; a messenger, Robert D. Suttice, who had worked previously in the office of the Court's Marshal; and two young honor graduates of the Harvard Law School. These two, David Filvaroff and Peter Edelman, had been selected as law clerks for Justice Frankfurter the preceding spring by Professor Albert M. Sacks of Harvard. Frankfurter's resignation had left them jobless shortly after their arrival in Washington late in the summer but Goldberg promptly relieved their unemployment. With one exception, the other Associate Justices had staffs identical to Goldberg's; Douglas preferred to have two secretaries and only one law clerk. The Chief Justice's personal staff was larger—three law clerks, two secretaries, and two messengers, plus, part time, the law clerk officially employed for retired Justices Stanley F. Reed and Harold H. Burton. The Chief Justice was also responsible for all the other employees of the Court and for the administrative office of all the federal courts.

The law clerks were all bright young men recently graduated from law school. (There has been one woman law clerk in the Court's history.) The jobs are eagerly sought each year by law school graduates all over the country. For the most part, the clerks had been at or very near the top of their classes at the nation's best law schools. Brennan and Frankfurter clerks always came from Harvard, the Justices' alma mater. Black always wanted at least one clerk from the South, and looked with some favor on tennis players. Harlan usually chose one clerk from

Harvard and one from a New York City law school. Douglas's clerk was always a graduate of a West Coast law school.

Every once in a while, someone attacks the Justices through their law clerks. During the peak of anti-Court sentiment in Congress in the late 1950's, some Congressmen suggested that appointments as clerks should be subject to Senate approval just as judicial appointments are. The clerks, the claim was, had a significant effect on the way the Court decided cases. It is obvious that no one is closer to the Justices when they decide cases than are their clerks. They frequently serve as sounding boards for views the Justices wish to try out, and they have an opportunity to express their views on particular cases. It is unlikely, however, that any clerk ever significantly altered the views of his Justice on a major issue. Nevertheless, the clerks can occasionally be significant in particular cases. In the first Flag Salute Case, Justice Stone was goaded by his clerks into writing an opinion instead of merely noting his dissent, the only one in the case. His opinion was so persuasive that, only three years later, three of his colleagues changed their minds and voted with him and two new Justices to overrule the former decision.

John P. Frank, an Arizona lawyer who once clerked for Black, has described the role of the clerks as "very much the product of the whim of their Justices." Frank added, "In general, it is the job of the clerk to be the eyes and legs for his judge, finding and bringing useful material." [2] Basically, this means research, and every Justice's clerks spend long hours in their office reading legal materials and writing memoranda. A few Justices have let their clerks do a large amount of opinion writing, while others let them do little more than comment on drafts. The miscellaneous tasks of the clerks are unpredictable. In the fall of 1962, at the age of seventy-six, Black was playing tennis on weekends and occasionally called on one of his clerks to fill in for doubles. Brennan sometimes taunted his clerks into joining him for his regular morning walks—walks that began at 5 A.M. and covered four or five miles. The Chief Justice often took his clerks to baseball or football games on warm Saturday and Sunday afternoons.

The idea of bringing young lawyers to the Court as clerks apparently originated with Justice Horace Gray in 1882. He paid them out of his own pocket until 1886 when Congress provided $1,600 a year for a "stenographic clerk" for each Justice.[3] Two of Gray's clerks later left a great imprint on the Harvard Law School and on American law, Samuel Williston and Ezra Ripley Thayer. Almost without exception, clerks have gone on to notable careers in law or in government. The Kennedy Administration in the fall of 1962 was sprinkled liberally with former law clerks: Assistant Attorney General Louis D. Oberdorfer; State Department Legal Advisor Abram J. Chayes; Deputy Assistant Secretary of State Richard N. Goodwin; Federal Communications Commission Chairman Newton N. Minow; Federal Trade Commissioner Philip Elman; Assistant to the Secretary of Defense Adam Yarmolinsky. White was the first law clerk to return to the Court as a Justice, but another of the men the President seriously considered for the seat, Paul Freund, had clerked for Justice Brandeis.

The clerks came to Washington in the summer of 1962 from all parts of the country—metropolises like New York, Washington, Cleveland, Denver, and San Francisco, and small cities or towns like Dos Palos, California; Janesville, Wisconsin; and Lafayette, Indiana. Eight of them were graduates of the Harvard Law School and four of the Yale Law School. The other law schools represented were Columbia, New York University, Stanford, Virginia, Mississippi, Indiana, and California. The preponderance of Yale and Harvard graduates recalled Frankfurter's statement about why the New Deal had been so heavily populated with Harvard Law School graduates: "If you want to get good groceries in Washington," he said, "you go to Magruder's, or in New York to Park and Tilford, or in Boston to S. S. Pierce. If you wanted to get a lot of first-class lawyers, you went to the Harvard Law School."[4]

For the clerks the year ahead might well be the most exciting year of their lives. Close association with a Supreme Court Justice invariably makes a deep impression on a young lawyer. The relationship is more than that of employer to employee, or even senior partner to young associate. The clerks share with their Justices long hours of decision. They are exposed to the processes by which nine men determine the great legal issues of the day. And nothing so exposes the inner workings of a man's mind as the process of decision-making. As the new clerks dug into the mound of cases already pending when they arrived in Washington, they found much to talk about. But they could talk about it only among themselves. Occasionally, a clerk would have lunch in the Court's cafeteria with old friends, but his conversation would be inhibited, because the Court's tradition of tight secrecy was quickly drummed into all its personnel. Ordinarily, the clerks ate lunch together in a private dining room, while the Justices ordered lunch from the cafeteria and ate in their chambers. Sometimes, however, a Justice would join his clerks for lunch in the cafeteria. A visitor there late in September could have seen Black and Harlan waiting patiently in the cafeteria line to select their food. Or, if he arrived at the Court early any morning, he could have seen Douglas eating breakfast there.

One of the first tasks assigned to most clerks was to go through the hundreds of cert petitions that had been filed during the summer. Some Justices had their clerks prepare a short memorandum on each petition describing the claims made and the decision of the lower court. These cut down the time the Justice had to spend in reaching his decision on each case as to whether the Court should hear it. In earlier years most of the papers filed at the Court were printed, but in the fall of 1962 more than half the cases awaiting action were petitions from prisoners in state and federal jails. These were often scrawled in longhand on prison stationery. As they arrived, each was assigned a number and referred to the law clerks of the Chief Justice. They deciphered the handwriting—no mean task in itself—and prepared a memorandum for all the Justices about each case. While most of these scrawled petitions were without merit, the Court occasionally found among them a case of great importance. One such case, which had been filed in the preceding January and would be heard during the coming term, was the protest of Clarence Earl Gideon that the State of Florida had denied him his constitutional rights by refusing to appoint a lawyer to defend him. When it took the case, the Court appointed an attorney for Gideon and expressly asked him to argue whether its 1942 decision that the states need not appoint counsel for all indigent defendants should be overruled.

During the first week in October the Justices met daily in one of the Court's conference rooms, going through their docket case by case. At these conferences, ordinarily held each Friday when the Court is in session, the Court makes its decisions. What goes on in that oak-paneled room is the Court's most tightly guarded secret. Rarely do the Justices talk about the conferences, and no one but a Justice has attended one in many, many years. However, in a speech in 1959 Justice Clark described them:

> Over the mantel facing the large rectangular conference table is a portrait of Chief Justice Marshall, the fourth Chief Justice by number but the first in stature. Around this table are nine chairs, each bearing the nameplate of a member of the Court. At the south end sits the Chief Justice, and at the north, Mr. Justice Black, the senior Associate Justice. On the sides, in order of seniority, sit the remaining Associate Justices. Bookcases from floor to ceiling line the walls containing all the opinions of the federal courts. Here the Court meets in conference at 11:00 A.M.

on each Friday during or preceding an argument week, and rarely does it rise before 5:30 P.M.

Only the Justices are present at conference. There are no clerks, no stenographers, no secretaries, no pages. This long-established practice is based on reason. The Court must carry on these Friday conferences in absolute secrecy; otherwise, its judgments might become prematurely known and the whole process of decision destroyed. We therefore guard its secrets closely. There must be no leak. . . .

Upon entering the conference room, each Justice shakes hands with those present, another custom begun by Chief Justice Fuller and hence dating generations back. We first take out our assignment sheets or lists of cases for the day. . . . The Chief Justice starts the conference by calling the first case on the list and discussing it. He then yields to the senior Associate Justice and on down the line seniority-wise until each Justice who wishes to be heard has spoken. There is no time limitation. The order is never interrupted nor is the speaker. Another tale going the rounds of the Court has to do with a conference of many terms back while the late Justices Harlan and Holmes were on the Court. Harlan was presenting his view of a case with which Holmes evidently did not agree. In the midst of Harlan's argument, Holmes interrupted with a sharp remark, "That won't wash! That won't wash!" Justice Holmes often greeted Justice Harlan as "my strong-hearted friend," but he had never chided him about his legal conclusions. Harlan, too, was strong-minded and never turned away from a fight. In this regard his opinions show that he wielded a wicked pair of horns and often got his adversary out on both of them. Holmes, on the other hand, was the rapier type that cut so quickly one did not know his head was off until he attempted to turn it. Fortunately, the Chief Justice at the time was Melville Fuller. He had already discussed the case and his position was similar to that of Harlan. When the diminutive but courageous, silver-haired Chief Justice realized that all was not well between his brothers, he quickly spoke up, saying, "That won't wash, eh! Well, I'm scrubbing away, anyhow." A tense situation passed over during the ensuing laughter.

After discussion of a case, a vote is taken. We each have available a large docket book, evidently, from its appearance, handed down to us by the first of the Justices. It has a hinge on its flyleaf which is kept locked. There we keep a record of the votes. Ever since John Marshall's day the formal vote begins with the junior Justice and moves up through the ranks of seniority, the Chief Justice voting last. Hence the juniors are not influenced by the vote of their elders![5]

In the conference, however, the Chief Justice can sometimes shape the outcome of the Court's work. Although the Chief is officially, so far as the decision-making process is concerned, only the "first among equals," he speaks first, outlining the case as he sees it. In so doing, he determines the manner in which the conference, at least initially, considers each case. Because almost every major case presents more than one issue and because the angle from which the issues are approached can affect the outcome, the Chief Justice's presentation is important. Also in the conference each Justice tries to persuade his colleagues to see the case as he does. Much of Black's major impact on the Court's decisions, for instance, has come through his long and closely reasoned presentations in conference.

The other major influence on the Court's work that a Chief Justice can wield also flows from the conference. After the Justices have voted on a case, the Chief assigns the task of writing the Court's opinion, unless he is in dissent, in which event the senior member of the majority makes the assignment. This often enables the Chief to write the opinions in the major cases himself if he so desires. The major opinions are normally distributed fairly evenly among the relatively senior Justices, but Warren often kept for himself those which promised to be condemned most vigorously. Since the personal imprint a Justice leaves on the law stems directly from the opinions he writes, this task of assigning them is a major responsibility. Chief Justice Stone, for example, rarely assigned major cases to Justice Frank

Murphy, who was made constantly ill at ease by that indication of lack of confidence in him.

During the first week in October, of course, there were no issues to be decided and no opinions to be assigned. Instead, the Justices turned to the 400 or so items that were on their conference list. A few of these were motions for reconsideration of decisions handed down the preceding year; such requests are often made but rarely granted. The other matters were appeals and petitions for certiorari that had accumulated over the summer. Most of these would be disposed of one way or another on October 8 when the Justices again sat in open court. Few of the petitions would be granted. During a full term the Justices have time to hear 140 to 150 cases argued, so they can hear only about 6 or 7 per cent of the cases brought to them. In addition to the sixteen argued during the preceding term, they had already agreed during that term to hear arguments in seventy-five new cases.

Among these seventy-five were many cases of national importance, and also many of interest only to specialists in specific fields of the law. One group of the first sort involved the sit-in demonstrations in the South where more than a thousand Negroes and some whites faced jail sentences for their parts in those protests against segregation at restaurants and lunch counters. Three cases involved the efforts of the National Labor Relations Board to apply American labor law to crews of ships registered under the flags of other countries; these efforts had already brought protests from five foreign nations. Another case involved the county-unit system under which Georgia had long selected its Democratic candidates for state and federal office.

It was clear that the stage was already set for an important term. The decision in the sit-in cases would anger either the civil libertarians or the segregationists. The Georgia voting case was likely to reopen wounds created by the Tennessee reapportionment case. The Colorado River water decision would chart the course for future development in the Southwest and the planning of the losing side would be seriously disrupted. The contempt-of-Congress cases would again bring the Court face to face with its congressional critics. The case of Clarence Earl Gideon and his plea for an attorney might bring forth once more the banner of states' rights. None of these cases would be easy to decide. In none of them was the answer clear nor would the result be free from criticism. But the Supreme Court sits to decide difficult cases; the easy ones never get there.

chapter 4

THE FIRST ARGUMENTS

ONLY A FEW SPECTATORS WERE IN THE COURTROOM ON OCTOBER 8 when Marshal Lippitt banged his gavel and the Justices—now nine in number—stepped quickly through the dark red velvet drapes. The preliminary work of the term had been finished in the conferences of the preceding week. Now the Justices were faced with a regular schedule for the next seven months. Each two weeks of arguments would be followed by two weeks of recess. Breaks from that routine would come at Christmas, when the Court would recess an extra week, and late in January when its recess was scheduled for four weeks. During argument weeks, the Justices would sit from 10:00 o'clock to noon and from 12:30 to 2:30 on the first four days, and meet in conference on Fridays. The Court would sit briefly on the first Monday of each recess period to announce decisions and hand down orders and would meet in conference on the last Friday of the period.

For many years the Court began public sessions promptly at noon. But at its first meeting in October, 1961, the Chief Justice suddenly announced that thenceforth the sessions would begin at 10:00 A.M. The break with tradition was such a surprise to the Court's staff that when the Justices adjourned that day Court Crier George Hutchinson announced, "This Court stands adjourned until 12 noon Monday next." A snicker swept down the bench and Stewart and Brennan whispered, "Ten o'clock, ten o'clock!" before the Crier caught his error and added, "I mean 10 A.M. Monday next."

October 8 was a typical day at the Court. When the Justices entered, dozens of lawyers were sitting in the courtroom. They had come from all over the country to be admitted to practice law before the Supreme Court. The admission requirements are minimal: an applicant must have been a member of the bar of the highest court in a state for three years, must produce letters of recommendation and a sponsor in Court the day he is admitted, and must pay a $25 fee. The fees are important to the Court because they are used to pay the expenses of cases involving persons too poor to pay them, usually criminal defendants. In addition to the right to practice before it, the Court gives each lawyer for his $25 an ornate certificate of membership in the Supreme Court bar. The certificate, framed and hung on the wall of a lawyer's office, looks impressive. In most instances the impression the certificate makes on his clients is the lawyer's only benefit from membership, since a minority of those admitted ever actually practice before the Court.

After all the waiting lawyers had been admitted that morning, the Chief Justice announced, "The orders of the Court have been filed with the Clerk and will not be orally announced." As two pages scurried around the courtroom, handing copies of the orders to Solicitor General Archibald Cox, the Court's official reporter Walter Wyatt, and the newsmen who sat at small desks just below and in front of the bench, the Chief Justice called, "Number 36. Wong Sun versus the United States."

Edward Bennett Williams, currently the nation's best-known criminal trial lawyer, moved to the counsel table on the left, quickly arranged his notes, and took his place at the lectern that stands directly in front of the Chief Justice's seat at the center of the bench. Solicitor General Cox gave the seat at the other counsel table closest to the lectern to one of his staff, J. William Doolittle, who would argue this case for the government. Williams had been appointed by the Court to represent Wong Sun and James Wah Toy, two San Francisco men who said they lacked the money to send an attorney to Washington to appeal their convictions for illegal possession of narcotics. The expenses of printing the record of the men's trial and the brief Williams wrote were paid from the accumulated $25 admission fees, but neither Williams nor the members of his firm who had worked on the case would be paid for their time and effort.

It took Williams almost ten of his allotted thirty minutes just to explain the complex facts of his case. It had all started at about 2:00 A.M. on June 4, 1959, when federal narcotics agents in San Francisco arrested a man named Hom Way for illegally possessing narcotics. Hom Way told the agents he had bought an ounce of heroin the night before from a man he knew only as "Blackie Toy," proprietor of a laundry on Leavenworth Street. About four hours later, as dawn was breaking, half a dozen federal agents went to a laundry at 1733 Leavenworth Street. James Wah Toy ran it, but nothing presented to the courts later identified him as "Blackie Toy"; the laundry was called "Oye's Laundry." One of the agents, Alton Wong, knocked at the door and told Toy that he wanted to pick up his laundry. Toy told him to come back at 8 o'clock and started to close the door. Wong then said, "I am a federal narcotics agent." Toy immediately slammed the door and ran down the hall toward his bedroom. Wong and the other officers broke open the door and ran after him, chasing him into a room where his wife and child were sleeping. As Toy reached into a nightstand drawer, Wong drew his pistol and placed him under arrest. The agents then searched the premises but found no narcotics. One agent said to Toy, "Hom Way says he got narcotics from you." Toy denied that he had narcotics but said, "I do know somebody who has." His name was "Johnny," and he lived at an 11th Avenue address. The agents immediately went to the house on 11th Avenue, found Johnny Yee in a bedroom, and arrested him. He took several tubes of heroin from a bureau drawer and surrendered them. Yee told the agents that Toy and a man he knew only as "Sea Dog" had brought the narcotics to him. Toy identified "Sea Dog" as Wong Sun and the narcotics agents promptly went to Wong Sun's house, searched it without finding any narcotics, but nevertheless arrested him. All three men were charged with violating the federal drug laws. They later made oral confessions to Agent Wong, but when Wong had the statements typed, the three men refused to sign them. At the trial of Toy and Wong Sun, the government's only evidence that they had illegally possessed narcotics was the heroin seized in Johnny Yee's bedroom, Toy's oral statements when he was arrested, and the unsigned statements of the two defendants.

There were many things wrong in this series of events, Williams told the Justices. The men he represented, Wong Sun and Wah Toy, had both been arrested illegally, he argued, and both their houses had been unreasonably searched in violation of the Fourth Amendment to the Constitution. But if there had been no more than this to the case it would have been a fairly simple one. The searches had produced no incriminating evidence, and the Ninth Circuit Court of Appeals had already ruled that the arrests were illegal. But Williams wanted the Court to lay down a new rule in criminal cases in the federal courts. He argued that if the arrests of Toy and Wong Sun were illegal, everything the police learned as a result of those arrests was barred as evidence against them. His argument would require extension of the "fruit of the poisonous tree" doctrine the Court had established years earlier. The doctrine originally prohibited the use against a defendant of evidence seized in violation of the Fourth Amendment's bar against unreasonable searches and seizures. Subsequently, the Court extended the prohibition to evidence uncovered as a result of other illegal police activity. The Justices did so because they believed that the federal courts could not, consistent with the requirements of due process of law, permit the federal government to win convictions by means of its own violations of its own laws. They had concluded from past experience that this was the only effective way to discourage the police from engaging in illegal conduct.

Williams argued that the prohibition should be applied to all evidence resulting from illegal arrests. The Justices were all aware, as Williams argued his case, of the fact that thousands of Americans are arrested illegally each year. Under the Constitution, police may never make an arrest unless they have "probable cause" to believe a felony has been committed and the man they are arresting committed it. Arrests based on mere suspicion are plainly unconstitutional, but Justice Douglas once said that 96,740 such arrests occurred in 1958.[1]

Doolittle argued for the government that if the Justices accepted Williams's argument they would place severe restraints on police work. Police must often make split-second decisions whether to arrest a particular man, and the line between "probable cause" and "suspicion" was so narrow that the best-intentioned officer might occasionally make an illegal arrest. To deprive the prosecution of the use of oral statements or other evidence resulting from such arrests would be unfair and unjust and would unreasonably inhibit law enforcement activity.

The case was the kind that had often brought the Court under heavy criticism. If it adopted the position for which Williams argued, it would strengthen the constitutional guarantee against arrests without probable cause and would force federal police to act more carefully. But its critics would then claim the Court was using "technicalities" to help criminals escape punishment. This dilemma had perpetually faced the Justices. A great number of its major decisions in the field of civil liberties have come in cases of this type. As Justice Frankfurter observed in 1950, "It is a fair summary of history to say that the safeguards of liberty have frequently been forged in controversies involving not very nice people."[2]

When the hour allotted to the case of Toy and Sun had expired, Williams and Doolittle gathered up their papers and left the counsel tables as the Chief Justice said, "Number 25. Presser versus the United States." William Presser, a leader of the Teamsters Union in Ohio, had been convicted of obstructing the work of the Senate Select Committee on Labor-Management Misdeeds by mutilating records the Committee wanted to see. His attorney argued that Presser's conviction should be reversed because the subpoena directing him to produce the documents had been issued in violation of the rules of the Committee and of the Senate. The government argued, among other things, that the validity of the subpoena was unimportant because Presser knew the Committee wanted the records and had a right to see them. Since he knew the Committee wanted the records, the government argued, he knowingly obstructed the investigation by destroying the records. The case, while quite different from most of those involving congressional investigating committees, might indicate how the two new Justices reacted to the activities of those committees.

While the Justices were listening to the arguments involving Toy, Wong Sun, and Presser, the Court's staff was sorting the morning's routine orders and preparing messages to tell attorneys what the Justices had done in their cases. In the press room on the ground floor, reporters were poring over the list of cryptic orders to see which were of interest to the general public. Altogether that morning the Court disposed of 385 cases. The Justices rejected outright the requests made in 363 of them. In some their decision meant someone had lost his appeal in a civil case. In others it meant a man would go to jail. In a few it meant the last avenue of appeal for a convicted murderer was closed and execution would follow. But in twenty-two cases the Justices agreed to decide the issues involved. Fourteen of these, including two that raised again the issue of religious exercises in the public schools, were scheduled for argument later in the year. The judgments of lower courts in four other cases were summarily reversed and in four more summarily affirmed. The

distinction between a summary affirmance of a lower court judgment and a refusal to consider a case at all is subtle but important.
By affirming, the Justices say the lower court was right. By
refusing to hear the case, they let the lower court's judgment
stand but indicate no opinion about whether it was right. Because of its tremendous case load, the Court cannot review even
all the cases the Justices think were wrongly decided. The Court
cannot see to it that justice is done in every case; its most important task, as Frankfurter often pointed out, is to establish the
basic rules of law under which lower courts administer justice.
Occasionally, of course, the Justices hear a case simply because
they think the lower court judgment is grossly unjust. But the
standard by which the Court usually chooses the cases it will
hear is the basic importance of the issues they raise. The votes
of four Justices are required for the Court's decision to hear a
case. In several cases on the order list this Monday one or two
Justices noted their opinion that the case should be heard, though
too few of their colleagues agreed.

One of the cases the Court rejected without comment was
Mississippi's request that it review the lower court order directing the enrollment of James Meredith at the University of Mississippi. This was the order under which Meredith had registered
at Ole Miss eight days before. Already the Supreme Court's
handling of the case had been criticized. Late in August Meredith's attorneys had asked Justice Black to set aside the latest of
a series of actions by Federal Circuit Judge Ben F. Cameron to
block the order directing Meredith's immediate enrollment. Black
promptly overruled Judge Cameron and reinstated the order
after noting the strange maneuvering within the Fifth Circuit
Court of Appeals. Early in July that court had ruled that Meredith must be admitted to Ole Miss for the September term.
Lawyers representing the University then asked Judge Cameron
to delay the effective date of that order, and Cameron, who had
not participated in the decision to admit Meredith, promptly

complied. On an application from Meredith's lawyers, the three judges who had decided the case ruled that Cameron was without power to block the order and dissolved his stay. Cameron, contending he had power, entered another stay. At this point all eight of Cameron's fellow judges on the circuit court agreed he was wrong. But Cameron persisted and Meredith's lawyers turned to Black, the Supreme Court Justice assigned to supervise the Fifth Circuit. Black pointed out that lower court orders are normally stayed pending appeal only if the losing party will be severely damaged by the order's enforcement or is very likely to win in the Supreme Court. Black said he thought there was little likelihood that the Court would hear the case, since only factual issues and not issues of law were involved. He could not see how Meredith's enrollment would severely harm the University while failure to enroll him immediately would mean his missing another semester. A number of Southern lawyers, including the outgoing president of the American Bar Association, promptly condemned Black and the Court for prejudging the case and denying Mississippi the benefit of argument. Some newspaper columnists joined the criticism, never recognizing that Black's action was actually a simple refusal to deviate from customary procedures.

Mississippi's case was only one of 363 that the Court had for one reason or another decided not to review. The fourteen it accepted and put on its calendar for argument, however, presented difficult legal problems. Two of them involved Bible-reading and prayer in the public schools, reopening the question of the relationship between religion and government. Maryland's highest court had ruled, 4 to 3, that it was constitutional for a school board to require Bible-reading and the Lord's Prayer as opening exercises. In neighboring Pennsylvania a three-judge federal court had ruled unanimously that a state law requiring daily Bible-reading in the public schools was unconstitutional. The constitutional issues in the two cases were identical and varied only slightly from those in the New York case decided the previous June. In addition to these two cases, the Court also agreed to hear arguments on the rules for school desegregation used by Nashville and Knoxville, Tennessee. Those rules provided that a student whose school had been desegregated could transfer out if he was a member of the minority race. The Court had been asked to hear many cases involving school desegregation since its 1954 ruling that segregation in public schools violated the Equal Protection Clause of the Fourteenth Amendment, but these were the first it had accepted.

While these cases, desegregation and prayer, were the ones that would attract public attention, the other eleven cases the Justices added to their docket illustrated the Court's broad jurisdiction. They involved such subjects as the immunity of the New York Stock Exchange from the antitrust laws; the power of a state to pass antidiscrimination laws affecting pilots on interstate airlines; Ohio's obscenity laws under which a theater manager had been convicted for showing *The Lovers*, a movie that had been shown in many other states and earned critical acclaim; the extent to which a shipowner was liable for injuries caused on shore by the condition of the cargo on board his ship; the power of a state to place a sales tax on goods sold inside its borders to out-of-state purchasers; the legality of lower rates requested by Eastern railroads for "piggyback" freight service to the South; and the constitutionality of a Kansas law that made the business of "debt adjusting" illegal. None of these issues was spelled out in the orders the Chief Justice had certified and given to the Clerk. The orders said only, for example, "No. 347. Charles Dickson Fair, etc., et al., Petitioners v. James Howard Meredith, etc. October 8, 1962. Petition for Writ of Certiorari to the United States Court of Appeals for the Fifth Circuit denied." The issues were explained only in petitions filed months earlier which were now being denied or granted.

As the Clerk's office worked through the order list that morning, the Justices went ahead with the arguments they had scheduled for the week. After the Presser case had used up its hour, they turned to the case of Charles Townsend, who had been convicted of murder in Chicago in 1955 and sentenced to death. Townsend's case was especially difficult because it involved the relationship between state and federal courts as well as the constitutionality of police procedures. In December, 1953, Jack Boone was found dead in an alley, his head smashed in with a brick. The police received a tip a few days later that Townsend knew something about the crime, and arrested him. A narcotics addict, Townsend began to suffer withdrawal pains several hours after his arrest and asked the police to help him. The police doctor gave him a shot, and a few minutes later Townsend relaxed and began to talk to the detectives. He calmly confessed to four murders and two other crimes. His confession of Boone's murder was the major evidence upon which the State of Illinois convicted him and sentenced him to death. After his conviction was upheld by the state supreme court, Townsend filed a petition for a writ of habeas corpus in the federal district court in Chicago. He said he was being held in jail unconstitutionally because his conviction was based on a confession made under the influence of a truth serum administered without his consent. The federal court refused to conduct a full hearing on Townsend's claim, but decided it by reviewing the record of his case before the Illinois state courts. Those courts had heard the evidence about truth serum fully and fairly, the federal judge said, and had decided against Townsend. The Supreme Court had agreed to review that ruling on two issues. One was whether it was unconstitutional to use Townsend's confession as evidence against him. The other was whether the federal district court should have held a hearing to find out if Townsend really was under the influence of a truth serum. The second was more complicated than the first. If the Justices said it should have held a hearing, the district court, and other federal courts in other cases, would have to hear evidence and decide issues that the state courts had already heard and decided. State judges would take offense at this, regarding it as a slur by the federal courts on their ability and desire to protect the constitutional rights of defendants. On the other hand, Townsend had asked the federal courts to decide whether he was imprisoned in violation of the federal Constitution. If the federal court held no hearing, it would be answering his question by assuming the fairness and accuracy of a hearing it did not conduct.

When 2:30 came around that afternoon, the Court adjourned until 10 o'clock the next morning although the attorneys in the Townsend case had not yet completed their argument. This practice of stopping for the day, or for lunch at noon, in the middle of a case can be disconcerting to the attorneys. On occasion, the Chief Justice has interrupted a lawyer in mid-sentence when the big clock in the courtroom said precisely 2:30. One old story about Chief Justice Hughes is that he once interrupted a lawyer in the middle of the word "to."

chapter 5

GOLDBERG'S FIRST OPINION

WHEN THE COURT MET ON NOVEMBER 5 AFTER ITS FIRST TWO-week recess, Mrs. Goldberg was sitting quietly in the box reserved for relatives and friends of the Justices. Her presence was unusual only because she was so early; the wives of some of the Justices attend Court frequently, but they rarely arrive until after the preliminary activities are over. Within a few minutes, however, it became clear why Mrs. Goldberg was there early that day. When the admissions to the bar were completed, the Chief Justice looked down the bench and nodded to Goldberg. He nodded back, looked down at the bench in front of him, and began to read his first opinion as a Justice of the Supreme Court.[1]

"I have for announcement the opinion and judgment of the Court in Number 42, the United States versus Loew's, Number 43, Loew's versus the United States, and Number 44, C. & C. Super Corporation versus the United States," Goldberg began. The cases were appeals arising out of the application of the antitrust laws to motion picture distributors. They had been argued only twenty days earlier and the speed with which Goldberg had produced the opinion was unusual. Did it mean the new blood on the Court would speed up the processes of justice?

Goldberg described the facts in the cases. Sometimes reading from his opinion, sometimes departing from it, he explained that they involved a practice called "block booking." This meant the distributors would put together a package of movies and offer the entire package for sale to a television station. In each package there would be some very good movies, some medium-quality ones, some "dogs." If the station wanted to show any of the movies, it had to buy the entire package. Goldberg pointed out that this meant a station wanting to show the good movies had to buy the bad ones whether it would use them or not. He used as an example a Washington television station. "To get 'Treasure of the Sierra Madre,' 'Casablanca,' 'Johnny Belinda,' 'Sergeant York,' and 'The Man Who Came to Dinner,'" Goldberg said, "WTOP also had to take such films as 'Nancy Drew, Trouble Shooter,' 'Tugboat Annie Sails Again,' 'Kid Nightingale,' 'Gorilla Man,' and 'Teargas Squad.'" After naming each third-rate film, Goldberg paused and the audience snickered.

As he went on to describe the history of the cases, Goldberg occasionally looked up at the audience and gestured with his hand as if he were on a lecture platform somewhere delivering a speech. He pointed out that a federal court in New York had decided that "block booking" violated Section 1 of the Sherman Act, the nation's basic antitrust law. Loew's and C & C. Super Corporation, both distributors, had appealed. The Justice Department, dissatisfied with the lower court's decree, had also appealed. As Goldberg plunged into the meaning of the antitrust laws and their application to this case, his audience began to stir a little restlessly. The issue, he pointed out, was not whether the distributors had engaged in block booking; they admitted that. The issue was whether this kind of tie-in sale should be judged by the law applicable to sales of copyrighted and patented material or the law applicable to sales of all other products. The difference between the two approaches was vital. If movies were treated as copyrighted materials, block booking would be presumed to restrain trade in violation of the antitrust laws. If they were treated as non-copyrighted material, the tie-in arrangement would be illegal only if each of the distributors was in a position to dominate a major part of the market for all first-run movies. The Justice Department, of course, had argued that motion pictures were copyrighted materials and should be treated as such by the Court. It was clear that block booking restrained trade, since the practice made it impossible for a station to buy only one movie or only first-rate movies. The distributor, of course, contended that the movies should be treated as non-copyrighted materials. Block booking might then be legal because no single sale, and perhaps not even all the sales combined, would affect the whole market for movies. But to win on this argument, the distributors had to convince the Justices that once a movie had been shown in the nation's theaters it lost the unique characteristics associated with copyrighted materials such as books and songs. Goldberg disposed of this point and of the case with one sentence: "A copyrighted feature film does not lose its legal or economic uniqueness because it is shown on a television rather than a movie screen."

Goldberg used almost thirty minutes to announce that decision, and sighs of relief, some of them audible, swept the courtroom when he finished. That afternoon some of his brethren on the bench suggested privately that he not be so long-winded in the future.

There is no particular pattern for announcing decisions to which Goldberg could have conformed and thus avoided the sighs of relief. The oral announcements vary from Justice to Justice, each man selecting the style that he likes best. Frankfurter always appeared to be speaking without notes, and he often delivered an oral opinion that sounded quite unlike his written opinion, although it usually meant the same thing. Whittaker, at the other extreme, read his opinions word for word when he first went on the bench, even including some of the footnotes. Later, he skipped some parts but still never varied from his written words. Brennan combines the two approaches, while Harlan is likely to outline the facts of the case briefly, announce the result, and then add, "Our reasoning is explained in an opinion on file with the Clerk. Anyone interested can read it there." The Court's oral announcements bother many who think the Justices' workload is too heavy for them to spend their time telling a usually half-empty courtroom about decisions they are releasing in written form at the same time. But oral announcements are an old tradition that the Court is reluctant to abandon. And sometimes the oral announcement tells much more about the way a Justice feels than does his written opinion. The written word cannot convey the strong emotion that is occasionally evident in the voice.

Goldberg's first opinion was a typical product of a first-class lawyer and a careful technician. The purpose of his opinion, as with all Supreme Court opinions, was to explain to judges and lawyers the reasoning by which the Court reached its decision. That reasoning is what makes the opinions useful. Technically, the Court's decision in a case applies only to the particular facts of that case and to the parties to it. But the reasoning outlined by the Court gives lower court judges a basis for deciding similar cases. The Court's effectiveness in guiding the development of American law depends on the quality and clarity of its reasoning and the willingness of lower courts to accept it. The lower courts are usually conscientious in their attempts to apply the Supreme Court's reasoning to cases presenting similar questions. But in some fields lower court judges who disagree with the Justices have refused to do so. For example, some federal district court judges and many state court judges in the South have openly flouted Supreme Court decisions on racial discrimination. Like many Southern lawyers they have argued, for instance, that the precedent of the school desegregation decision does not control almost identical cases before them, but applies only to the four school systems involved in that particular decision. It can be argued that their theory is technically correct, but it would destroy the legal system if pursued in all cases. It would mean that almost no case was governed by a prior decision. It would mean that a Supreme Court decision barring one state from collecting an unconstitutional tax would not prevent another state from collecting an identical tax until the Supreme Court said that it was unconstitutional in the other state. Since the Justices are physically able to rule on only a minuscule percentage of all court cases brought in the nation, such a situation would make their work almost useless. The Supreme Court has had experience with this kind of situation in the patent field. The Patent Office and lower courts regularly ignored the strict requirement of novelty that the Court was trying to enforce on patentable inventions, and Justice Jackson said in 1949, "I doubt that the remedy for such Patent Office passion for granting patents is an equally strong passion in this Court for striking them down so that the only patent that is valid is one which this Court has not been able to get its hands on." [2]

Not all Supreme Court opinions, of course, are notable for superb reasoning or brilliant language. Every opinion goes through a process once described by Justice Clark:

> When one starts to write an opinion for the Supreme Court of the United States, he learns the full meaning of the statement of Rufus Choate that "One cannot drop the Greek alphabet to the ground and pick up the Iliad." It takes the most painstaking research and care. . . . In the average case an opinion requires three weeks' work in preparation. When the author concludes that he has an unanswerable document, it is printed in the print shop in the Supreme Court building and circulated to each of the Justices. Then the fur begins to fly. Returns come in, some favorable and many otherwise. In controversial cases, and all have some touches of controversy, the process often takes months. [3]

Goldberg's first opinion had been carefully done. His reasoning followed precisely from point to point and each premise was well supported by past decisions of the Court. This is not always the case. Justice McReynolds was accused of writing opinions by scribbling away until he came to a tough spot in the argument, then drawing a line down the page and starting on a new point. The opinion Chief Justice Hughes wrote in the case upholding invalidation of contract clauses requiring repayment in gold has been compared, not unreasonably, with a train going through the Rocky Mountains—you knew where it had been and where it was going until it entered a tunnel; then everything went black and the train suddenly came out the other end going in the opposite direction.

Writing, of course, is an art, and writing legal opinions is a very specialized form of that art. Not all Justices are good at it. John P. Frank, a careful student of the Court, once divided the writing styles of the Justices into four categories: legal lumpy, legal massive, rock-bottom contemporary, and legal lucid.[4] For an example of "legal lumpy," he quoted Justice Shiras:

> "Whether, if the power of the state to fix and regulate the passenger and freight charges of railroad corporations has not been restricted by contract, there can be found, by judicial inquiry, a limit to such power in the practical effect its exercise may have on the earnings of the corporations, presents a question not free from difficulty."[5]

From an opinion by Justice (later Chief Justice) Stone he took his example of "legal massive":

> "Apart from the cases involving historic public callings, immemorially subject to the closest regulation, this court has sustained regulations of the price in cases where the legislature fixed the charges which grain elevators, Brass v. North Dakota, 153 U.S. 391; Budd v. New York, 143 U.S. 517; and insurance companies might make, German Alliance Ins. Co. v. Lewis, supra; or required miners to be paid per ton of coal unscreened instead of screened, McLean v. Arkansas, supra; Rail & River Coal Co. v. Yaple, 236 U.S. 338; or required employers who paid their men in store orders to redeem them in cash, Knoxville Iron Co. v. Harbison, 183 U.S. 13; Dayton Coal & I. Co. v. Barton, 183

U.S. 23; Keokee Consol. Coke Co. v. Taylor, 234 U.S. 224; or fixed the fees chargeable by attorneys appearing for injured employees before workmen's compensation commissions, Yeiser V. Dysart, 267 U.S. 540; or [and so on]." [6]

His illustration of "rock-bottom contemporary" was from Chief Justice Vinson:

> ". . . our inquiry in this case is narrowed to determining whether this particular offense involves moral turpitude. . . . Without exception, federal and states courts have held that a crime in which fraud is an ingredient involves moral turpitude. . . . In every deportation case where fraud has been proved, federal courts have held that the crime in issue involved moral turpitude. . . . In the state courts, crimes involving fraud have universally been held to involve moral turpitude. . . . The phrase 'crime involving moral turpitude' has been without exception construed to embrace fraudulent conduct." [7]

While only a lawyer, if indeed anyone, could read these passages for enjoyment, some of what Frank called "legal lucid" ranks with the best of American literature. Justice Holmes, a philosopher as much as a jurist, produced many a felicitous phrase during his twenty-nine years on the Court. All lawyers and many laymen know the one from his opinion in *Buck v. Bell*. A Virginia law required the sterilization of a feeble-minded daughter of a feeble-minded mother who had already produced one illegitimate and feeble-minded child. Holmes summed up the facts and the law and added, "Three generations of imbeciles are enough." [8] The law was constitutional. Occasionally, Holmes turned his pen on his fellow Justices. A majority of the Court once upheld the refusal to permit a woman to become a naturalized citizen who would not, because she was a Quaker, swear to bear arms in the country's defense. Holmes concluded his brief dissent with biting sarcasm:

> . . . recurring to the opinion that bars this applicant's way, I would suggest that the Quakers have done their share to

make the country what it is, that many citizens agree with
the applicant's belief, and that I had not supposed hitherto
that we regretted our inability to expel them because they
believe more than some of us do in the teachings of the
Sermon on the Mount.[9]

It is a rare day when such eloquent bitterness appears in a
Supreme Court opinion. The last Justice to produce anything
comparable was Robert H. Jackson, who died in 1954. He had
directed the same skill with words at Justice Black's opinion for
the Court upholding a New Jersey law authorizing local school
boards to pay for the transportation of children to parochial
schools. Black eloquently stated the meaning of the First Amendment and the strict line of separation it drew between church
and state, concluding: "The First Amendment has erected a
wall between church and state. That wall must be kept high and
impregnable. We could not approve the slightest breach. New
Jersey has not breached it here." Jackson's long dissent contained
a literary analogy:

> In fact, the undertones of the [Court's] opinion, advocating
> complete and uncompromising separation of Church from
> State, seem utterly discordant with its conclusion yielding
> support to their commingling in educational matters. The
> case which irresistibly comes to mind as the most fitting
> precedent is that of Julia who, according to Byron's reports,
> "whispering 'I will n'er consent,'—consented." [10]

Of the Justices on the Court when the 1962 term began, only
Black and Stewart had produced styles of opinion writing clearly
their own. Black's opinions, particularly his dissents, were
often explorations in depth into the philosophical and historical
underpinnings of the American system of government. They
were fascinating documents for students of government—lucidly
and literately written—but lawyers often complained they
were excursions into what the law ought to be rather than what
it is. Stewart, the junior member of the Court until White's ap-

pointment, had quickly shown his ability to produce a clever phrase and his delight in using it. When the Court upheld the constitutionality of the Sunday Blue Laws, he filed a very brief dissent:

> Pennsylvania has passed a law which compels an Orthodox Jew to choose between his religious faith and his economic survival. That is a cruel choice. It is a choice which I think no State can constitutionally demand. For me this is not something that can be swept under the rug and forgotten in the interest of enforced Sunday togetherness. I think the impact of this law upon these appellants grossly violates their constitutional right to the free exercise of their religion.[11]

He read the words "enforced Sunday togetherness" with emphasis and a grin.

Not all decisions of the Court, even in cases that have been argued, are announced with opinions. On Tuesday of the week after Goldberg delivered his first opinion—the Court did not sit on Monday, Veterans Day—the Chief Justice announced that the conviction of William Presser was affirmed by an equally divided Court, Goldberg having disqualified himself. Goldberg publicly gave no reason for excusing himself from the case (the Justices rarely do) but it probably lay in his previous connections with the labor movement. The Court did not announce, nor does it ever in such situations, how the eight Justices had voted. But their even division in this case produced a great deal of speculation. Presser had been convicted of mutilating records that a congressional committee wanted to see, and the decision in his case had been expected to indicate the general attitude of the Court's two new members toward the activities of congressional committees. There were substantial questions about the way the committee had conducted the investigation that led to Presser's conviction. Since Goldberg did not vote, the 4-to-4 decision almost certainly meant White had voted with Harlan,

Clark, and Stewart to affirm the conviction; Warren, Black, Douglas, and Brennan could be assumed to have voted together and for reversal. White, therefore, might be expected to join the wing of the Court that would permit congressional committees wide latitude in their investigations. If this hypothesis was correct, Goldberg would cast the crucial vote in future cases growing out of congressional investigations and would determine the direction to be taken by the law in this controversial area.

On the same day the Court upheld Presser's conviction, the Justices frustrated the nation's tax experts by refusing to hear four cases involving the meaning of the word "gift" in the Internal Revenue Code. The question in all four cases was the same, but diametrically opposite answers had been given by the lower federal courts. Since one of the fundamental tasks of the Court is to resolve such differences, the cases had seemed to demand a hearing and decision by the Justices. But, with only Warren dissenting, they refused to do so. The problem in these cases was whether a corporation was making a "gift" to the widow of one of its officers when it paid her a substantial sum of money after his death. For some years prior to 1960, the Tax Court had ruled that such payments were gifts and were not taxable income. That year the Supreme Court had grappled with a case involving the meaning of "gift," coming up with an opinion that almost no one thought clarified matters. After that the Tax Court and one federal circuit court of appeals decided that under the Supreme Court's decision such payments to widows were not gifts but were additional compensation for the services the deceased officers had rendered to the corporation. They ruled that the payments were income upon which the widows must pay income taxes. The courts of appeals in two other circuits, however, had decided the same Supreme Court decision meant that such payments were gifts. As a result of these conflicting decisions and the refusal of the Supreme Court to resolve them, the impact of the national tax laws on identical payments to widows would depend on where the widows happened to live.

As usual, there was no explanation from the Justices for the refusal to hear the cases. One reason may have been their great dislike for tax law; none of them was a specialist in that very technical field, and their decisions in it almost always draw heavy criticism from the tax law experts. Another may have been a feeling that the Supreme Court ought not spend its time interpreting an ambiguously written law when Congress is in a better position to clarify it. Perhaps some of the Justices yearned for action along the lines suggested by Dean Erwin Griswold of the Harvard Law School in 1960:

> But basically, the Court's problem comes from the number of cases of extreme complexity and difficulty which, in the public interest, have to be decided. Since these cases are inescapable, the Court should be protected from having to decide other cases of lesser magnitude. A number of years ago I urged that there should be a separate Court of Tax Appeals to which all nonconstitutional tax cases should go for final decision. That seemed a good idea to me then, and it seems even better now. The same approach could be taken in a considerable number of other areas when constitutional questions are not involved.[12]

Griswold's comments highlighted the broad range of matters that eventually reach the Supreme Court. Those involving the broad questions of public policy and the meaning of certain provisions of the Constitution are the ones that reach public attention. But these make up only a small fraction of the Court's work. It spends much time on questions in three other areas that are never as exciting and dramatic but are just as important. One of these areas, perhaps the most crucial in a federal system of government, is balancing competing demands of the national and state governments: Does a particular state tax interfere with free commerce between the states? Does a particular state law conflict with acts of Congress in the same field? How do state laws comport with federal constitutional guarantees of individual rights? Justice Holmes regarded this as the most fundamental part of the Supreme Court's work. A federal system is the most difficult kind of government to operate successfully, and without a body to settle the disputes that arise inside it, the system might fly apart because of internal conflicts. Holmes once said:

> I do not think the United States would come to an end if we lost our power to declare an Act of Congress void. I do think the Union would be imperiled if we could not make that declaration as to the laws of the several States. For one in my place sees how often a local policy prevails with those who are not trained to national views and how often action is taken that embodies what the Commerce Clause was meant to end.[13]

Beyond questions of that type, the Court must often decide what Congress meant when it passed a law that is clearly constitutional: What is a gift? Does certain conduct by a labor union violate the national labor laws? Congress rarely writes laws that are crystal clear. Laws are written in generalities, and it is the courts—ultimately the Supreme Court—which must decide whether Congress intended for these generalities to apply to the peculiar facts of a specific situation. As Professor Freund once put it, Congress makes law wholesale while the Court makes law retail. A third kind of case that the Supreme Court frequently encounters involves the procedures used in lower federal courts. These are essentially technicalities, of little interest except to lawyers, yet they can determine who wins and who loses a lawsuit.

Cases involving each of these areas are before the Court every month. In the three-day period following their action in the Presser and the tax cases, the Justices heard arguments on six different issues. They spent the remainder of Tuesday and part of Wednesday on the Arizona-California water dispute. After lunch Wednesday, the Justices turned to a narrow procedural question: Was a notice of appeal, filed while the trial court was considering a motion to vacate its judgment, valid? Later in the afternoon the Court started in on a matter of great interest to law enforcement officers: Could a federal court block a state official from testifying in a state criminal trial about information gotten while cooperating with federal officials in an illegal arrest and search? On Thursday the Court listened to arguments on three more new questions: Must South Carolina's courts enforce a Virginia court order affecting the custody of children living in South Carolina regardless of what the South Carolina judges think is best for the children? Can a gasoline company cut its prices to a single service station operator, in order to help him defend himself in a price war, without violating the antitrust laws? Can New York constitutionally condemn property after giving notice of its action only by posting notices in the area to be condemned and running newspaper advertisements, or must it make a real effort to inform the property owners? On Friday the Justices went into conference to decide how they would rule on these questions and on the dozens of other matters before them.

chapter 6
ETHICS AND LAW

EARLY IN NOVEMBER CHIEF JUSTICE WARREN SLIPPED OFF TO
New York to deliver the major address at the Louis Marshall
Award dinner of the Jewish Theological Seminary of America.
It was not unusual for the Chief to make a speech; he and the
other Justices make a good many of them each year. But this
speech was unusual. It was front-page news in New York the
next morning, and Warren's office was flooded with requests
for reprints. His first paragraph set the tone of what he had to
say:

> In civilized life, Law floats in a sea of Ethics. Each is
> indispensable to civilization. Without Law, we should be at
> the mercy of the least scrupulous; without Ethics, Law
> could not exist. Without ethical consciousness in most
> people, lawlessness would be rampant. Yet without Law,
> civilization could not exist, for there are always people who
> in the conflict of human interest, ignore their responsi-
> bility to their fellow man.[1]

Until recently, Warren pointed out, no one dreamed of consulting an expert before getting married or divorced. Now, the
services of professional marriage counselors are widely sought.
Perhaps, the Chief Justice suggested, the nation needs counselors
on ethics to advise those faced with major decisions on what
course of action would be morally right and what would be
morally wrong. The Chief Justice mentioned an example used
by Judge Rifkind of what happens when a major corporation

decides to enter a new business venture. The Board of Directors meets, and the experts are called in to report. One by one, the engineer, the treasurer, the salesman, the personnel manager, the lawyers use their expertise to explore the implications of the venture. ". . . all kinds of experts are present," Warren said, "except for one expert—the expert in ethics, who can suggest whether the whole plan as conceived was socially useful, was right, was appropriate under the circumstances. . . .

"Is it fantastic," he asked, "to suggest that there is an urgent need in our troubled times for the development of the profession of the counselor in ethics, having the same relation to inter-personal conduct, beyond the Law, that the lawyer has to conduct that is subject to review in the courts?"

The Chief Justice answered his own question. "The developments of this century indicate that this need is no fantasy at all. . . . The search for ethics has been pursued since ancient times. Is it not obvious that all of us need ethics counselors?"

The Chief Justice's comments raised more problems than they solved. Underlying his suggestion that Americans needed help in making the right decisions were several troubling questions: Have Americans become so confused by the complexities of modern life that they base their decisions on something other than what is right? Has the emphasis on the idea that the nation lives under a rule of law brought people to believe that whatever is legal is also right? How closely do our laws conform to our ideals of what is right and what is just? Have religious leaders lost their standing as spokesmen for morals in their communities, either through their own failings or through those of modern society?

Answers to those questions would tell much about the morality of Americans. They were questions that had long bothered many detached observers of modern life. But in recent years they were questions that had become increasingly troubling to those who watched the drama of everyday life played out in the courtroom, for it is to the courtroom that many Americans come seeking an answer as to what is right. Is it right to take short cuts on income tax returns? Is it right to pad expense accounts? Is it right to mislead someone into marriage? Is it right to buy property cheaply knowing the seller is unaware of its true value? Is it right to obey—barely—the letter but avoid the spirit of laws governing business? All too often Warren had seen those questions underlying disputes before the courts. The answer the courts give is directed not to the question of what is right but to the question of what is legal. Yet that answer is often taken to provide the sanction of morality to a questionable practice. Law and ethics, the Chief Justice pointed out, are not synonymous. "Not everything which is wrong can be outlawed, although everything which is outlawed, is, in our Western conception, wrong." Society could not—witness the prohibition era—put all its changing ethical standards in statutes. "Indeed, we feel that we should not. One of the purposes of civilized society is to produce men capable of making righteous decisions and adhering to them. To compel obedience in all areas of life would be to reduce men to automata, incapable of making their own moral decisions and defeating the very purpose of civilization itself."

The same problems had been troubling other members of the Court. A year earlier, Justice Clark had suggested to a group of corporation lawyers that they ought to reconsider the role they play in formulating business policy. In addition to advising on the law, he said, these lawyers should help the business community "develop a corporate conscience." Clark's comments resulted from his reflections about the great conspiracy in the electrical manufacturing business to evade the antitrust laws. For years before they were caught, top officials of twenty-nine firms had conspired to fix prices in clear violation of the law. Some of them, leaders in their churches and communities, admitted later that they had known what they were doing was illegal but accepted it as a fact of corporate life. They had brushed aside whatever ethical problems may have existed, in their efforts to increase the earnings of their companies.

It was with all this in mind that the Chief Justice suggested the creation of a new profession of advisors on ethics. Ministers, he said, already were overburdened, but they or someone else must take on the task of analyzing the problems of the individual in the modern world. He said:

> I can conceive of a school dedicated to the purpose of training such professionals, becoming the center of research in the field of moral standards, trying to resuscitate the glories of Aristotle, of Maimonides, of St. Thomas Aquinas and of Spinoza; and yet different from their ways of research in its concern with concrete problems of conduct, and training people to help themselves and to help others solve concrete issues of personal behavior. . . .
>
> The businessman, the labor leader, the politician or the college executive may fear that with such an ethics counselor at his elbow, he might be discouraged from undertakings he has much at heart. But what in fact is the alternative to such discouragement of what is contrary to the public good, or the long range good of mankind, or to simple compassion for the individual? Is it to proceed headlong as we are proceeding now, deifying Success as the sole goal in life, and constantly putting greater emphasis on quantity rather than on quality in what we achieve? And if we proceed in this manner, is it not obvious that within a reasonable time—not too long—the whole world, emulating us Americans, even if it does not love us, will adopt the very standards which we have adopted? And when that happens, will it not turn out that we, like Brutus, Hamlet, Macbeth and King Lear, have brought on ourselves quite avoidable disaster?

This speech marked one of those rare occasions when an American public official chose to talk about the deep philosophical and moral problems that confront the nation. Most officials are men of action, too busy with their daily tasks to reflect on the basic problems of society. But Justices of the Supreme Court, cut off by their jobs from much of the pressure of daily life, are able to contemplate the philosophy that underlies America and the tremendous impact with which modern technology has affected the concepts written into the Constitution. They have an unusual opportunity to participate in, and yet be detached from, the many problems that superficially involve only enforcement of the laws but in reality cut deep into more fundamental issues.

The speech told a great deal about Earl Warren. Ten years earlier he would never have dreamed of making it. In the fall of 1962 he was still the "big, hearty, healthy Californian" whom newspapers had mentioned twenty years before as a likely Republican candidate for President. But internally Earl Warren was a different man now. The imprint of the Supreme Court on him had been deeper than his imprint on it. He was still the glad-handing politician with a firm handshake and quick smile. But the opportunities to meet people were fewer now as he lived a "sedentary life." That life gave a man a chance to read and reflect that is normally denied to the active politician, and Warren's reflections appeared from time to time in his speeches.

Sitting in his chambers one day with a group of newsmen, the Chief Justice recalled some of the changes in his life a telephone call had made. The call, from President Eisenhower, came on the last Tuesday night in September of 1953. Warren, then in his fourth term as Governor of California, was told his appointment as Chief Justice of the United States would be sent to the Senate the next day. The Court's new term would begin the following Monday, President Eisenhower said. Could Warren be there when it did? "I worked night and day—Wednesday, Thursday, Friday and Saturday," Warren recalled. "I got on a plane Sunday afternoon, got here Sunday night and was on the bench Monday morning. It was a great change."

Adjusting to the quiet, contemplative life of a Supreme Court

Justice was difficult. Warren said, "It would be a shock to any-body to make that change as quickly as I did." Like Goldberg, he found his staff strangely small. As Governor, he had many assistants and he did "very little real spade work." Others wrote his speeches, did his research, and executed his orders. As Chief Justice, he had one secretary (he soon added a second), three law clerks, and two "very old" messengers, one of whom had worked for the Court before it moved from its old quarters in the basement of the Capitol back in 1935. Much of the task of research and writing could not be delegated. Then, there was the change in social activities. As Governor, he was on the road almost every night, making speeches and repairing political fences. "We go out very little now as a matter of choice," he said. "I find you either have to stay out of social activities or go over your head. I just can't do this kind of work and be out a number of nights a week at social affairs." One problem, he admitted, was that people asked questions about the Court and its decisions that he should not answer. "If you went to all these affairs, you'd be in trouble," he said. "I don't go."

The greatest change, however, was from being a politician to being a judge. "I find it different—greatly different. No one could have a background of such activities as I had without oc-casionally having a nostalgic feeling for it, particularly when there are exciting things going on in the country and in the world." A few minutes later, to make sure no one misunderstood, he added, "I'm not one who feels I'm missing out on politics, because I had a great many years of it. After I had been Gover-nor of California for eleven years, I was ready to do something else. It's a hard life to be in politics for eleven years. Sometimes now I wonder how I got through all those years." But, watching Warren carefully, one could occasionally detect a longing for that old political arena. He let himself go for just a moment one day when he was talking to Saul Pett of the Associated Press. Did Warren ever wish he could defend the Court against its critics? The Chief's dark blue eyes lighted up and his big hand slapped the desk. "Oh boy!" he said. "Sometimes it makes you cringe to see what other people write and say." Then he disappeared back into the quiet, detached shell that almost all the Justices wear almost all the time.

What of the impact of Warren on the Supreme Court? It was the "Warren Court" now, and its critics referred to him as the leader of that bunch of judges who were ruining the nation. Warren had come to it at a turning point in American constitutional law. The school desegregation cases were already before the Court when he arrived in the fall of 1953, and other issues, almost as controversial and just as difficult, were coming over the horizon. The first major opinion he chose to write for the Court was the one holding racial segregation in the public schools unconstitutional, and the barrage of bitter attacks began promptly. Throughout his nine years, Warren had been a lightning rod for the Court, absorbing much of the criticism that might have been directed with equal or greater fervor and justice at his colleagues. Much of the criticism was hard to take, based as it was on a complete misunderstanding or no understanding at all of what the Court was doing. But Warren had restrained his natural political instinct to fight back; the Court's tradition permitted no such rebuttals. As a result, he ignored an essay contest sponsored by the John Birch Society early in 1962 on "Why Earl Warren Should Be Impeached." He also ignored the billboards that sprouted across the country calling for his impeachment and the mass of critical letters that flowed into the Court. He even ignored a threat on his life made in 1958 after the Little Rock schools were desegregated. The only difference that threat made was that the guards at the Court were increased and police kept watch over him and Frankfurter, who had also been threatened, for several weeks.

Warren's opinions at first bore the stamp of a man who was more a public figure than a judge or philosopher. His opinion in the school desegregation cases was short and clear, devoid of legalisms and complex reasoning. It was written with the knowledge that it would be reprinted and widely read by the general public, for it must go down in history as the most important single action of the Court since Reconstruction. But the fact it was such a document brought Warren criticism from some legal scholars. The criticism—that it lacked careful craftsmanship of the sort that had marked the work of two of his three immediate predecessors, Chief Justices Stone and Hughes —was substantiated in some of his later opinions. His opinion in the contempt-of-Congress case involving John T. Watkins went far beyond the legal issues in the case and delved into the proper role of congressional investigating committees. The opinion was useful in one way; it brought on a wave of discussion about the activities and procedures of those committees. But it was also mischievous because it misled the public about what the Court was actually deciding and because it opened the Court to valid criticism—in essence, that it was not minding its own business— which was immediately picked up by the Court's enemies and carried to extremes. Warren produced the same kind of sweeping opinion two years later when the Court struck down the Defense Department's Industrial Security Program on a narrow ground. In later years, however, his opinions lost some of their sweeping language and took on a considerable degree of analytic polish.

Despite the influence a Chief Justice can have on his Court through his prerogatives of speaking first on each case in conference and assigning the authorship of the Court's opinion when he is in the majority, the influence Warren has had inside the Court can be easily overestimated. In a Court composed of, as Frankfurter once said, "nine free men," it is difficult to think that any one man dominates the group, particularly a group composed of such strong-minded men as Black, Frankfurter, Douglas, Harlan, and Clark.

In his role as Chief Justice, however, Warren brought several innovations to the Court. He turned a traditionally dull and boring admissions ceremony into a brisk and pleasant daily interlude. Warren speaks individually to each of the twenty or thirty lawyers who appear on a normal day, often saying, "Mr. ———, I congratulate you and welcome you to the bar of this Court." He gave a feeling of warmth to the marble and velvet chamber where cold dignity often reigns. Warren also worked hard to improve the administration of all federal courts. He lobbied on Capitol Hill for bills to increase the number of federal judges, and he spurred lower court judges to greater work in an effort to make the federal courts models of efficiency rather than horrors of delay.

The warm, smiling public picture of Warren, the politician, may sometimes be deceiving. Some of his employees consider him a slave driver who shows little concern for their personal welfare. His law clerks often work the longest hours of all and are regularly in their offices late in the evenings and on Saturdays and Sundays. Warren showed his temper early in 1962 in two of the most extraordinary displays of judicial anger ever witnessed in Washington. It had been clear for some time that he did not like the tactics often engaged in by Justice Frankfurter during oral argument. Frankfurter often treated attorneys as if they were his old law students, driving them into verbal corners and humiliating them with questions beyond their ability to answer. There were days when other Justices had difficulty asking their questions because the attorneys were too busy coping with Frankfurter. More than once, Warren had broken into these exchanges to urge that a line of questioning be dropped.

Frankfurter had apparently also driven the Chief Justice to desperation by expanding his written opinions when he announced them orally. Frankfurter did that in a routine case one day in March, 1962, with the remark, not in his written opinion,

"I know what the Court has said but I don't understand the meaning of it." Warren snapped back with a restatement of his view of the case—but no one will find it in the official reports, because not a word was recorded. Just a month later, Frankfurter lectured his fellow Justices for upsetting a murder conviction. They were "turning a criminal appeal into a quest for error," he said bitterly. When he finished, the Chief Justice leaned forward and said, "I must say that although I did not file an opinion in this case, that was not the dissenting opinion that was filed. This is a lecture. It was a closing argument by the prosecutor to the jury. It is properly made, perhaps, in the conference room but not in the courtroom. As I understand it, the purpose of reporting an opinion in the Court is to inform the public and not for the purpose of degrading this Court. I assure you that if any opinion had said those things I would have much to say myself. But unfortunately the record will not show it."[2]

Such public exchanges are rare. How often they occur in the conference room no one but the nine Justices knows and none of them ever tells.

chapter 7

THE FIRST SHARP DISAGREEMENTS

THE MORNING OF JANUARY 14, 1963, WAS CLEAR AND COLD IN Washington. The President was to deliver his State of the Union message to a joint session of Congress at noon. The Supreme Court had broken with its normal routine and announced that it would recess so the Justices could walk across the Capitol grounds and join Congress to hear the President's speech. Other affairs of state had crowded the Court out of the newspapers for several weeks. The Cuban crisis had come and gone. An election had been held and the new Congress had just begun work.

In the basement of the Court building that morning it was clear very early that this would be an unusual day. The small printing plant in one corner of the building had been busy all weekend, and now Bert Whittington, the Court's public affairs officer, pulled a cart loaded with stacks of opinions into the elevator, rode up one floor, and trundled it around to his office. As he stacked the papers away in a locked cabinet, one reporter after another wandered in and asked, "How's it look, Bert?" The noncommittal reply was, "Pretty good." Later, as a Justice announced the Court's opinion upstairs in the courtroom, Whittington would distribute copies of all the opinions in that case to the waiting press. In past years the Court had announced only a handful of decisions each Monday, letting most of them accumulate until late May and early June. This time it looked as if the Justices had been working hard over the Christmas holidays to cut into the backlog of cases.

That morning the group of lawyers awaiting admission was dominated by twenty from nearby Montgomery County, Maryland, who were sponsored by their state attorney general, Thomas B. Finan. When he had welcomed them all to the Supreme Court bar, the Chief Justice looked down the bench toward Justice Goldberg. Goldberg, bent over the papers on his desk, missed the nod until he was nudged by Justice Stewart. Then he looked up abruptly and began: "I am privileged to announce the opinion of the Court in Number 56, Sun Oil Company versus the Federal Trade Commission."[1] This was the case involving selective price-cutting, the practice by which major gasoline companies helped filling stations compete in local price wars, usually started by stations not affiliated with any major distributor and selling non-standard brands of gasoline. The Federal Trade Commission had ruled that the practice was illegal under the Robinson-Patman Act's bar against price discrimination that tends to lessen competition. This was so, it said, because a large oil company could absorb the loss incurred by one station in order to drive competing stations out of business. The Sun Oil Company had contended that its price cuts to one dealer in Jacksonville, Florida, were legal under the law's exemption of good-faith efforts to meet competition. In the Court's view, neither the FTC nor Sun Oil was clearly right. Goldberg said that if Sun had cut its prices to meet similar cuts made by another gasoline wholesaler, its action would be legal. But if it had cut them solely to help its station meet the prices offered by another station which had no similar help from its wholesaler, the cuts would be illegal. With that, the Court upheld the FTC's decision but said Sun Oil could ask the Commission to reopen the case if it had evidence to show what situation actually existed. Goldberg made a point of saying that the Justices were not themselves approving the wisdom of such a distinction. "It's not our business as a Court to substitute our economic predilections for a decision made by Congress."

Goldberg described the case in some detail, gesturing as he spoke and again obviously enjoying the opportunity to confront an audience, even the sparse one on hand that morning. The abrupt change from the active public life of a Secretary of Labor to the quiet, withdrawn existence of a Justice was showing. Mrs. Goldberg was again in the courtroom to hear her husband. Soon she was joined by Marjorie Brennan, whose husband had the second decision to be announced that morning. It was in the case from Virginia involving its laws against the solicitation of business by lawyers.[2] The NAACP had been encouraging Negroes in Virginia to bring lawsuits against school segregation, referring them to lawyers on its staff or on the staff of the NAACP Legal and Educational Defense Fund and then paying much of the cost of the litigation. Virginia said this put the NAACP in the business of promoting lawsuits. While practices of this general type are outlawed by most states through statutes prohibiting solicitation of business by lawyers and control of litigation by anyone other than the "real party in interest," Virginia had recently broadened its statute to be sure the activities of the NAACP were outlawed. The NAACP, Virginia said, solicited business for its lawyers and then controlled the litigation. The Court said that, as it was applied to the NAACP, the statute was unconstitutional. Brennan explained that the encouragement the NAACP and its lawyers gave to Negroes by urging them to contest in court various denials of their constitutional rights fell under the protection of the Free Speech Clause of the First Amendment. He said the Virginia law presented "the gravest danger of smothering all discussion looking to the eventual institution of litigation on behalf of the rights of members of an unpopular minority." This was so because the law made it a crime to advise a person of his rights and then refer him to a particular lawyer. Not all the Justices agreed with Brennan. White, who also thought that the law was unconstitutional, dissented from parts of Brennan's opinion. Harlan, joined by Clark and Stewart, disagreed totally. He said the Court was treating Virginia's objection to the NAACP's activities in "too facile" a manner, and that the decision "will cut deeply into accepted notions of state regulatory power over the practice of law."

This was a decision that illustrated the strain on the law brought about by the civil rights crisis. Virginia had passed the law as part of its unsuccessful program of "massive resistance" to desegregation. The rest of its resistance package had been struck down as unconstitutional either by its own supreme court or by lower federal courts. But this law had given those courts trouble. In the context of its passage, the law was clearly aimed only at the activities of the NAACP; it was drafted with the purpose of driving the NAACP out of the state. If it had been held constitutional, the law would have made much more diffi-cult the task of informing poor, illiterate Negroes of their rights and helping them exercise those rights. In addition, such a ruling might have enabled Virginia to disbar several of the Negro attorneys in the state who were most active in civil rights cases. Just as the intentions of the legislature are important in deter-mining the proper application of a law of unquestioned constitu-tionality, they can be weighty evidence of the unconstitution-ality of a law carefully drafted in innocuous language. Vir-ginia's law, passed in another era with entirely different aims, might have stood the test of constitutionality. Although this was the rationale relied upon by Douglas in a concurring opin-ion, it was not mentioned by Brennan in the majority opinion. He had made the decision turn on another ground, but without the context explained by Douglas, Brennan's opinion was un-persuasive.

It was 11 o'clock by the time Brennan completed his an-nouncement of the Court's decision. Elizabeth Black, the Jus-tice's strikingly attractive former secretary whom he had married six years after the death of his first wife, joined the other two wives in the reserved box.

Brennan also had the third decision of the day. It was in the first case argued when Court began in October—that of Wong Sun and James Wah Toy.[3] As Brennan began to read his opinion, those listeners who were given copies flipped through the pages to find out how the case had come out. They quickly learned that the Court had reversed the two convictions by a 5-to-4 vote and had established the new rule in criminal cases that Edward Bennett Williams had urged. A dissatisfied look crossed the face of Solicitor General Cox as he discovered the result. The Court's majority had agreed with the Ninth Circuit Court of Appeals that the arrests of both men were illegal. All the officers knew when they arrested Toy, Brennan said, was that a man who had never been an informer before, Hom Way, said a "Blackie Toy," who had a laundry on Leavenworth Street, had sold him narcotics. There was no evidence to tie "Blackie Toy" with James Wah Toy except the fact that he also operated a laundry on Leavenworth Street, but it was called "Oye's" laundry, not "Toy's." This amount of information, Brennan said, did not meet the constitutional requirement that the police have "probable cause" before making an arrest.

The Court's ruling about the legality of Toy's arrest was only its starting point. The crucial part was its decision about the admissibility of the evidence resulting from that arrest. The evidence consisted of statements Toy made in his bedroom immediately afterward, the narcotics seized in Johnny Yee's room to which Toy then directed the agents, and the unsigned confessions Toy and Wong Sun had made to Agent Wong several days later. Brennan dealt with each of these bits of evidence in turn as the case became even more complex than it had seemed.

The statements Toy made in his bedroom could not be used as evidence, Brennan said, because they were the "fruits" of the illegal arrest. Years before, the Court had held that evidence seized in an illegal search cannot be used to incriminate the person from whom it was seized. Originally, the rule barred only physical, tangible evidence and the statements by police officers of what they had seen during their illegal invasion of a man's home or office. In fact, in 1928 the Court had ruled specifically that the Fourth Amendment did not protect verbal evidence the way it did material evidence. But that decision, on a 5-to-4 vote with Justices Holmes, Brandeis, Butler, and Stone dissenting, had been eroded over the years. Taking note of that erosion, Brennan said that a decision of the Court three years earlier indicated that the Fourth Amendment "may protect against the overhearing of verbal statements as well as against the more traditional seizure of 'papers and effects.' " There was no reason for the Court to make a distinction between the two, he said, so far as the rule barring illegally seized evidence from trials was concerned. "Nor do the policies underlying the exclusionary rule invite any logical distinction between physical and verbal evidence. Either in terms of deterring lawless conduct by federal officers . . . or of closing the doors of the federal courts to any use of evidence unconstitutionally obtained . . . the danger in relaxing the exclusionary rules in the case of verbal evidence would seem too great to warrant introducing such a distinction." As a result, Brennan said, the bedroom statements of Toy were inadmissible as evidence against him.

Turning to the narcotics found in Yee's room, Brennan said these, too, should not have been used as evidence against Toy. The prosecutor had admitted the agents would never have found them except for Toy's statements in his bedroom. Thus, the narcotics had come into the government's hands solely because of the illegal action of the agents.

With Toy's original statements and the narcotics out of the case, the only evidence remaining against him was the unsigned statements he and Wong Sun had made to Agent Wong after their arrest. Wong Sun's statement could not be used against

Toy because of a line of earlier precedents barring the use of an out-of-court declaration made after arrest against the declarant's partner in crime. That left only Toy's unsigned statement and it, alone, could not support a conviction without corroborative evidence.

That disposed of Toy's conviction, but the Court still had to rule on Wong Sun's appeal. He, too, had been arrested illegally, Brennan said, but that fact had no bearing on his appeal. His illegal arrest produced no evidence. Even though the narcotics seized in Yee's room could not be used as evidence against Toy, they could be used against Wong Sun. The difference was that the agents seized that material because they had illegally invaded Toy's rights; Wong Sun could not claim the narcotics were seized through any invasion of his own rights. Thus the narcotics could be used to corroborate Wong Sun's unsigned statement. But because the judge had also relied on what Toy had said to corroborate Wong Sun's statement, Wong Sun was also entitled to a new trial. Toy's statement could not be used against Wong Sun just as Wong Sun's statement could not be used against Toy.

The case was incredibly complex but it illustrated the rules the Court has developed to protect the rights of individuals. If the government agents had obtained a warrant for Toy's arrest or one to search his room or one to search Yee's room, the case would have been quite different. But their failure to do that or to be sure they had "probable cause" to arrest Toy had resulted in this tangle.

In a sharply worded dissent, Clark ripped into Brennan's opinion. The Court had made a "Chinese puzzle" out of a simple case, he said, and "dashed to pieces the heretofore standards of probable cause necessary . . . to make an arrest." The knowledge police had when they went to Toy's laundry was sufficient to justify his arrest and it was reinforced when Toy ran from the door. Because the arrests were legal there was no need for the

Court to go into the question of whether the statements should have been excluded from their trials. Clark's opinion was joined by Harlan, Stewart, and White.

The two Kennedy appointees had split in the first 5-to-4 decision of the term. It was possible, but dangerous, to predict from that division that Goldberg would join Black, Warren, Brennan, and Douglas in giving broad scope to the guarantees of the Bill of Rights, while White would adopt the narrower view that had theretofore prevailed. This was the issue that most seriously divided the Court at the time the two new Justices were appointed. It was the views of those four about the Bill of Rights that precipitated complaints that the Court was elevating individual rights so high as to hinder the effective solution of crime.

With Toy and Wong Sun disposed of, the Court turned to a minor tax fraud case involving the Shotwell Manufacturing Company of Chicago.[4] The company and two of its officers had been convicted of failing to report income they received during 1945 and 1946 on black-market sales of the candy they made. The basic issue in their appeal was whether the Fifth Amendment's guarantee against self-incrimination barred the use of confessions made by the two officers to an Internal Revenue agent. They had told the agent that they had deliberately misstated the facts on their tax returns to conceal their black-market operations. They told him they were making the confession under a Treasury Department policy then in effect that no taxpayer would be prosecuted criminally who told the Revenue Service he had cheated before an investigation into his returns was begun. When government agents checked the story, they found that the men were telling only half the truth. They neglected to confess that they and a third man had pocketed between $300,000 and $400,000, said in their confession to have been spent on supplies. Because they had lied in their confession, the government claimed, they could not benefit from the voluntary disclosure policy. The defendants claimed they would never have told the government agents anything if the policy had not existed, and argued that since they had relied upon the policy, the government should not be allowed to disregard it and prosecute them. For a majority of the Court, the government's argument was more persuasive. Harlan announced their opinion, which accepted the principle that if the government used promises to persuade a man to confess, it could not use his confession against him in violation of the promises. If the two men had told the truth, the Fifth Amendment's guarantee against self-incrimination would have protected them. But the two men had given a false story designed to obtain immunity from prosecution and yet to conceal the true amount of the taxes they owed. In that situation, Harlan concluded, the confession was not the result of the government's promise of immunity but was the result of the desire of the two men to avoid both prosecution and taxation. The two must serve their three-year prison terms.

The tax case created little interest among observers until Black began to read a dissent. He and Warren and Douglas did not agree with the Court's views. As Black spoke, his voice began to rise. "There's no past opinion of this Court, weak or strong, unanimous or nonunanimous, or any other kind of opinion which supports what the Court is doing here today," he said with his anger growing more obvious. As he spoke, Mary Clark, Mary Ann Stewart, and Marion White came into the courtroom and looked up in surprise at the sound of his voice. What was wrong with this case, Black said, was that an agent of the government had assured the two men they would not be prosecuted if they confessed. The Fifth Amendment forbids the use of any confession obtained as a result of such a promise. To evade this the Court had reached the "astonishing conclusion" that the promise had not induced the confession. Its way of reaching that conclusion "lops off a significant part of the protection the Fifth Amendment has always been thought to offer." Slightly flushed, and pausing to emphasize words not in his written opinion, Black concluded, "This weakening of the Bill of Rights is being done by this Court, not by the amending process, on this 14th day of January, 1963. We would not do the Fifth Amendment this way."

There was no sound in the courtroom except for Black's voice as he finished. The audience, realizing the depth of feeling with which he spoke, was spellbound. Then Harlan moved in his chair and began to speak again. "I also have for announcement the opinion and judgment of the Court in . . ." he began. The tension broke and the audience stirred. A few minutes later the Chief Justice recessed Court so the Justices and their wives could go to the Capitol and listen to the President's speech.

As the Justices left the courtroom they chatted amiably. The sharp, almost bitter, disagreement that had dramatized the morning on the bench seemed to have disappeared. A rough fighter in the courtroom, Black was a kindly man off the bench. He had voiced many harsh criticisms in the past of the views of Frankfurter, his principal antagonist on the Court, and now he was voicing them against the views of Harlan. But when Frankfurter left the Court, Black said to him, "We're going to miss you on the Court, because we need you. When some of my friends say to me, things will be easier on the Court now, I tell them they couldn't be more wrong."[5] The same kind of feeling apparently exists between Black and Harlan.

The history of the Supreme Court in the years since the end of World War II has been, in large part, the history of Frankfurter and Black. The two men, who were the senior Justices in experience on the Court after the retirement of Justice Reed in 1957, had adopted sharply differing philosophies. Frankfurter was the exponent of judicial restraint, Black the exponent of judicial activism. These two approaches to the Court's role in government were the opposite sides of a coin. Charles Black, a professor of law at Yale, once wrote:

You may say that the line between prudent restraint and courageous decisiveness is hard to draw. Of course it is hard to draw; it is impossible to draw with anything like concise logical precision. In this it resembles the line between not eating enough and eating too much. The essential thing to keep in mind is that sickness and even death inhere both in malnutrition and in obesity. The sloganeers of judicial restraint see only one danger. They are like the man in Chesterton who loved the noble color red, and who proceeded to paint the town—houses, lampposts, and all—uniformly with this color.[6]

Charles Black, it should be added, has been a Hugo Black supporter in the seemingly endless battle among the law professors in speeches and in the pages of the law reviews.

Upon Frankfurter's retirement, the task of rebutting Black's philosophy logically fell to Harlan. Harlan agreed with Frankfurter's views on judicial restraint and on the Bill of Rights. His writing style was careful and precise, yet it could be forceful. He was already unique in the Court's history as the only descendant of a Justice to become one. His grandfather, John Marshall Harlan, served twenty-nine years as a Justice and his dissenting opinions in the late nineteenth century in segregation cases were now being adopted by the Court as the correct view of the law.

These two men, Black and Harlan, were a study in contrasts. Before being appointed to the Court, Black was a politician's politician and Harlan a lawyer's lawyer. Black grew up in the rural South, Harlan in New York City. Black never finished college, Harlan was a distinguished student and a Rhodes scholar. Harlan looked like a Justice—tall, serious-faced, dignified—while Black looked more like the lively little old man next door.

If Frankfurter's ranking among the outstanding jurists of the twentieth century seemed to him like a dream, Black might well say that his ranking in that category seemed miraculous. The trail he had followed from a rural farmhouse in Clay County,

Alabama, to the Supreme Court had wound through strange places and strange events. It certainly was not a path one would expect to lead to the Court. Black's life was full of paradoxes. Once a poorly educated youth whose two-year law school course ended when he was twenty, at seventy-six he was a broadly educated man whose writings showed an intimate knowledge of philosophy, history, and literature. Once a hard-hitting, highly partisan politician who championed President Roosevelt's plan to "pack" the Court, now he was a thoughtful jurist who staunchly defended the Court, ignored the bitter attacks on himself, and used his remarkable talent for political infighting only inside the Court. Once an eager congressional investigator who ran roughshod over the rights of witnesses, now he regularly denounced congressional committees for abusing witnesses. Once a member of the Ku Klux Klan whose appointment was attacked on the ground that he was a bigot, now he was one of the strongest defenders of minority groups ever to sit on the Supreme Court. Once a police court judge with a minimum of legal training, now he was the leader of a major school of American legal thought and an innovator in constitutional law.

All these paradoxes were hidden behind Black's deceptively mild appearance. Over the years his black hair had turned to white and thinned noticeably, but his blue-gray eyes still sparkled and his Alabama drawl persisted. More than one lawyer had discovered that two or three soft questions from Black could cut the heart out of his argument. More than one lawyer had heard Black begin, "Now, as I understand you," and then make the argument more forcefully and more clearly than the lawyer had been able to. This ability to cut through the morass that tends to surround legal issues and to define the problem quickly was one of Black's strong points on the bench. Another characteristic that set him apart was his desire, and his ability, to write opinions that laymen can understand. One of his former law clerks, John P. Frank, said: "Black has an impression that some people other than lawyers may actually read the Supreme Court reports. When a paragraph is turned to his satisfaction, he has a way of saying with gusto: 'Now they'll understand that,' and 'they' are some unidentifiable general readers."[7]

Black's primary contribution to the Court, however, has been in the realm of ideas. It was in that realm that he and Frankfurter battled and it is there that he and Harlan continued the struggle. Black's dissent in the *Shotwell* case illustrated the depth of his feelings about the Bill of Rights. When he said, "We would not do the Fifth Amendment this way," it sounded as if he were talking about a living thing that must be handled with utmost care. In fact, he does feel that way about the guarantees of the Bill of Rights. To him they are the soul of American freedom. His task as a Justice, as he sees it, is to protect every bit of that soul against all enemies. Where he differs from other Justices in regard to the Bill of Rights is in his interpretation of those guarantees and the vigor with which he defends them, particularly those found in the First Amendment. His view has been quite accurately described by Professor Edmond Cahn of the New York University Law Center as "The 'Firstness' of the First Amendment." The Amendment says that Congress shall make no law establishing religion or prohibiting its free exercise, or abridging freedom of speech or of the press or the rights to assemble peaceably and to petition the government. In 1960 Black said in New York:

> The phrase "Congress shall make no law" is composed of plain words, easily understood. The Framers knew this. The language used by Madison in his original proposal was different, but no less emphatic and unequivocal. . . .
>
> Neither as offered nor as adopted is the language of this Amendment anything less than absolute. . . . To my way of thinking, at least, the history and language of the Constitution and the Bill of Rights . . . make it plain that one of the primary purposes of the Constitution with its amendments

was to withdraw from the Government all power to act in certain areas. . . .[8]

It is his use of that word "absolute" that has separated Black's views from those of many of his colleagues, past and present. He believes that Congress lacks power to make any law that in any way abridges any of these First Amendment rights, and that the Court has not only the power but also the obligation to declare unconstitutional any such laws that Congress may pass. A classic example came in 1951 when the Court had to rule on the constitutionality of the Smith Act legislation which made it a crime to advocate the overthrow of the government by force and violence.

Black said the Smith Act was unconstitutional because it abridged the right of free speech. A Communist had a right to advocate the overthrow of government and could be arrested only when he went beyond advocacy and started acting. A majority of the Justices, however, approached the First Amendment with a different attitude. They said no right could be "absolute," but each had to be balanced against the other rights involved in specific situations. The government's right to protect itself from illegal overthrow had to be weighed against the abridgment of free speech incurred by restricting advocacy of such illegal overthrow. Taking note of the danger of the international Communist conspiracy that Congress had mentioned as its reason for passing the Smith Act, a majority of the Justices decided that danger was sufficiently great to justify the restrictions on free speech. In a bitter dissent, Black said:

> Public opinion being what it now is, few will protest the conviction of these Communist petitioners. There is hope, however, that in calmer times, when present pressures, passions and fears subside, this or some later Court will restore the First Amendment liberties to the high preferred place where they belong in a free society.[9]

The majority of the Court also used the "balancing" test in other areas where governmental regulation touched on First Amendment rights. In one of those, when congressional investigating procedures were involved, Black explained the conviction that underlay his feeling about the right of free speech:

> The First Amendment means to me, however, that the only constitutional way our Government can preserve itself is to leave its people the fullest possible freedom to praise, criticize or discuss, as they see fit, all governmental policies and to suggest, if they desire, that even its most fundamental postulates are bad and should be changed. . . . Our Constitution assumes the common sense of the people and their attachment to our country will enable them, after free discussion, to withstand ideas that are wrong. To say that our patriotism must be protected against false ideas by means other than these is, I think, to make a baseless charge.[10]

Language like that from Black can incite anger in some of the other Justices, particularly Harlan, just as absolute as Black's interpretation of the First Amendment. On one such occasion Harlan announced that he would depart from his normal practice and read his opinion verbatim because he feared if he spoke extemporaneously he would say something he did not intend.

The greatest single innovation in Black's philosophy, however, is his view that the Bill of Rights protects the people against the state governments as well as against the federal government. The Court rejected this view early in its history but the idea recurred after the Fourteenth Amendment was adopted. One clause of that amendment said that "No State shall . . . deprive any person of life, liberty, or property, without due process of law." In a 1947 opinion Black argued that the intent of those who wrote the Fourteenth Amendment had been to incorporate through it, as "due process of law," all the guarantees of individual rights in the entire Bill of Rights. He was bucking a strongly entrenched traditional view, but he got three members of the Court at that time to agree substantially with him. Several years earlier, the Court had rejected the idea, ruling instead that the Fourteenth Amendment's Due Process Clause barred the states from encroaching only on those individual rights that are essential to "civilized decency" and "fundamental liberty and justice." Black objected because this left it up to the Court to decide what parts of the Bill of Rights were "fundamental." He wrote:

> [The provisions of the Bill of Rights] may be thought out-dated abstractions by some. And it is true that they were designed to meet ancient evils. But they are the same kind of human evils that have emerged from century to century wherever excessive power is sought by the few at the expense of the many. In my judgment the people of no nation can lose their liberty so long as a Bill of Rights like ours survives and its basic purposes are conscientiously interpreted, enforced and respected so as to afford continuous protection against old, as well as new, devices and practices which might thwart those purposes. I fear to see the consequences of the Court's practice of substituting its own concepts of decency and fundamental justice for the language of the Bill of Rights as its point of departure in interpreting and enforcing that Bill of Rights.[11]

Again and again Black has brought up that argument. Douglas agrees with him and it appeared as if both Warren and Brennan might. But a majority of the Court never has. Instead, they have used the Due Process Clause as a method of applying some of the guarantees of the Bill of Rights to the states, one at a time.

It sometimes seemed strange to recall that October 4, 1937, the day Black took his seat on the Court, was christened "Black Monday" by the nation's liberals. On that day many of those whose counterparts later vigorously supported Black's views wore black armbands to mourn his ascension to the bench. Their condemnation was based on the fact that he had once been a member of the Ku Klux Klan.

Black's appointment to the Court by President Roosevelt had come as a great surprise. Despite much criticism—the New York *Herald Tribune* said he showed "not the slightest qualification" for the post—Black was confirmed quickly by the Senate and went to Europe on vacation. While he was gone it became known that as a young politician in Alabama he had been a member of the KKK. Demands were made, both on Capitol Hill and across the nation, for his immediate resignation. He had been confirmed only because he concealed his past, his critics said. An ex-Klansman was unfit to sit on the Supreme Court. He would be intolerant. He would be prejudiced against all minority groups. When Black returned from Europe, he made one radio speech: "I did join the Klan. I later resigned. I never rejoined." He denied that he was prejudiced. "When this statement is ended, my discussion of the question is closed."

By 1962 no one doubted that Black had lived down that Black Monday. In fact, his most bitter enemies were the modern-day, white-collar Klan, the Southern White Citizens Councils. Black now rarely visits Birmingham, where he spent many years as a police court judge and as a successful trial lawyer before entering politics and representing Alabama in the United States Senate for almost ten years. Even his son had left Birmingham when the criticism brought on him by his father's activities became too great to bear. As examples of bias in favor of Negroes and all minority groups, his present critics point to his votes in racial discrimination cases and his decisions defending the rights of accused criminals. The two were combined in one case early in his career as a Justice when the Court sharply reprimanded the State of Florida for the brutality its police used to obtain confessions from four young Negroes. Black, speaking for the Court, wrote:

> Under our constitutional system, courts stand against any
> winds that blow as havens of refuge for those who might
> otherwise suffer because they are helpless, weak, outnum-
> bered, or because they are non-conforming victims of preju-
> dice and public excitement. Due process of law . . . com-
> mands that no such practice as disclosed by this record
> shall send any accused to his death. No higher duty, no
> more solemn responsibility, rests upon this Court, than
> that of translating into living law and maintaining this con-
> stitutional shield deliberately planned and inscribed for the
> benefit of every human being subject to our Constitution—
> of whatever race, creed or persuasion.[12]

The next day President Roosevelt suggested pointedly that the
newspapers which had said Black was a bigot now owed him an
apology.

The most fundamental disagreement, however, between Black
and other members of the Court, at first particularly Frankfurter
and now Harlan, was over the role of the Court in government.
Black opposed Frankfurter's attitude of great self-restraint and
deference to legislatures. His view was that the Court's task of
deciding what laws were constitutional permitted it to defer to
no one, whatever the reason or whatever the result. This flowed
directly from his view that there were "absolutes" in the Constitution. While Frankfurter and Harlan believed that the times
and circumstances could be relevant to the constitutionality of
a law, and the Justices could look to Congress for help in weigh-
ing their effect, Black could look only to the Constitution. There
could be no deference under his view, particularly when individual liberties were involved, and the Court's decisions were
its and its alone to make.

chapter 8

JUSTICE AND THE STATE COURTS

"HARD CASES MAKE BAD LAW" IS AN OLD LEGAL ADAGE. THE basic principle of good law, of course, is that it establishes rules to which men can conform their actions and by which controversies can be decided in an equitable and fairly predictable fashion. But regardless of how good a particular rule or principle is, the situation inevitably arises in which its intellectually pure application produces a result that offends the sense of justice. One of the controversies that divide American judges and legal scholars into different schools of thought revolves about this dilemma. The "Harvard School"—perhaps so called because its chief exponent, Justice Frankfurter, was so closely connected with the Harvard Law School—often criticizes Black and Douglas for being "result-oriented." By that, they mean those two Justices are more concerned with seeing that justice is done in a particular case than in seeing that sound general rules of law are established. The Supreme Court, they argue, should be less concerned about the justness of the result in any one case than about the need for rules and procedures that lead to just results in the maximum number of cases. This was the point Justice Holmes made when he wrote, "I have said to my Brethren many times that I hate justice, which means that I know if a man begins to talk about that, for one reason or another he is shirking thinking in legal terms."[1] The "Yale School"—the name reflects more than traditional rivalry; Roscoe Pound's theories of "sociological jurisprudence" found their earliest acceptance at the Yale Law

School—argues that the Harvard approach takes the heart and the justice out of law. They look with disdain on the idea, once stated by Frankfurter, that the Supreme Court exists to establish rules of law, not to provide justice. To Justice Black, that idea removes the spirit of justice while leaving its forms intact; he once remarked, "It takes all the heart out of the law." But to Black's opponents, his approach destroys the forms of justice without which its spirit can accomplish nothing. Every Justice insists that his philosophy permits him to support both the spirit and the forms of the law, but the differences in their fundamental views sometimes show through in particular cases. Thus the old adage has real meaning; a hard case, where strict application of existing rules would produce an unconscionable result, is often resolved by bending those rules or, sometimes, by creating a new rule.

Early in January the Justices heard a case that, to some of them at least, fit the adage. It involved Charles Noia, who had served more than twenty years in a New York prison for a murder committed in 1942. His case presented unusually difficult questions about the relationship between federal and state courts and might leave a deeper mark on the American federal system than any other case of the 1962–63 term, yet it was unheralded. When the Chief Justice called, "Number 84, Edward M. Fay, Petitioner, versus Charles Noia," only twenty-one spectators were in the courtroom.

William J. Siegel, an assistant district attorney of Kings County, New York, began his argument with a sentence that lay the issue bare. "New York is here in this Court seeking to reverse a decision of the Second Circuit Court of Appeals which we believe has seriously infringed the sovereignty of the State of New York."

The case was not a pretty one. Noia, along with Santo Caminito and Frank Bonino, had been charged with the murder of Murray Hammeroff, a storekeeper in Brooklyn, during a robbery. Noia had told the police he pulled the trigger. The jury that convicted all three men of first degree murder recommended life imprisonment instead of death in the electric chair. When the men came up for sentencing, Judge Brancato readily accepted the recommendation for Caminito and Bonino but to Noia he said: "I have thought seriously about rejecting the recommendation of the jury in your case, Noia, because I feel that if the jury knew who you were and what you were and your background as a robber, they would not have made a recommendation. But you have got a good lawyer, that is my wife. The last thing she told me this morning is to give you a chance." Noia went to Sing Sing with those words in his ears. Although Caminito and Bonino filed appeals, Noia chose not to do so. Years later, he testified that he did not appeal because he had run out of funds and wanted to be a financial burden on his family no longer. His lawyer testified that no appeal was filed because Noia was afraid that, if the conviction was reversed, he might be convicted again and sentenced without having a judge's wife intercede for his life. Caminito and Bonino were unsuccessful in their appeals but they did not give up. Time after time they tried to win their freedom. Finally, in 1955, Caminito got a hearing in a federal district court in New York on his claim that his confession, the basic evidence against him, had been coerced. At that hearing the facts were spread on the record.

Caminito was arrested on May 11, 1941, at 6 P.M. From 9 o'clock that night until 2 o'clock the next morning he was questioned by five or six police officers. Then he was locked in a cell that contained only a wooden bench—no bed, no blankets, no spring, no mattress. Eight hours later, the questioning was resumed. It lasted all day with several detectives taking turns. During the day members of Caminito's family, some of his friends, and an attorney called at the jail in efforts to find out what had happened to him. They got no information and no one was allowed to see him. During that day the detectives decided that if they were going to get Caminito to confess, they would have to try something unusual. As a result, three new detectives, two women and one man, were brought into a room where Caminito and Noia and Bonino were sitting. The three detectives pretended to be eyewitnesses to the murder, and each identified the men as the ones who had committed it. About 9 o'clock that night Caminito confessed. Six hours later, after he had been in jail for thirty-three hours, he was officially placed under arrest. Later that day he was taken before a judge who told him he had a constitutional right not to talk to the police unless he wanted to. After almost two days of questioning, that standard warning seemed a rather empty gesture.

These circumstances, Caminito contended, made his confession inadmissible as evidence because it was obtained by violations of his constitutional rights. The Supreme Court had ruled years earlier that a confession was admissible only if it was voluntarily made. The deterrent effect of this rule on police third-degree methods was recognized as desirable, but a more important reason for the rule was the inherent unreliability of a coerced confession. Even an innocent man might confess to a crime to stop a beating or to escape a bright light in his eyes or to sleep after several days and nights of questioning. Over the years the Supreme Court had worked out a rule for determining whether a particular confession was coerced. Simply stated, the rule is that a confession is coerced and hence inadmissible at trial if the will of the suspect has been overcome by the procedures used by the police or if the confession was not the product of a rational intellect or a free will.

After hearing the facts of the situation under which Caminito confessed, the federal district judge ruled that his confession had not been coerced. But his claim was received very differently on appeal to the Second Circuit Court of Appeals. It said, "All decent Americans soundly condemn satanic practices, like those [in this case], when employed in totalitarian regimes. It should shock us when American police resort to them, for they do not comport with the barest minimum of civilized principles of justice. . . ."[2] The evidence compelled the conclusion that Caminito had confessed only because of "satanic" coercion. Therefore, his confession could not be used against him and he was entitled to a new trial. After the Court of Appeals ruled, the State of New York decided that it must release Caminito. Without the confession it had no case against him.

A few weeks later, Bonino asked the New York Court of Appeals, that state's highest court, to reopen his case. It did so and ruled that since Bonino's treatment had been the same as Caminito's, his confession too had been coerced. Bonino was thereupon released.

At that point Noia filed a petition in the New York courts asking for similar treatment. Since both the state and the federal appellate courts had said there was no difference in the way the three men's confessions had been extracted by the police, Noia reasoned that the courts should now treat all three of them the same and order his release, too. It was then—fourteen years later—that his decision not to appeal his conviction in 1942 came back to haunt him. The New York courts agreed that Noia's continued imprisonment was unjust but said their procedures provided no way of doing anything about it. Because Noia had not appealed his conviction, his case had never been in the appellate courts so they had no jurisdiction to reopen it.

Sorely disappointed by this reception in the state courts, Noia turned to the federal courts. He filed a petition for the ancient writ of habeas corpus, a court order that requires a jailer to produce his prisoner and prove that his imprisonment is legal.

This move brought to the fore one of the most subtle concepts of American government, that of federalism. Under the federal system, two sets of courts exist side by side. Most cases originate in the state courts and run their courses there. Decisions of state courts can be appealed to the United States Supreme Court only if questions of federal constitutional rights or federal law are involved. Cases can originate in federal courts if they present questions of federal law or if the litigants are citizens of different states. The habeas corpus jurisdiction of the federal courts can disrupt this neat division of labor. To determine whether the writ should be granted the federal courts must examine the criminal proceedings in state courts to see whether the requirements of the federal Constitution have been met.

The federal district court in New York turned Noia down. Under federal law, it said, a petition for habeas corpus by a man in a state jail could be entertained only after the prisoner had exhausted all the remedies provided by the state. Since Noia had failed to appeal in 1942, he had failed to exhaust his state remedies. Thus, Noia was trapped. The New York courts could not release him because he had not appealed, the federal court could not act until after he appealed, and under New York law he could no longer appeal because the thirty-day period in which a conviction can be appealed had expired fourteen years earlier.

Once again, the Second Circuit Court of Appeals saw the situation differently. It said the writ should be issued and Noia should be freed because he was in prison in violation of the Constitution. His conviction by use of a coerced confession had been unconstitutional, and the court would overlook his failure to exhaust his state remedies because the circumstances were so unusual.

That decision struck New York law enforcement officers like a thunderbolt. There was no precedent for it. Always before, the federal courts had refused to review the claims of state prisoners unless they had exhausted all state remedies. Always before, the courts had held that to exhaust his remedies a prisoner must take every opportunity available to him at any time to get his conviction reversed. The reason for those rulings went to the heart of the federal system. The states in that system are sovereign in many areas, including criminal law. Each establishes its own criminal rules and its own methods of applying those rules, so long as they do not conflict with the federal Constitution. Federal courts had deferred to the state rules, even when federal judges did not like them, because such deference was thought essential to recognition of the states' prerogatives and maintenance of a proper balance between the two sets of courts. State court judges are sensitive about the jurisdiction of the federal courts under writs of habeas corpus. Under those writs, a federal judge can evaluate the proceedings in a state court to see whether they met the requirements of the federal Constitution. State court judges resent having their decisions subject to review not only by their own appellate courts but also by federal trial courts; it suggests that state courts are inferior and do not consistently conduct themselves properly. The rule that all state remedies must be exhausted before a prisoner turns to the federal courts is designed to minimize the number of habeas corpus insults inflicted on the state trial judges by giving the state a full opportunity to correct its own errors. Many of the New York judges reacted to the decision of the Second Circuit Court of Appeals in Noia's case the way that court's dissenting member did. "If this is to be the rule of law, is not a reappraisal of our criminal procedure in this field called for?" said dissenter Leonard Moore. "If the delicate balance of the State-Federal relationship is to be upset, possibly the majority's approach is best, namely, upset it dramatically. . . . And in fairness to the two distinguished appellate courts in New York, would it not be better to advise them that in any case before them involving a coerced confession they are but puppets whose strings may be cut at any time by the keen edge of the 'Great Writ.' "[3]

In its request that the Supreme Court review the decision, the State of New York adopted Judge Moore's reasoning. It argued that the decision had destroyed part of the structure of the federal system. "It is our respectful submission that in the case at bar the sovereignty of the State of New York has been disregarded. . . ," the petition said.

As he argued the issue before the Justices, Assistant State's Attorney Siegel tried to make it clear that while he thought the Circuit Court's decision was wrong as a matter of principle, he agreed that something should be done for Noia. In response to questions by Brennan, Siegel admitted that New York would not attempt to try Caminito and Bonino again. They were free men. "We would be ready to do here what we have done in other cases," Siegel said. "If this man, Noia, ever made an application to the State of New York, we could work out some sort of arrangement to put him on a parity with Bonino and Caminito. . . . We don't like this situation either, even though it's not the fault of the people of New York." Joseph J. Rose, speaking a few minutes later for New York's attorney general, agreed. His office would not object to executive clemency if Noia sought it.

As the Justices listened to the case and questioned the lawyers, it was clear that the issue troubled them. Without doubt Noia was being held in jail as the result of an unconstitutional conviction. But did the federal courts have power to order his release? And if they did, should they exercise it? The balance of the federal system was involved. New York was entitled to run its courts and its criminal law as it saw fit, provided only that its requirements were consistent with the guarantees of the federal Constitution. Nothing in that system conflicted with the Constitution, and if Noia had followed the example of Caminito and Bonino and taken advantage of all the opportunities that system gave him, he would already be free. Since he had failed to use the procedures New York law provided, he was in prison. Should the federal courts leave him in prison because of that failure, deferring to state law as they had always done in the past? Or should they modify or abandon their old rule so that

Noia's unquestioned constitutional right to freedom would be vindicated?

For years the difficulties abounding in their habeas corpus jurisdiction had troubled the Justices. Twenty years earlier the Court had said that unless a man convicted in a state court not only took all available appeals in the state courts but also petitioned the Supreme Court for certiorari, he could never protest his conviction in the federal courts by habeas corpus. The Circuit Court's ruling in Noia's case conflicted directly with the doctrine of that case. During the Noia argument, Justice Clark remarked that some of the earlier decisions had given the Justices great difficulty. Many drafts of one opinion were exchanged before the decision was finally announced, he said, and they produced "often more heat than light." Just four years before Noia's case was argued, the Court had divided sharply in the case of Leslie Irwin, an Indiana murderer. It had decided in his favor by a vote of 5 to 4, and the attempt in Brennan's opinion to answer some of the many questions about federal habeas corpus jurisdiction had satisfied no one. When Professor Henry Hart of Harvard attacked it as one that produced grossly inadequate guidance for other courts, Brennan struck back in a public speech. That speech made it clear that the opinion was ragged because Brennan had difficulty getting the fifth and crucial vote. Stewart had finally joined the opinion but would not accept all Brennan's original ideas. Thus the views the two new Justices adopted in Noia's case might go far toward determining the shape of the federal-state relationship in this area of criminal law.

But the appropriate use of writs of habeas corpus was only one of many problems involving state criminal proceedings that faced the Justices. Another of those problems was argued the next week. Clarence Earl Gideon's laboriously scrawled petition had been received by the Court more than a year earlier. Gideon wrote that he was in jail in Florida unconstitutionally because he had been denied legal counsel at his trial. Gideon was arrested in Panama City, Florida, and charged with breaking into the Bay Harbor Poolroom with intent to steal liquor from the bar. When his case was called, Gideon told the judge he was not ready for trial because he did not have a lawyer. The judge asked Gideon if he wanted to hire a lawyer and Gideon said he had no money. "Your Honor," he added, "I request this Court to appoint counsel to represent me in this trial."

"Mr. Gideon," said the judge, "I am sorry, but I cannot appoint counsel to represent you in this case. Under the laws of the State of Florida, the only time the Court can appoint counsel to represent a defendant is when that person is charged with a capital offense. I am sorry but I will have to deny your request to appoint counsel to defend you in this case."

The trial proceeded. Gideon called witnesses in his own defense, questioned them, and tried to cross-examine the witnesses for the state. The jury found him guilty and the judge gave him the maximum sentence, five years in prison.

Late in May of 1962 the Supreme Court announced that it would hear Gideon's appeal and appointed Abe Fortas, one of Washington's most able lawyers, to represent him. The Court asked Fortas and the lawyers for Florida to argue whether *Betts v. Brady* should be overruled. That decision had been controversial from the day it was announced in 1942. It said the federal Constitution required a state to provide a poor man with a lawyer only where special circumstances would make a trial without counsel "offensive to the common and fundamental ideas of fairness."[4]

The Sixth Amendment says, "In all criminal prosecutions, the accused shall enjoy the right . . . to have the Assistance of Counsel for his defence." While the Court had previously interpreted this to mean that the federal courts must appoint a lawyer to defend every person charged with crime who could not afford to hire one, it had applied a different standard to the states. That difference arose from the interpretation the Court's majority had placed on the Due Process Clause of the Fourteenth Amendment. If the majority had adopted Black's view that the Due Process Clause incorporated all the guarantees of the Bill of Rights, the same standards would have applied in federal and state courts. But the majority's view was that the Due Process Clause required the states to recognize only those protections in the Bill of Rights necessary to the fundamental principles of liberty and justice. In a line of cases beginning in 1932, the Court decided that in certain circumstances a trial could not provide due process, could not provide fundamental fairness, unless the defendant was given an attorney. By the time Gideon's case was argued, it was clear that the state must provide defense counsel if a death sentence might be imposed. Other special circumstances that might require appointment of a lawyer included youth, ignorance, or mental instability or subnormality on the part of the defendant and the presence of unusually difficult legal problems in the case. While the existence of such special circumstances depended on the peculiar facts of each particular case, and in theory there could be cases where the state court need not appoint counsel, the Justices had found special circumstances in every case they had reviewed since 1950.

In this area of law, as in the habeas corpus field, the major problem was one of federalism. The Court could, if it chose, reverse its past course and adopt Black's view that the Fourteenth Amendment incorporated the guarantees of the Bill of Rights. Or it could rule that due process now required the presence of an attorney in every case in which the defendant wanted one, thereby overruling *Betts v. Brady*. Or it could continue as it had in the past and deal with the problem through the special circumstances rule. The question was: Should the Supreme Court impose upon the states this particular minimum standard in criminal trials or, with due respect to state prerogatives in the federal system, should it permit them to develop such standards and systems as they thought best?

Fortas began his argument for Gideon with the words: "If you study the record perhaps you will share my feeling, a feeling of despondency. This record does not indicate that Clarence Earl Gideon is a moron or a person of low intellect. This record does not indicate that the trial judge or the prosecutor of the State of Florida were derelict in their duty. They tried to help Clarence Earl Gideon. But to me the record indicates the basic difficulty in *Betts v. Brady*."

Justice Harlan interrupted. Was the real point in *Betts v. Brady* that the demands of federalism outweighed the right to a fair trial?

"I believe," replied Fortas, "that this case dramatically illustrates the point that you cannot have a fair trial without counsel. I believe that a criminal court is not properly constituted without a judge, counsel for the prosecution, and counsel for the defense." In an adversary system of justice like that of the United States, he added, the attorney for the state presents the best case for conviction he can, while the defense attorney does his best to get his client acquitted. The system rests on the belief that the best way to find the truth is to have two sides, equally matched, fight out the points in dispute before an impartial jury.

"No," said Justice Harlan. "It isn't quite so simple as that. . . . I think you've got to argue this on the basis of federalism."

"I think we can agree that a man does not have a fair trial if he is tried without a lawyer," Fortas began.

Douglas interrupted. "The Constitution doesn't say a state can have a system of law that denies a man a fair trial, does it?"

Fortas said the Fourteenth Amendment's Due Process Clause required a fair trial. "There has been a tendency because of the pull of federalism to forget what really happens." What Florida had done, he said, was to charge Gideon with a crime and then say, "There, Clarence Earl Gideon, defend yourself. Apply the doctrine of *Mapp v. Ohio*. Construe this statute of the State of Florida. Cross-examine witnesses. Call your own witnesses. Argue to the jury."

Fortas recalled that Clarence Darrow, one of the greatest criminal trial lawyers in American history, was once charged with tampering with a jury. "The first thing Clarence Darrow realized was that he had to have a lawyer."

Harlan kept returning to the problem of federalism. Should the Supreme Court require the states to appoint counsel or should the states be free to do as they saw fit?

Fortas went into the history of the right to counsel in American courts to argue that considerations of federalism should not govern this case. He pointed out how the Justices had undermined *Betts v. Brady* with the special circumstances rule.

"How long has it been since we've failed to find special circumstances?" Justice Stewart asked. "I think in the four and a half years I've been here we've never failed to find them."

"That's what's wrong," Fortas said. "It's wrong as a matter of federalism. . . . How can a judge look at a defendant and tell if there are special circumstances? How can he tell in advance of trial whether the defendant is stupid or a moron? The trial judge can't know before the trial whether the special circumstances requiring him to appoint a lawyer exist and after the trial it's too late to appoint one."

Fortas pointed out that forty-five of the fifty states already required that a lawyer be appointed in every criminal case. Only Alabama, Florida, Mississippi, North Carolina, and South Carolina did not, and Florida did in its four largest counties. He noted that the attorneys general of twenty-two states had filed a brief in the case as friends of the Court—*amici curiae*—saying that *Betts v. Brady* was "an anachronism" that should be overruled. "My point is that we may be comforted in knowing this constitutional movement represents a deliberate change . . . and it represents a change that has the overwhelming support of the bench, of the bar, and, even, of the states."

The Court had authorized a third hour's argument in this case, and half of that time went to J. Lee Rankin, who spoke for another *amicus curiae*, the American Civil Liberties Union. As Solicitor General under Eisenhower, Rankin had argued many criminal cases on behalf of the Government. Now he was arguing for a defendant. "It's time, long past, that our profession [of lawyers] should stand up and say we know, from our day-to-day experience, that a layman can't get a fair trial by himself," Rankin said. "It is enough of a fiction to claim that the ordinary lawyer . . . can present a case fairly against the skilled prosecutor. Court procedure is just too complex for the layman to master."

"Isn't that the assumption of the legal profession?" Justice Stewart asked. "Florida wouldn't let Gideon represent anyone else [in its courts]."

To argue its case, the State of Florida had sent Bruce R. Jacobs, a twenty-seven-year-old, crew-cut assistant attorney general. He began by telling the Justices that 65 per cent of the prisoners in Florida's jails had not been represented by counsel at their trials. To require counsel in all cases would put a heavy burden on the taxpayers. A man can get a fair trial without counsel, he said, if the trial judge takes pains to help him throughout the trial.

Justice Brennan remarked that four cases from Florida similar to Gideon's had been heard by the Supreme Court in recent years. All four convictions had been reversed on the grounds the judges should have appointed lawyers. "That's a 100-per-cent record," he added.

Jacobs admitted it was, but argued that it was better than a new rule requiring the automatic appointment of lawyers. "We contend it's better for this Court to reverse them on a case-by-case basis. It still allows us to make our own rules."

Pursuing his argument that it was possible for a man to get a fair trial without counsel, Jacobs said that the prosecutor and judge always leaned over backwards to help a defendant without counsel to defend himself. He pointed out that in federal courts a defendant could waive his right to counsel and insist on defending himself. If a layman could never adequately defend himself, waiver meant an unfair trial. Surely the Supreme Court wouldn't permit that in the federal courts!

Stewart broke in. "I suppose a man has a right under the Constitution or as an individual to insist on an unfair trial," he said.

It was clear that Jacobs was arguing to a friendly but not very sympathetic group of judges, and his closing comment helped his position not at all. Just before he yielded some of his time to George D. Mentz, he told the Justices that if they ruled the poor must be provided with lawyers at state expense, the decision would lead to the state providing them funds for investigations, appeals of their convictions, and even psychiatric examinations. That, he said, "would be requiring the states to follow a program of socialism, a welfare program."

Mentz, an Alabama assistant attorney general, admitted that "it would be desirable" for all the states to appoint lawyers to represent the poor in all cases. But this was a state problem, he said, not a federal one. In his state there were thousands of criminal trials every year and only a few complaints about the state's refusal to provide free counsel.

Stewart asked if it were customary in Alabama to appoint lawyers to defend the poor. Mentz said it was not. He explained that judges tried hard to see that defendants without lawyers got fair trials.

"I assume all that you're saying is true," Stewart said. "But the judge's job is to be a judge, not a defense counsel."

When Mentz concluded his argument, the fate of Clarence Earl Gideon joined that of Charles Noia in the hands of the nine

THE MAKING OF JUSTICE

Justices. Each man had much in his favor. Neither the Justices nor the New York officials thought the continued imprisonment of Noia was just, and the constitutional issue he raised had received a sympathetic hearing. Gideon, too, clearly had much support on the Court for his constitutional argument. But Gideon had one major advantage in the active support of almost half the state attorneys general and the fact that almost all the states had already accepted on their own initiative the procedure for which he argued. On issues involving the state-federal relationship that kind of support for a constitutional change is important to the Court.

Less than a month before, the Assembly of the States had quietly begun a campaign to rebuke the Justices and remove much of the Court's power because of its handling of state-federal relations. The Assembly, an offshoot of the Council of State Governments, is composed of delegates from every state, usually from the legislatures. It met in Chicago in mid-December and agreed to work for the adoption of three amendments to the federal Constitution. Two of the three were aimed directly at the Supreme Court. The third was intended to make the state legislatures more powerful. They were:

1. A proposal to create a "Court of the Union" composed of the chief justices of each state's highest court. It would have jurisdiction to override the Supreme Court in all cases concerning state-federal relations.

2. A proposal to overturn the Court's reapportionment decision by an express reservation to the states of all matters involving the apportionment of state legislatures. This would mean a state could divide its legislative seats among its citizens in any manner whatsoever and the federal courts could not intervene.

3. A proposal to change the procedure for amending the Constitution. Amendments can now be initiated either by a two-thirds vote of each house of Congress or by a constitutional convention called by Congress at the request of two thirds of the state

legislatures. Once so proposed, an amendment becomes effective when it has been ratified by, at the option of Congress, the legislatures of or conventions in three fourths of the states. The Assembly of the States proposed giving the legislatures of two thirds of the states power to initiate amendments without any congressional action.[5]

The central theme of all three proposals was that the federal government was too powerful and must be curbed. But a more subtle theme ran through the last two. If the federal courts were deprived of jurisdiction over reapportionment cases, there would be no way in which the control held by rural, usually conservative politicians over many states' legislatures could be broken. The Assembly of the States was composed largely of conservative politicians. Beyond that, the proposed change in the amending process would make it possible for state legislatures to bypass Congress completely. Congress tends to be far more liberal than the average state legislature.

The first proposal was, of course, a vote of no confidence in the Supreme Court. It meant that the Court's decision would not be final in cases like those of Noia and Gideon. The chief justices of all the states could be convened to decide whether the Supreme Court had ruled properly. No one explained how a case could be argued before fifty men, or how any body of law could develop from a court whose membership would be so unstable and which would rule on only a few cases a year. The absurdity of the proposal became clear when in more than a dozen states no member of the legislature would introduce it.

While no one in Washington expected any of these proposals to receive national support, they did point to some fundamental problems. It was true that the federal government was becoming more powerful while state governments were becoming relatively less important. It was true that the Supreme Court, in cases akin to Noia and Gideon, had curtailed the freedom of states to devise their own systems of procedure. But these developments rested, at least in part, on the failure of many states to meet their own responsibilities, to face problems like those in *Noia* and *Gideon*. No lawyer, for example, can seriously contend that a defendant in a criminal trial has as good a chance of being acquitted without a lawyer as he does with one. Most states had recognized this and acted voluntarily. But five had refused to face the problem. Particularly in Gideon's case, the question before the Court was like the one Congress often faces in appropriating money for health and welfare problems. Should it act to help citizens of states whose state governments refuse to meet standards that the rest of the nation regards as minimal?

chapter 9

THE ATTORNEY GENERAL COMES TO COURT

As THE JUSTICES STRODE THROUGH THE VELVET CURTAINS ON THE morning of January 17, Attorney General Robert F. Kennedy occupied the place at the counsel table normally reserved for Solicitor General Cox. In his morning coat and striped trousers the Attorney General looked like a nervous and uncomfortable young bridegroom. The long lock of hair that usually jutted over his forehead was carefully combed. His fingers drummed impatiently on the table. For two weeks Kennedy had left the Justice Department to his subordinates and the Presidency to the President in order to prepare for this day. This was not just his first argument before the Supreme Court; it was his first appearance in any court as the lawyer in charge of the case.

It has become traditional for every Attorney General of the United States to argue at least one case before the Supreme Court during his term of office. Kennedy and his staff had carefully selected the case he was to argue. Because an Attorney General's appearance before the Court is so rare, immediate public attention is directed toward the case he chooses to argue. This case was important but it was not complex. Its significance was as much political as constitutional. The issue was the constitutionality of the Georgia county unit system of primary elections. Because it was a new issue for the Court and little prior law was involved, Kennedy did not have to concern himself with the details of dozens of old cases, a task that usually confronts a lawyer about to argue before the Justices.

The Georgia case was the first result of the Court's decision the preceding spring that the apportionment of seats in a state legislature is a subject fit for judicial scrutiny. It had been filed in federal court in Atlanta by Morris Abram, an Atlanta lawyer who had long fought for a fair division of legislative seats in his state, just a few hours after the Justices announced their decision in April. The county unit system was one of two devices that Georgia's rural politicians had used to keep control of the state government. The other was an apportionment of seats in the legislature that severely short-changed Atlanta.

In most states, malapportionment had given the rural leaders control only of the legislature; the governor and other officials were elected by the popular vote of the entire state and usually were concerned about protecting the interests of the major cities. But under Georgia's county unit system the rural counties were able to control the executive branch of government as well as the legislative. Each county was assigned a number of unit votes for the nomination of Democratic Party candidates. The contender who received a majority of the popular vote in each county won all of that county's unit votes. Because no county had more than six unit votes and none fewer than two, it was possible for a candidate to lose the statewide popular vote and still win the nomination. In Georgia, of course, the Democratic nomination is tantamount to election. As a result, the three smallest counties in the state, with a total population of 6,980, had as large a say in the election of state officials as Atlanta's Fulton County, with a population of 556,326. In fact, it was possible for a candidate to win the Democratic nomination by getting a little more than half the votes in counties containing only 22.2 per cent of the state's population. The advantage this gave the small, rural counties had been underlined by the success of the late Gene Talmadge, who rarely campaigned in the cities and won election by criticizing Atlanta in the boondocks.

Even closer to the hearts of Atlanta voters, however, was the situation involving their Congressman, James C. Davis. Davis had twice won renomination to Congress on the basis of county unit votes despite running behind in the popular vote. His district was composed of three counties, Fulton, with six votes for its 556,326 residents, and DeKalb and Rockdale, with eight votes for their 267,354 residents. Davis had once lost Fulton County by 50,000 votes but won the nomination by carrying the other two counties by a total of fewer than 10,000 votes.

Before Abram filed his case in 1962, four other lawsuits had challenged the county unit system. In 1946 a federal court in Georgia upheld the system as constitutional and the Supreme Court dismissed an appeal. The Court's action, closely following its refusal to allow the federal courts to intervene in congressional apportionment matters, was taken as indicating that the Justices considered the county unit system a part of the "political thicket" in which it thought judicial intervention inappropriate. Four years later, in *South v. Peters*, a federal court again upheld the constitutionality of the county unit system. The Supreme Court summarily affirmed that decision, Black and Douglas dissenting. If it now ruled that the county unit system was unconstitutional it would have to overrule *South v. Peters*. The third and fourth challenges to the county unit system, filed subsequent to that case, were dismissed by lower courts.

Despite this history, the reaction in Georgia when Abram filed his suit showed that local lawyers and politicians thought the system was in danger. Even while the federal trial court, composed of three judges as required when a case directly attacks the constitutionality of a statute, had the case under advisement, the Georgia legislature amended the system in a desperate effort to save it. But the change, designed to give Atlanta and other urban areas more unit votes, was unsuccessful. Both the old and the new system, the judges ruled, unbalanced the election in favor of rural residents and discriminated against those who lived in urban areas. This, they said, was a denial of "equal protection" of the laws guaranteed by the Fourteenth Amendment. The three judges thought, however, that a county unit system could be used in state elections if it did not discriminate against any particular class of citizens. They drew a parallel between the county unit system and the allotment of votes to states in the federal electoral college or the division of seats in the United States Congress. In neither of these bodies is the number of seats or the number of votes assigned to the states in precise proportion to the number of their voters or citizens. A county unit system that varied no more from true equality than those two bodies would be constitutional, the judges said. This ruling set a standard that might be used for judging reapportionment cases as well as county unit cases. The constitutional principles applied by the three-judge court in Georgia were the same as those used by the Supreme Court when it ruled that an apportionment system was unconstitutional if it "invidiously discriminated" against a particular group of voters. The basic question that remained in reapportionment cases was how unfair a system could be without being invidiously discriminatory. The judges in Georgia had provided an answer. If the Supreme Court were to accept their answer, this case would be a guide in all future apportionment cases.

B. D. Murphy, a deputy attorney general of Georgia, explained all these facts to the Justices as the argument began. In a slow drawl Murphy outlined the development of the county unit system from the good old days when the state legislature selected the Democratic Party's nominees for all offices. Suddenly he was interrupted by Justice Stewart. "There is not involved here legislative reapportionment as such, is there?" Murphy agreed that apportionment was not in question, only the county unit system.

As Murphy went on, the Solicitor General began to whisper

to Kennedy, apparently passing on the ideas that occurred to him as the discussion progressed.

Murphy explained to the Court that, because of the decision of the three judges below, Georgia had elected its state officials and its Congressmen a few months earlier by popular vote. Representative Davis had finally been defeated.

"Now that you've tried the popular vote, does the Democratic Party want to return to the county unit system?" Justice Brennan asked with a grin.

"We think the Democratic Party ought to have a right to select any method of nominating candidates that it wants," Murphy replied.

Stewart asked if the lower court decision would block the Democrats from using a nominating convention instead of a primary. "A dozen Democratic leaders could meet in a smoke-filled room and pick the nominees," he said.

When Murphy replied, "That's what the Republicans do," the Justices joined in the laughter that spread through the courtroom. As it subsided, Brennan asked, "Is that because there are only as many Republicans as there are offices to be filled?" Murphy's answer was lost in the louder laughter.

A few minutes later, the Court recessed for lunch. When it returned at 12:30, the courtroom was jammed and the seats reserved for friends of the Justices were full. The Attorney General's wife, Ethel, was there, as was his mother, Mrs. Joseph P. Kennedy, and two of his sisters, Jean Smith and Eunice Shriver. Four of the Attorney General's then seven children had front-row seats in the general audience. In addition, Dorothy Goldberg and Marion White had come to listen. Mrs. White was sitting with her four-year-old daughter Nancy when the Justices came back on the bench. A big grin spread across the little girl's face as her mother held her up to see her father. After Justice White noticed her and smiled, Mrs. White led her from the courtroom and returned alone a few minutes later.

E. Freeman Leverett, another deputy assistant attorney general from Georgia, had taken over the argument for his state just before lunch. He attempted to justify the county unit system in constitutional terms. He argued that Georgia had adopted the system to provide a balance between urban and rural forces.

"Do you think it is unconstitutional for rural votes to have seven and a half times the power of urban voters in your state?" Goldberg interrupted to ask.

"As far as the Constitution is concerned, no, sir," Leverett replied. "Now, I'm not talking political science and I hope the Court won't talk political science."

"Let's talk in constitutional terms," Goldberg said. "Why do you think it is constitutional?"

"Simply because it has never been the law before . . . that equal population requires equal votes," Leverett said. He argued that when the Constitution was written, the English system of representation by districts was chosen over the French system of one man, one vote. The plain words of the Constitution barred equality. "There is no such equality of one man, one vote in the House of Representatives or in the Senate or in the electoral college or in the process of amending the Constitution."

Stewart interrupted. "I thought we had before us here an amendment adopted a hundred years later." The Fourteenth Amendment under which the lower court had ruled was adopted in 1868.

Leverett returned to his basic argument that the federal government was not a pure democracy and that the states were not, therefore, required to be purely democratic. Goldberg pointed out that the items Leverett said made the federal system not completely democratic were written into the Constitution as compromises between the states. And Stewart added, "Georgia wasn't created by several counties getting together and creating a state, was it?"

Leverett agreed. But he insisted that Georgia gave counties great autonomy and chose the county unit system deliberately as the system that best met its needs. If this system were unconstitutional, he argued, it would be extremely difficult for a state to devise a system in which representation could be precisely equal. "How close to precise representation must a state come?" he asked.

"There is one easy formula. One man, one vote," Goldberg said. "You used that in the last election. Did anything bad follow from that?"

"Nothing except that the express desire of Georgia's lawmaking body was frustrated," Leverett said.

"You're saying that it's enough if the legislature just says it wants to favor a rural county, aren't you?" Justice White asked.

"Yes, sir," Leverett replied.

"Wouldn't you get the same result if the legislature just said every rural voter can cast three votes?"

"Yes, sir."

"Would it be the same thing if the votes were weighted for the city?"

"Yes, sir."

"Why should rural areas be preferred?"

Leverett suggested it was probably to prevent the people in heavily populated cities from voting great portions of the state tax money to urban projects and neglecting the rural areas.

In concluding his argument, Leverett said that the Constitution required only that a state legislature have some "recognizable, identifiable policy" in the way in which it chose to apportion votes in a county unit system or seats in its legislature. "If there's any basis to it at all," he said, "that ends the inquiry by courts into the system."

In the basement of the court building the four youngest Kennedys present had gathered near the candy and soda-pop machines. Kathleen, Joseph, Robert, and David, aged eleven, ten, eight, and seven, had all come to hear their father argue his first case. A reporter asked them what they thought of the case so far. Kathleen replied for the group: "They talk an awful lot."

When the red light came on in front of Leverett to tell him his time was up, he was replaced by Abram.

The reason for apportioning seats in state legislatures, Abram said, was to give minorities some representation. But no such justification applied to voting. "The only purpose of this system," he said, "could be to see that a minority prevails."

Abram attempted to tell the Justices some of the facts of life in Georgia politics. If neither candidate in a statewide race for Governor got a majority of the county unit votes, a run-off between the two would follow. "It's tough in a run-off to be the man who got the majority of the [popular] vote," he said.

"Do you think it would be bad politically to be known as the man most of the people wanted as Governor?" Stewart asked with a tone of amazement.

"It would be death, sir," Abram said. He explained that Atlanta had long been plagued by anti-urban and anti-Negro attitudes in Georgia's small counties. A candidate who swept Atlanta would be at a disadvantage because he would be tagged in all the rural counties as the favorite of the Negroes and the city slickers.

As Abram continued his argument, the crowd in the courtroom gradually increased. Dozens of reporters who seldom set foot in the building filled up the seats reserved for the press in the north corridor separated from the courtroom only by marble pillars and bronze screens. Television crews set up their equipment outside the building to catch the Attorney General and the Kennedy clan as they left the building. The Court does not permit photographs, or even sketches, to be made during its sessions.

Abram said he started his constitutional argument from the premise that voting is a personal right. A state, he said, cannot make arbitrary classifications between voters in order to give some votes more weight than others, though it can establish a general classification of who is eligible to vote.

"Can a state classify as eligible voters only those who paid taxes?" Stewart asked.

"I think it might," Abram responded.

"Eighth-grade education?"

"Yes."

"Literate?"

"Yes."

"How much property he owns?"

"That is historically permissible," Abram said. "How it would be decided today, I don't know."

Stewart asked about a plan that would give every college graduate five votes, every high school graduate three votes, and every grade school graduate one vote. Abram said that would be unconstitutional. "All I'm saying is that once you have determined what is the proper classification for voting, the vote of one man cannot count for more than the vote of another."

Abram said he did not want to talk about legislative reapportionment. This was a voting case, he insisted, not an apportionment case. "The worst that can happen if this Court upholds the court below is that everybody in Georgia can have a vote." The Justices could not uphold the Georgia county unit system, he concluded, "until you say that two plus two equals eight and fifty cents is change for a dollar. . . . I think a qualified voter is a qualified voter is a qualified voter. And a vote is a vote is a vote."

As Abram was finishing his argument, Mrs. White got up from the box reserved for special visitors and left the courtroom. She returned a minute later accompanied by the President's wife, Jacqueline. At about the same time, Edward Kennedy, the junior Senator from Massachusetts, appeared in the area behind the special box. The Kennedy family had turned out almost its entire Washington delegation to hear Bobby argue his first case.

When Abram concluded, Kennedy moved to the lectern. He said the United States had intervened in this case "to restore some confidence in representative government." The Georgia system, he said, was a "gross and arbitrary discrimination" that violated the Equal Protection Clause of the Fourteenth Amendment.

"We are not against a country unit system as such," the Attorney General said, but the United States was against discrimination against urban voters. "We are not saying that under all circumstances every vote must be given the same weight."

As he talked, the Attorney General pecked on the lectern with one finger. His bold, loud, and staccato delivery betrayed his nervousness. He told the Justices that Georgians should be granted a "free and unencumbered" vote. "The kind of invidious practice existing in Georgia now strikes at the very heart of the United States." If the right of a citizen to vote cannot be protected, then "the whole fabric of the American way of life is irreparably damaged." Raising his hand in the probing movement his brother had made well known, Kennedy said, "This case will have an effect on millions of Americans who have been disenfranchised in whole or in part." The system in Georgia, he said, reminded him of the old days. "We used to have a saying in my city of Boston, 'Vote early and vote often.' If you live in one of the smaller counties of Georgia, you've just got to vote once to accomplish the same result."

In general, Kennedy's argument supported the decision of the lower court. He told the Justices that not all county unit systems were unconstitutional. But when the Chief Justice asked, "Do you believe there is any system of weighting the votes that is constitutional?" Kennedy admitted that he had difficulty in thinking of a system that made sense. Warren's question, like the others put to Kennedy, was fairly easy. The Attorney General met none of the sharp questioning that sometimes fills the courtroom. But most Attorneys General have not been questioned at all when they appeared to argue. Kennedy had let it be known that he wished to waive that courtesy.

Harlan asked him if the Court could strike down the Georgia system without setting up some standard by which other county unit or reapportionment systems could be judged.

Kennedy thought it could. "For the Supreme Court to set up a standard for various states is impossible," he said. "The people of the states know their background and problems. As for Georgia, we feel that as men of good will, the legislature will pass a law that is fair. . . . We think it is clear that the ideal is 'one man, one vote'; that if there is any departure from it, it should be to further the electoral process."

"Isn't the logic of your position that all county unit systems are bad?" Goldberg asked. "Why doesn't the Government have the courage of its convictions?"

"We have the courage, Mr. Justice," Kennedy replied. "I just don't think it's necessary to say it now. It might be that there are states where legislatures would come up with a system making some sense."

"But you can't conceive of that?"

"But I can't conceive of that."

When Kennedy's thirty minutes ended, the Justices turned to the next case and the spectators drained out of the courtroom. Ethel greeted Bobby with a kiss on the cheek as he stepped into the corridor. Pushing back his hair, he said with a grin, "I'm glad it's over." All the other Kennedys and their friends swarmed around, telling him what a fine job he had done. Solicitor General Cox joined in offering his congratulations. To many in the courtroom who had no reason for great personal loyalty to the young Attorney General, however, his performance left something to be desired. The mass turnout of his relatives with their inevitable press entourage had threatened to make the courtroom more a spectacle than a place for serious debate.

Then, too, Kennedy had not really addressed himself to some of the most difficult points in the case. He had not talked about how the Justices could square the lower court's decision with their holding thirteen years earlier in *South v. Peters*. Nor had he grappled with the basic problem of how far an electoral system could deviate from pure representation and still be constitutional. Those were questions Cox would have discussed if he had argued the case for the government. But Kennedy had taken a different tack. He had argued in broad terms, treating the county unit system almost as a political scientist would treat it. His arguments dealt mainly with policy, though the Court usually deals with technicalities. Cox later said this was a deliberate choice by the Department of Justice. A Solicitor General could not do it, Cox said, but an Attorney General could appropriately present that kind of argument.

Cox's comments reflected the peculiar role of the Solicitor General. He is the third-ranking official of the Department of Justice, but he has responsibilities to the Supreme Court and to the rest of the government as well as to the Justice Department. He decides which lower court decisions the government will appeal to the Court. He decides what position the government will adopt in the cases the Court chooses to hear. He decides which attorney will argue that position. The traditions of the office are high, and the Justices expect each man who holds it to live up to them. They expect the Solicitor General to bring to the Court only cases of major importance and to be candid about the facts and law in each case, even when complete candor means revealing that the government has been wrong. They also expect him to present them with solid legal and constitutional arguments for the position he takes in each case. Thus it would be inappropriate for a Solicitor General to present an argument based more on policy and political considerations than on legal reasoning. In the county unit case, the government had presented that part of its argument in its brief which Cox had filed.

Cox had, of course, spent many hours preparing Kennedy for his appearance. But Kennedy's courtroom manner was quite different from that of his Solicitor General. Cox had spent much of his life as a professor of law, and sometimes gave the impression that he was teaching the Justices as he once taught students. This occasionally irritated some members of the Court, but it was clear that on some subjects even the Justices might learn something from a Cox lecture. On labor law, for example, Cox is one of the nation's experts. He had taught it for years at Harvard and had written innumerable law-review articles on it. When Senator John F. Kennedy became deeply immersed in labor legislation, Cox spent months in Washington, helping draft the new law and sitting at Kennedy's side on the Senate floor as it was debated. This long experience gave Cox a depth of knowledge in that field unsurpassed in the country. In other fields of the law Cox used the knowledge accumulated in years of teaching and research to weave together forceful presentations. Kennedy, when he argued the county unit case, had none of this depth, either of specific knowledge or of general philosophy of the law. As a result, his argument was tied closely to the facts of the case, which he had mastered down to the last statistic, and to the immediately relevant law. If Cox had argued the case, the discussion would probably have roamed far afield from Georgia and its peculiar situation.

Cox was appointed Solicitor General largely because of his work on the 1960 labor legislation and his political activities in support of President Kennedy's 1960 campaign. He was the coordinator of a group of university faculty members who contributed ideas, position papers, and drafts of speeches to the campaign. Almost all his predecessors as Solicitor General had similar records of political activity and most, like Cox, had distinguished careers in the law. Several had gone on to become

Supreme Court Justices or judges of federal appellate courts; four later became Attorneys General.

The Solicitor General, of course, does not argue all the cases in which the government appears nor does he prepare all the briefs that are filed. He has a select staff of ten lawyers, composed principally of able young men, honor graduates of leading law schools. In addition, he can use the legal offices of all departments and agencies of the federal government.

Since the Solicitor General occupies a position quite different from that of most lawyers, he rarely argues a case in which he believes his client—the government—is wrong. An ordinary lawyer's opinion of the merits of his client's case is properly discussed only with the client, who is entitled to have his case fully argued. But the Solicitor General owes a duty to the Court not to bring it insubstantial cases. Occasionally, the candor required of the Solicitor General leads to requests being filed by a government agency without his signature. When this happens, the eyebrows of all those at the Court go up. In one notable case Solicitor General Simon Sobeloff refused to handle the government's appeal in a security matter. Attorney General Herbert Brownell signed the papers himself and sent another lawyer up to argue the case, which the government lost. This apparently had no adverse effect on Sobeloff's relationship with Brownell, however, since he was appointed a federal judge thirteen months later. While such showdowns are rare, the power that the Solicitor General wields behind the scenes is tremendous. Shortly before the arguments in the county unit case, the Solicitor General's office became involved in discussions with the Air Force over the dishonorable discharge of an airman. He had been convicted of rape in the Oklahoma courts and immediately discharged. But when the conviction was reversed on appeal, the airman demanded reinstatement and sued in the Court of Claims for back pay. He lost there and petitioned the Supreme Court for certiorari, which was granted. Cox signed the government's papers only after the Air Force admitted it was partially wrong and agreed to remove the "dishonorable" from the discharge. Later, after studying the case further, Cox persuaded the Air Force it was totally wrong and a settlement of the back-pay claim was reached just before the case was to be argued.

Sometimes, however, the Solicitor General's views do not prevail over those of lawyers elsewhere in the government. In the spring of 1962 Cox had been unable to get all government agencies to agree on a single position in a case involving the confidentiality of reports made to the Census Bureau by manufacturers. The law provided that the files of the Census Bureau were confidential and would not be shown to any other government agency. The Federal Trade Commission had wanted to see the reports of the St. Regis Paper Company, and tried to subpoena the duplicate copies St. Regis had kept in its files. When the matter came before the Supreme Court, the FTC and the Antitrust Division of the Department of Justice insisted that the reports could be subpoenaed; the Census Bureau and the Bureau of the Budget disagreed. Faced with this dilemma, Cox argued both sides of the case fully and persuasively. Then he said that since the government was so badly divided, he thought that as Solicitor General he had an obligation to tell the Justices his personal views about the issue, which were contrary to those of the Antitrust Division. At this, Justice Frankfurter spluttered angrily, "How do you expect us to decide this matter if you can't even get an agreement inside the Justice Department?"

"Oh, Mr. Justice," said Cox with a broad grin, "if the dispute were only inside the Justice Department, I'm sure I could settle it."

chapter 10

THE MIDWINTER RECESS

FOUR DAYS AFTER THE COURT HEARD ARGUMENTS IN THE GEORGIA county unit case, it began its midwinter recess. During the next four weeks the Court scheduled no public sessions and only one conference. The rest of the time the Justices were free to work on the opinions they had been assigned, prepare for the arguments yet to be heard, or spend a few days resting. Some Justices like to get away from Washington during the winter. White and the Robert Kennedys had gone to Colorado to ski at Christmas, and now Black went to Florida with hopes of getting in some tennis. As is usual at the end of January, most of the term's work still lay ahead. Seventy-three cases had been argued and the Court would hear an additional seventy-odd before June. Twenty-seven of the cases argued had been decided, leaving a backlog of five opinions of the Court per Justice, plus whatever dissents or concurrences they felt compelled to write.

The two new Justices had made little noticeable impact on the decisions of the Court so far, but their effect on the atmosphere in the building had been noticeable indeed. One big change was the simple matter of getting Goldberg settled in the chambers assigned to the junior Justice. The three-room suites, like the seats on the bench, are assigned according to seniority, and the retirement or resignation of one Justice often triggers a moving day for his juniors on the Court. The two junior Justices, in particular, are usually anxious to move because only seven suites of offices are located behind the big, bronze doors that seal the

Justices off from the public; the other two suites are just outside
the "golden gates" on a public corridor. Douglas, however, the
rugged individualist, had chosen not to move up the line of
chambers as he moved up from junior Justice in 1939 to third
senior in 1962. Most of the chambers are very much alike, and
moving was too much bother, so he remained outside the golden
gates as, over the years, twelve less senior Justices moved behind
them. But Frankfurter's retirement entitled Douglas to the corner
suite of the second senior Associate Justice, and he decided to
take it. When Goldberg took over the offices Douglas vacated
there was a marked change in their appearance. Douglas had
filled the three oak-paneled rooms with mementos of his many
journeys to faraway places, and his chambers were obviously
those of a world traveler. Goldberg turned the offices into a small
art gallery, full of his wife's paintings. On the wall across from
his desk was an abstract painting in which could be identified,
among other things, the Preamble to the Constitution. In his secretary's office was one painting he particularly liked to show
visitors. It was Dorothy Goldberg's impression of one of the
memorable occasions in her husband's life, his appearance before
the Supreme Court on May 13, 1952, on behalf of the United
Steelworkers Union. Five weeks earlier, only hours before the
union was to go on strike against the nation's major steel mills,
President Truman seized the mills, placed them under federal
control, and ordered the workers back to their jobs. Goldberg
found himself on the same side as management, for a change, and
they fought the seizure through the courts, winning before the
Supreme Court, which held the President's action unconstitutional. A Goldberg legend was born of his argument as *amicus
curiae*. Because the issue was so important, the Justices had given
unlimited time for argument. When counsel for all sides finished
what they had to say, the Chief Justice gave them the thanks of
the Court for their hard work in getting the case briefed and
argued in record time. Many spectators, unaware that compli-

ments are not infrequently given by the Court, thought Goldberg was being praised for a job extraordinarily well done. It has been said ever since that Goldberg's argument was one of the best in modern times.

After four months on the Court, Goldberg was suffering a bit from the inhibitions of his new job. His social life was much slower than when he was Secretary of Labor, both because he needed to work at home some evenings and because the Justices are traditionally somewhat aloof. As he put it, "The Secretary's phone never stops ringing; the Justice's phone never rings—even his best friends won't call him."[1] Of course, the things that a Justice can talk about or do with propriety and those that a Secretary of Labor can do are quite different. It is a difference well understood by lawyers and by most residents of "official" Washington, but one that some newcomers never seem to grasp. High-ranking government officials are accustomed to having other officials and private citizens second-guess their decisions and urge particular courses of action upon them, and the cocktail parties and dinners for which Washington is famous are enlivened by these discussions. But such conversation, particularly regarding matters pending before the Court, is out of place with the Justices. When Justice Brennan was new in Washington he was once dumfounded by Eisenhower's Postmaster General, Arthur Summerfield, who cornered him at a party to complain about the Court's handling of obscenity cases and to talk about a case then before the Court. When the school desegregation cases were pending, one naïve soul asked Justice Black how the Court was handling them. Black, an old Washington hand, looked around with a blank stare and replied, "School cases? What are they?"

Appointment to the Court does not, however, cut a man off entirely from his friends. White regularly brings some of his old associates in the Department of Justice to the Court, more often than not meeting them in the Court's gymnasium. New lines were painted on the gym's floor after White was appointed to make it serve as a paddle tennis court, and he puts it to good use. Every now and then, Perry Lippitt dashes out of the Marshal's office in response to a one-word call from White: "Upstairs." That means it's time for exercise. Early in White's term a law clerk to another Justice was working late and, he thought, almost alone, when he heard a rhythmic thumping outside his office. Curious, he opened his door to see White dribbling a basketball down the long corridor on his way to the gym. White is so energetic he even impresses the special police on duty at the Court. "You know," a guard said one day, "he drives in here every morning and hits those stairs three at a time." White, whose office is two very long flights of stairs up from the basement garage, rarely uses the elevator.

Few of the other Justices are so athletically inclined. In a speech after his initiation into the Phi Alpha Delta legal fraternity that winter, Goldberg said, "As a new brother, I think I should tell you some of the innermost secrets of the Supreme Court. The Court is sorely divided. There is one group that believes in an active judicial philosophy; Justices Black, Douglas, and White are addicted to physical exercise. The middle wing, which believes in moderate exercise, consists of the Chief Justice and Justices Clark and Brennan. And then there's the third group—Justices Harlan and Stewart and myself."

During the winter White's career as a star football player was recalled again and again. In December *Sports Illustrated* picked him for its twenty-five-man Silver Anniversary All-American team. A few days later, he received the Gold Medal of the National Football Foundation and the Distinguished Citizen Award of the Maryland "M" Club. In January he was presented with the Mr. Sam Award of the District of Columbia Touchdown Club as the government official who had contributed most to the status of athletics in 1962. Never before had the sports-minded felt so close to the Supreme Court. But, then, never before had one of their own been a Justice.

White's sports prowess did not create any problems for the Court (beyond the suddenly expanded use of the athletic facilities in its third-floor gym and exercise room), but his former relationship with the Department of Justice did. To spectators who had known him as Deputy Attorney General, it seemed a bit strange for White to be questioning Robert Kennedy when he argued the county unit case. A year before, Kennedy was asking White's counsel and making the decisions himself. White, of course, disqualified himself in all cases in which he had been involved while in the Department of Justice. Whether a Justice should step out of a case is traditionally left to his own conscience and good judgment. The rule of thumb that most of them have accepted is that a Justice should abstain from any case with which he has had personal contact or in which his impartiality might be questioned. But he is free to sit as long as he thinks he can approach the issues with an open mind and without reflecting on the impartiality of the Court. The Justices seldom explain their reasons for stepping out of a case or for staying in one. Their actions are rarely questioned. In the mid-1940's, however, the Court suffered through one of its most bitter internal battles when Jackson thought Black should disqualify himself in a case and Black refused to do so. In that case a lawyer who had been one of Black's partners many years earlier was representing one of the parties.

The problems of disqualification are most difficult for those Justices who, like White, have worked in the Department of Justice. The Department is the largest single litigant before the Court, appearing in more than a third of the cases argued each year. Immediately after World War II, the Court was crippled because President Roosevelt had appointed so many Justice Department officials to it. When a major antitrust case involving the Aluminum Company of America reached the Court, four Justices disqualified themselves because they had previously been involved in the matter. That left the Court without its quorum of six Justices. To meet the problem, Congress passed a special law giving jurisdiction of appeals in such cases, which ordinarily go directly to the Supreme Court, to the three senior judges of the circuit in which the case was tried. In the *Alcoa* case this meant the appeal was decided by a very distinguished panel consisting of Learned Hand, Augustus N. Hand, and Thomas W. Swan. In ordinary cases, however, lack of a Supreme Court quorum requires automatic affirmance of the lower court's decision.

Of the eight men Roosevelt appointed to the Court, Reed, Murphy, and Jackson came directly from the Department of Justice. In the years since, only Clark and White were in the Justice Department immediately before coming to the Court. Clark has often been accused of carrying to the bench the attitudes of a prosecutor developed during the twelve years he spent in the Justice Department, first in the Antitrust Division, later as head of the Criminal Division, and finally as Attorney General. He alone dissented in 1957 when the Court upset the convictions of a group of second-string Communist leaders, placed some restraints on the activities of congressional investigating committees, and gave defendants in criminal trials a right to compare statements government witnesses made to the FBI with their statements in court. In some instances the criticism the Court received for those decisions could be traced directly to the language of Clark's dissents. His opinion in the *Jencks* case, for example, contained the grossly inaccurate statement that "those intelligence agencies of our Government engaged in law enforcement may as well close up shop, for the Court has opened their files to the criminal and thus afforded him a Roman holiday for rummaging through confidential information as well as vital national secrets."[2] Liberals decided Clark was a man who placed little weight on the rights of individuals because of his fears that the Court's emphasis on individual rights was leading the country to disorder and destruction. But in 1961 Clark cast the deciding vote and wrote the Court's opinion when it barred state courts from accepting as evidence in criminal trials materials that had been gathered by means of unconstitutional searches and seizures. The fact that Clark wrote that opinion may well have muted criticism of the decision by law enforcement groups that had often described Clark as the only Justice who really understood the problems of law enforcement. As these cases imply, it is difficult to predict with assurance Clark's position on any issue presented to the Court for the first time. Unlike Black or Frankfurter, he has not delineated a jurisprudential theory of the Constitution that might indicate how he stands on undecided issues.

Clark has, however, made major contributions to American law in his work off the bench. He spends a great deal of time on problems of administration of justice in the lower federal courts, urging that ways be found to speed up the judicial process and that training programs be instituted for new judges. Any time anyone has a project that may improve the courts, Clark is the Justice who will be glad to discuss it and lend it his support if it is worthy. As this interest in law at the level where it affects the greatest number of Americans may suggest, Clark is one of the friendliest members of the Court. He likes to play the poor country boy from Texas who can't always follow the sophisticated talk of his Washington neighbors. In 1961 he began a speech in typical fashion, explaining that he was speaking extemporaneously "because I found several words I couldn't pronounce in the speech written by my Harvard Law clerk." Nobody who knows Clark takes that corn-fed attitude seriously; it veils the keen mind of a man who knows what he wants and how to get it.

chapter 11

THE LAW IS NEVER STILL

"THE LAW MUST BE STABLE," DEAN ROSCOE POUND ONCE WROTE, "but it must not stand still."[1] Without stability, the law would be unpredictable and the decision in every lawsuit would turn on the whim of the judge or the jury. But if the law never changed, it would quickly prove inadequate in a dynamic modern society. Law in the United States, of course, is much more than the statutes passed each year by Congress. The courts' interpretations of those statutes are law. So is the Constitution. So are court decisions interpreting it. And so is the "common law," the great body of judicial decisions on questions to which no statute or constitutional provision applies. The common law originated in decisions of early English judges and was brought to America during the colonial period. Since then, the decisions of judges in each state have added to the common law of that state, so that now, although most of the states have "common law," that law can be very different in, say, New Hampshire and Nebraska. In all its aspects, the law is constantly changing, and one of the tasks of the Supreme Court is to keep those changes within the framework of basic constitutional principles.

No thoughtful jurist would now deny that judges make law although in the past many conscientious judges firmly believed that they simply "found" the law in the statutes and the old cases. The common law, which is entirely judge-made (though some of its rules have been modified by legislation), governs a great many of men's ordinary affairs—contracts, the meaning of wills, liability for harm inflicted on others. In addition, many of the words and phrases used in statutes find their specialized meanings in the common law. In interpreting the Constitution, judges also make law. Chief Justice Hughes once said, "We are under a Constitution, but the Constitution is what the judges say it is. . . ."[2] He went on to explain the limitations on judges, but what he had said was, in a very real sense, true. Because the Supreme Court has the last word on the Constitution, no one else can say precisely what its more vaguely worded clauses mean until the Justices have spoken. And they, of course, sometimes change their minds. The judges also make law in the area of statutory interpretation. By defining what an Act of Congress or a state law really means, the judges often set the limits to the law's application.

All three of these law-making functions were demonstrated on the day in February when the Justices returned to the bench after the midwinter recess. They clarified, to some extent, the power of Congress to take away American citizenship and to do so they interpreted the Constitution. They refused to believe that Congress intended to authorize the National Labor Relations Board to regulate labor activities on ships manned by alien crews and registered in foreign countries; in doing so, they set a limit that Congress had not expressed on the operation of the national labor laws. And they continued a long process of creating law to protect railroad employees.

Goldberg opened this sequence by announcing the Court's decision in two citizenship cases.[3] In each case the Court was called upon to decide the fundamental question of whether Congress had power to divest an American of his citizenship because he remained outside of the country during time of national emergency in order to evade the draft. In 1944 and again in 1952 Congress had passed laws doing just that.

The cases involved Francisco Mendoza-Martinez and Joseph Henry Cort. Mendoza-Martinez, whose parents were Mexican, was an American citizen because he was born in California. In 1942 he went to Mexico to evade the draft and stayed there until 1946. A month after his return to California, he pleaded guilty to draft-dodging and was sentenced to prison for a year and a day. He served the sentence and then lived in California undisturbed until 1953 when the government told him he would soon be deported. Because he had left the country to evade the draft, the government claimed, he had automatically lost his citizenship under the 1944 Act of Congress. As an alien, he could be deported.

Cort was also a native-born citizen. After receiving his medical degree from Yale University in 1951, he went to England to do research at Cambridge University. He was told to return home by his draft board but refused, claiming that he would be prosecuted for his political beliefs if he returned. He had been a member of the Communist Party while a student at Yale. Subsequently, Cort moved to Czechoslovakia where, in 1959, he applied for a new American passport. His application was rejected because he had lost his citizenship when he refused to return and be drafted.

The difficulty of the cases lay in the fact that the Constitution confers citizenship on all persons "born or naturalized in the United States" but says nothing about how that citizenship can be lost. Noting this, Goldberg said that there are "imperative obligations" of citizenship that Congress can compel a citizen to fulfill. "One of the most important of these is to serve the country in time of war and national emergency. The powers of Congress to require military service for the common defense are broad and far-reaching, for while the Constitution protects against invasions of individual rights, it is not a suicide pact." He pointed out that the government claimed the Acts of Congress involved in these two cases were valid not only as an exercise of its power to make war and to regulate foreign affairs but as an exercise of its inherent sovereignty. Attorneys for Cort and

Mendoza-Martinez, on the other hand, said the Acts were beyond the reach of those powers and, in addition, imposed cruel and unusual punishment on draft-dodgers in violation of the Eighth Amendment. Before turning to previous decisions of the Court on this subject, Goldberg mentioned the "grave practical consequences" of the deprivation of citizenship. Cort would be a stateless person without membership in any national entity; he would have no government to turn to when he needed help. Mendoza-Martinez, who was also a Mexican citizen, would not be in quite so difficult a situation.

Once before, the Supreme Court had dealt with the power of Congress over citizenship. In 1958 six Justices said Congress had power to take citizenship away from native-born Americans in some situations. Black, Douglas, and Whittaker dissented, arguing that Congress had no power to revoke citizenship. The Court then voted, 5 to 4, that a law taking citizenship away from Americans who voted in an election in another country was constitutional. Black, Douglas, and Whittaker were joined in dissent by the Chief Justice, who thought that voting in a foreign election merely for local, not national, officers was not an indication of a change of allegiance for which citizenship could be revoked. In another case decided the same day, the Court had held unconstitutional a law taking citizenship away from those dishonorably discharged from the military forces during wartime for desertion. In that case, Brennan had joined Black, Douglas, Whittaker, and Warren in voting against the law. Brennan, who had thought the power entrusted to the federal government to avoid embarrassment in international affairs was sufficient to allow Congress to revoke the citizenship of those who participated in foreign elections, could not find a similar justification in cases of desertion. The result of this split on the Court was to leave the power of Congress in the citizenship area quite unclear and to make it impossible to predict how the Justices would divide in the draft-dodgers' cases.

In his opinion for the Court, Goldberg said there was great similarity between the case of the deserters and that of the draft-dodgers. The real aim of the Act of Congress, he said, was to punish the draft-dodger, not to help the government wage war or conduct foreign affairs. It was punishment without an indictment and without a trial. Since the Fifth and Sixth Amendments to the Constitution guaranteed that no person would be punished without those safeguards, he concluded, the Act was unconstitutional. As he announced the decision from the bench, Goldberg remarked, "My distinguished predecessor in this seat [Holmes] once said, 'A page of history is worth a volume of logic.' " Then he traced the history of the Act and its forerunners from 1865 to 1944 to substantiate his view that Congress had intended the law as punishment. In an appeal for public understanding, Goldberg made clear that draft-dodgers could still be punished. An American living abroad cannot assert many rights, he pointed out, and must come home to enjoy most of them. When he comes home, he can be sent to prison for draft-dodging. In addition, Goldberg pointedly commented, the Court had not said Congress could not increase the penalty for draft-dodging.

Black and Douglas, while joining in Goldberg's opinion, noted that they still believed Congress lacked power ever to deprive a native-born American of his citizenship. Brennan filed a concurring opinion to say that he now had doubts about the wisdom of his basic vote five years before that Congress did have that power. But this case did not require him to resolve those doubts.

As Goldberg finished his announcement, he swung around in his chair and cupped a hand under his chin to watch Stewart announce the principal dissent. Stewart, joined by Clark, Harlan, and White, said Goldberg was misreading the legislative history of the Act. He agreed that the 1865 Act of Congress had been passed as a measure to punish draft-dodgers. But the history of that Act was not relevant to the intent of Congress in 1944 and

1952, he said, and there was nothing in the background of those Acts to show they were intended to punish draft-dodgers. Congress could be understood to have said that those who left the country to evade the draft disassociated themselves from the nation. Permitting international draft-dodgers to claim American citizenship, he added, might have an adverse effect on the morale of those who were drafted or were about to be. Denationalization was a reasonable way to deal with this problem. Agreeing that withdrawal of citizenship was a "drastic measure," Stewart said it was justified as far as these men were concerned. "It is hardly an improvident exercise of constitutional power for Congress to disown those who have disowned this Nation in time of ultimate need."

Harlan also wrote a brief dissent and he announced it with a hard, harsh tone to his voice that conveyed an unusual sense of anguish. He said he wanted to "underscore" what Stewart had said. "It seems extraordinary to us that there is any doubt of the power of Congress, to borrow a phrase from my brother Stewart, 'to disown those who have disowned their Nation.' "

It was readily apparent that all the answers to the citizenship problem were not in. Goldberg's opinion disposed of the cases on a narrow ground. It did not say that Congress lacked power to deprive a draft-dodger of citizenship as part of the penalty for the crime of leaving the country to evade the draft. Such a statute would get around Goldberg's objection that Cort and Mendoza-Martinez were punished without indictment and jury trial, but it would raise the question whether denaturalization was a cruel and unusual punishment barred by the Eighth Amendment. Nor did Goldberg's opinion deal with the extent of congressional power to deprive native-born Americans of citizenship. It left that question for another day, and Brennan's concurrence indicated that he, at least, was not so sure now as he had been in 1958 that Congress had such power. Still a third question that remained open was whether there could be a difference in the position of a native-born citizen and that of a naturalized one. This question was referred back to the lower courts by an order filed the same day.[4] It was raised in the case of Angelika Schneider, who was born in what is now West Germany, came to the United States with her family when she was four years old, and gained citizenship when her mother was naturalized eleven years later. She grew up in the United States, graduated from Smith College, and spent two years studying abroad. There she met Dieter Schneider, a German lawyer, whom she married in 1956 and with whom she has lived in Germany ever since. In 1959 the State Department refused to extend her passport and demanded that she surrender her naturalization certificate, saying she had lost her citizenship by living in the country of her birth for three years. She asked the federal district court to convene a three-judge court to hear her claim that the Immigration and Nationality Act, which provided for such denaturalization, was unconstitutional because it discriminated unreasonably between naturalized and natural-born citizens. The federal district court refused, saying that there was no substantial question about the constitutionality of this statute. The Supreme Court disagreed, and in a terse *per curiam* opinion directed that the case be heard by a three-judge court.

By deciding the *Cort* and *Mendoza-Martinez* cases on the narrowest possible ground, the Court was following its long history of avoiding as many issues as possible and deciding such issues as it had to face in a way that would not block further development of the law. Two quite different factors lie behind this policy. One rests on the Constitution, which limits the judicial power of the United States to "Cases" and "Controversies." The Court has long held that it has no jurisdiction to give advisory opinions, such as might be requested by Congress on the constitutionality of proposed legislation. This means that a statute like the one involved in Mendoza-Martinez's case can lie around for twenty years, or even more, before it ever reaches the Supreme Court. When an Act does reach the Court under constitutional challenge, the other factor comes into play, and the Justices use any available alternative ground to dispose of the case without deciding the constitutional question. They feel that holding a law unconstitutional is a drastic step that should be used only as a last resort. This enables the Court to avoid unnecessary confrontations with Congress, with the President, and with state governments. Inevitably a decision by the Court branding some action unconstitutional sets up a wave of resentment, and avoidance of this wave wherever possible is the better part of valor. Thus the Court's decision, though it held this particular method of denaturalization unconstitutional, did not say Congress was barred from trying some other method. Whether Congress would do so was quite problematical.

In some areas of law, however, the Court's problem is not that Congress has acted but that it has ignored a problem. One of these that has caused the Justices considerable anguish over the years involves the liability of railroad and steamship companies for their employees' injuries. Most industrial employees in the nation are now covered by state workmen's compensation acts. But many years ago, before workmen's compensation laws became prevalent, Congress passed the Federal Employees Liability Act and the Jones Act to liberalize the rules in negligence cases brought against their employers by railroad workers and seamen. When these statutes were new, they gave the railroad and maritime workers a substantial advantage over their industrial counterparts. But workmen's compensation laws, based on the philosophy that on-the-job accidents are inevitable and should be treated as a cost of doing business, made payments to injured workers automatic. No longer did the workers have to prove that anyone had been negligent. Thus in recent years the railroad and maritime workers have been at a substantial disadvantage, since they must still show that their employers' negligence caused their injuries. The obvious solution is to amend the FELA and the Jones Act, but only Congress can do so, and it has not seen fit to act. The Court has handled this inequity by reducing almost to the vanishing point the amount of evidence of negligence needed to submit one of these cases to the jury, knowing full well that juries almost always decide against railroads. Immediately after the citizenship cases were disposed of, Justice White announced a decision that illustrated what the Court was doing.

This case involved James Gallick, who had worked for the Baltimore & Ohio Railroad in its Cleveland yards.[5] On August 10, 1954, Gallick was working on a section of track in downtown Cleveland that ran beside a pool of stagnant water. The pool, littered with dead rats and pigeons, had been there for years and, like several other pools and the nearby Cuyahoga River, was swarming with all kinds of insects. As Gallick walked down the track, one of the insects crawled up his leg and bit him. He crushed the bug, dropped it on the ground, and forgot about it. Subsequently, the bite became infected, his doctors could not discover how to treat it, and he lost both his legs. If Gallick had been covered by workmen's compensation, he would have been supported by the company for the rest of his life because he was totally disabled. But he was covered only by the FELA, and before he could make the railroad pay anything, even medical bills, he had to go to court and prove that its negligence caused his injury. Under the normal law of negligence, this would have required Gallick to show that the railroad company owned or controlled the pool of water, knew about its unsavory condition, and knew that someone was likely to be injured because of it, and that his injury was the result of the railroad's failure to correct the situation. All Gallick could prove was that the railroad knew a vermin-infested pool was on its property and that his injury may have been due to the bite of a bug that may have come from it. The jury awarded him $450,000. However, the Ohio Court of Appeals reversed that judgment on the grounds that the railroad's negligence was purely conjectural and even the jury said there was no reason for it to anticipate that its stagnant pool would cause injury to anyone.

This case was typical of the FELA and Jones Act matters that reach the Supreme Court. The question was whether the Ohio appellate court was justified in saying that as a matter of law there was insufficient evidence to support the jury's verdict. In most negligence cases the decision of the Ohio court on this point would be decisive because the formation of the rules in these cases is normally left to the states. As a matter of pure negligence law, there was insufficient evidence for the jury to return a verdict for Gallick. But in FELA cases, which are based on an Act of Congress, federal rather than state law is always applied even though employees like Gallick may sue in either state or federal courts. Thus the Supreme Court, which determines all questions of federal law, sets the standards of evidence. In his opinion for the Court in Gallick's case, White said a majority of the Court thought the Ohio court was wrong. The only question the courts could ask, he said, was whether it was possible for any reasonable man to decide that Gallick's injury was due in any part to the negligence of the railroad. If the answer to that question was yes, the entire problem was up to the jury.

Harlan, Stewart, and Goldberg dissented, and in a brief statement Harlan pointed out the whole trouble with FELA and Jones Act cases. "Heartrending as [Gallick's] accident has turned out to be," he wrote, "I think this case should not have been brought here. It involves no unsettled questions of federal law calling for decision by this Court. . . . The case has necessarily required an inordinate amount of time, which the Court can ill afford in the present state of its docket. . . . [It] affords a particularly dramatic example of the inadequacy of ordinary negligence law to meet the social obligations of modern industrial society. The cure for that, however, lies with the legislature and not with the courts."

This is the kind of case that infuriates the legal purists. Frankfurter believed so strongly that the Court should not spend its time on FELA and Jones Act cases that for several years before his retirement he refused to participate in them. It is quite clear that the Court has been distorting the law of negligence to provide a solution to the problem of workers not covered by workmen's compensation laws. It has done this under the pretense that to do otherwise would be to deny these workers the right to have a jury decide their claims. The result is that the workers have a remedy, but the remedy requires time-consuming litigation and is much more costly to employers. A workmen's compensation award to support Gallick for the rest of his life would have fallen far short of the $450,000 the jury gave him.*

Gallick's case was an example of what can happen when Congress is unconcerned about problems in the law. The Supreme Court would have been spared hours of work, the railroads would have been saved millions of dollars, and the railroad workers would have been better protected if Congress had seen fit to pass a workmen's compensation law for them. Another decision, announced a few minutes after Gallick, illustrated, on the other hand, what can happen when Congress passes a law without considering all its ramifications. In this instance, the ramifications had brought the National Labor Relations Board and the State Department into direct conflict and had brought protests to the United States Government from the governments of Great Britain, Canada, Honduras, Panama, and Liberia.

The case involved an assertion of jurisdiction by the NLRB over labor matters on board ships owned by the United Fruit Company and carrying bananas from Honduras to the United

* Both Gallick and the attorney who represented him died shortly after the Supreme Court reinstated the $450,000 judgment. Presumably the money, after hospital bills and attorneys' fees (probably at least $150,000) were paid, went to Gallick's heirs.

States.[6] The ships were registered in Honduras, flew the Honduras flag, and had crews composed almost totally of citizens of Honduras. The Labor Board ruling was the outgrowth of a long struggle between the two major United States maritime unions and the American owners of ships flying foreign flags. By registering their ships elsewhere, the owners escaped the high wage scales and stringent regulations imposed by the unions. The owners called the foreign flags "flags of necessity" since without them, they said, American shipping could not remain competitive in the world market. The unions called them "flags of convenience" that made shipping more profitable and put American seamen out of work. The attraction of these foreign flags was demonstrated by the bulk carrier fleets of the world. As of June 30, 1961, the capacity of tankers and ships carrying dry bulk cargoes registered in Liberia was twice that of the same kinds of ships registered in the United States. For years these ships had been treated, for legal purposes, as those of the country where they were registered; the law followed the flag.

The Labor Board decided it had jurisdiction over the crews of these ships because of the language Congress used when it passed the National Labor Relations Act in 1935 and the Taft-Hartley Act in 1947. Those Acts gave the Board jurisdiction over labor matters "affecting commerce," and it defined commerce to include "trade, traffic, commerce, transportation or communication . . . between any foreign country and any State, Territory, or the District of Columbia." Read literally, the language gave the Board power to decide labor problems arising on any ship carrying traffic to or from any American port. The Board said even it didn't think Congress really meant the Act to be that sweeping. Instead of claiming jurisdiction on all ships engaging in American commerce, the Board ruled that it would take jurisdiction only over ships that had many relationships with the United States. It included among these relationships the real ownership of the vessels and the amount of time they spent in American trade.

The Board's assertion of jurisdiction raised ticklish questions of foreign policy. Solicitor General Cox had told the Supreme Court, "In the opinion of the responsible government officials, the assertion of NLRB jurisdiction . . . would embarrass the United States in the conduct of its international relations." It could lead to reprisals against American shipping, he said, and could create serious problems for the Defense Department. Ships that belonged to American companies were considered part of the pool available for defense purposes even though they were registered in other countries; if the NLRB really had jurisdiction over their labor affairs, Cox said, the Defense Department feared the ships would be sold to foreign owners and become unavailable in time of war. While admitting that a literal reading of the law gave the Labor Board jurisdiction, Cox urged the Court to restrict that jurisdiction as much as possible.

The Court had no real trouble with the case, and the opinion Clark announced was unanimous except for Goldberg, who abstained, presumably because he had contact with the case as Secretary of Labor. Clark pointed out that no one disputed the power of Congress to apply American labor law to crews of foreign flag ships at least while the ships were in American waters. The question was, he said, whether Congress intended to exercise that power. The evidence concerning what Congress intended to do was scanty. It was clear the Court could read the Act either way and support its decision by logic. "The presence of such highly charged international circumstances," Clark wrote, "brings to mind the admonition of Mr. Chief Justice Marshall in *The Charming Betsy* . . . (1804), that 'an act of Congress ought never be construed to violate the law of nations if any other possible construction remains. . . .' " With that as a premise, the Court said that Congress never intended its broad language to mean what it actually said. Until Congress unmistakably said that the NLRB had jurisdiction, the Court added, the Justices would rule otherwise.

Time and again, the Supreme Court confronts the same kind of problem. Did Congress really mean what it said? Or what did Congress mean by this equivocal language? Sometimes this difficulty occurs because Congressmen never thought of the problems that would arise. Other times it occurs because Congress was so badly divided that only an imprecise, ambiguous law could be written. On every such occasion, the task of the courts is to fill in the gaps and to try to discover the intent of Congress. Judge Learned Hand once wrote of this problem:

> There is no surer way to misread any document than to read it literally; in every interpretation we must pass between Scylla and Charybdis; and I certainly do not wish to add to the barrels of ink that have been spent in logging the route. As nearly as we can, we must put ourselves in the place of those who uttered the words, and try to divine how they would have dealt with the unforeseen situation; and, although their words are by far the most decisive evidence of what they would have done, they are by no means final.[7]

Sometimes the Court is successful in reading the mind of Congress. Sometimes it is not. In either event, Congress has a quick remedy if it does not like what the Court has done. It can change the law. But Congressmen sometimes find it more useful to condemn the Court for distorting the will of Congress than to change the law. One of those situations in the mid-1950's gave some Congressmen a useful tool with which to attack the Court. The issue then was whether Congress, in making it a crime to conspire to overthrow the United States Government by force, had intended its law to override all state laws on the same subject. Because of the Supremacy Clause in the Constitution, any state law that conflicts with an Act of Congress is unconstitutional.

That Clause says, "This Constitution, and the Laws of the United States which shall be made in Pursuance thereof . . . shall be the supreme Law of the Land . . . any Thing in the Constitution or Laws of any State to the Contrary notwithstanding." From this Clause has arisen a doctrine known as "pre-emption." When Congress passes a law, it may pre-empt the subject covered by its law, thus barring all state laws on the same subject. In the case of the anti-subversion legislation, Congress had said nothing about pre-emption. The Supreme Court, considering the problems that would arise if every state, as well as the federal government, set its police to pursuing subversives, decided Congress had intended to pre-empt the field of subversion. The outcry, both in Congress and in some of the states, was that the Court had deliberately misread the intent of Congress in order to protect Communists. Congress, however, seemed quite content to let its members berate the Court for thwarting its intent and never bothered to change the law. It could have overridden the Court's decision simply by passing an Act saying it had not pre-empted the field.

chapter 12

BANKS AND THE LAW

ALTHOUGH THE GENERAL PUBLIC'S ATTENTION TENDS TO FOCUS on the Supreme Court's work in the areas of civil rights and criminal law, the Court's impact on American business, year after year, is tremendous. Almost half the cases decided by the Court relate to some aspect of business activity—the legality of state and federal taxes, the constitutionality of state regulations placed on corporations with interstate operations, the meaning of the national labor laws, the limitations placed on business activities by a wide variety of federal statutes.

Over the years, the attitude of the Court toward governmental regulation of business has changed markedly. For many years prior to 1937 the Court often struck down both federal and state efforts to regulate business practices on the grounds either that the regulations deprived businessmen of property without due process of law or that they were beyond the powers granted to Congress by the Constitution. Since the late 1930's, however, it has been a rare occasion when the Court has ruled that Congress overstepped its power in attempting to regulate business or that state legislation violated the Due Process Clause of the Fourteenth Amendment. Less rare have been the occasions when state regulations have been struck down on the grounds either that they conflicted with federal regulations or that they unconstitutionally impinged on the free flow of interstate commerce.

The most potent single weapon of the federal government in its regulation of business is the antitrust laws. The Sherman Act was the first, passed in 1890 to stop the pyramiding of control of industrial enterprises in mammoth corporations and trusts. This Act outlaws "every contract, combination in the form of trust or otherwise, or conspiracy, in restraint of trade or commerce among the several states." This Act also makes it a crime for any person to monopolize or attempt to monopolize "any part of the trade or commerce among the several states, or with foreign nations." Underlying the Sherman Act was a fear that monopoly power could be used by large corporations to set prices at high levels and produce unconscionable profits. For example, it would be illegal under the Sherman Act for the automobile companies to agree to set a minimum price of, say, $2,500 on every automobile manufactured in the United States. It would also be illegal for General Motors to buy up all the other auto companies so that it could totally dominate the market and eliminate all competition. The basic theory, of course, is that a free market economy operates best only when there is substantial competition among sellers. The Act is designed to protect that competition and to bar arrangements that might seriously impair it.

By its terms the Sherman Act bars every contract, combination, or conspiracy that restrains interstate trade or commerce. The Supreme Court, however, narrowed the Act in two respects soon after it was passed. One dealt with the types of business covered by the law. Like most federal legislation regulating business, the Sherman Act is based on the clause of the Constitution that gives Congress power "to regulate commerce ... among the several states." Because the Court decides what the words of the Constitution mean, the Justices have the last say on what corporations are engaging in the commerce that Congress can regulate. In the last years of the nineteenth century and the early ones of the twentieth, the Court limited the reach of laws like the Sherman Act by taking a narrow view of what constituted "commerce." The other limitation the Court placed on the

Sherman Act came when the Justices said it barred only "un-reasonable" restraints of trade. Ever since, it has been up to the courts to say what restraints are "unreasonable." After a brief round of enthusiasm, during which the antimonopoly provision was used to break the oil and tobacco trusts, these two limita-tions, combined with a marked lack of enthusiasm in the De-partment of Justice for bringing enforcement suits, made the Sherman Act peculiarly ineffective for a number of years.

In 1914 Congress passed the second major antitrust law, the Clayton Act, which in effect specified some practices that un-reasonably restrained trade. Its provisions, plus those of the Federal Trade Commission Act of the same year and the Robin-son-Patman Act of 1936, placed substantial restrictions on the activities of corporations beyond those that could be deemed monopolistic or combinations or conspiracies to restrain trade. The Clayton Act, for example, barred certain practices that might lead to a substantial lessening of competition. It outlawed, if they lead to a substantial lessening of competition, such things as discriminatory price-cutting, the practice involved in the Sun Oil case in which Justice Goldberg wrote his first opinion, and tie-in sales requiring a retailer to buy one product of a manu-facturer which he may not want in order to be permitted to buy another product which he does want. The FTC Act went even farther. It prohibited "unfair methods of competition" and thus reached practices that the Sherman and Clayton Acts would have left untouched.

From the viewpoint of businessmen, the various acts often seem to conflict. They argue that the Sherman Act was designed to protect competition but that the Robinson-Patman Act pro-tects competitors at the expense of competition. By this they mean that the Robinson-Patman Act prohibits some of the busi-ness practices that, if they were permitted, would result in lower prices. The Act clearly does have that effect and sometimes works to keep prices at a level high enough to let inefficient companies stay in business. On the other hand, the provisions that protect these inefficient competitors also serve to stop a few major corporations from driving smaller (and less efficient) ones out of business and thus reaching a position in which they could dominate the market and set their prices arbitrarily.

The two provisions of the antitrust laws that are of the greatest concern to businessmen are those involving price-fixing and mergers. The Sherman Act makes it a federal crime to conspire to fix prices and, as top officials of several electrical manufacturers learned in 1961, price-fixing violations can result in prison sentences. The anti-merger provisions of the antitrust laws are called into action by the Justice Department several times each year in an effort either to block proposed mergers or to break up established company ties. As contrasted with its attitude in earlier years, the Supreme Court has recently been sympathetic to the efforts of the Justice Department in this area. In the 1950's the Court decreed that Du Pont must dispose of the great blocks of General Motors stock it had held for years. Its reason was that Du Pont's holdings were so large as to unduly restrict the competition that might otherwise have existed for the sales to GM of products Du Pont made. In 1962 the Court barred a merger between the Brown Shoe Company, which primarily makes shoes, and the G. R. Kinney Company, which sells them, because that merger might unduly lessen the competition between shoe manufacturers by giving Brown an assured market. As a result of these and other decisions, every businessman contemplating expansion of his business, by buying another company either in the same industry or in a related industry, must consider the impact on his plans of the antitrust laws.

Soon after the Kennedy Administration took office, the Justice Department attempted for the first time to apply the antitrust laws to the field of banking. The Bank Merger Act of 1960 makes mergers of national banks insured by the Federal Deposit Insurance Corporation subject to the approval of the Comptroller of the Currency. Before he makes his decision on each merger, the Comptroller must ask the opinion of the Justice Department, the FDIC, and the Federal Reserve Board. In November, 1960, the Philadelphia National Bank and the Girard Trust Corn Exchange Bank decided to consolidate. The Philadelphia National was that city's second largest (and the nation's twenty-first largest) bank with assets of more than a billion dollars. Girard, a state bank, was Philadelphia's third largest with assets of about $750 million. Each of the three other government agencies advised the Comptroller that this consolidation would have an adverse effect on the banking business in the Philadelphia area. Their reports showed that the new bank would have 36 per cent of all assets and deposits of banks in that area and 34 per cent of all loans. This, they said, would reduce competition among banks in Philadelphia so much that the consolidation should not be approved. But the Comptroller ignored their opposition and approved the merger. He later explained that the consolidated bank would be "far better able" to serve Philadelphia because its lending capacity would help attract new industry to the area. The over-all effect on competition would not be unfavorable, he said, because there were adequate alternative banking facilities in Philadelphia and because of the "beneficial effects of this consolidation upon international and national competition."

The day after the Comptroller approved the consolidation, the Department of Justice filed an antitrust suit to stop it. It claimed that the consolidation would violate Section 1 of the Sherman Act and Section 7 of the Clayton Act. The Sherman Act section is the one declaring illegal all contracts, combinations, and conspiracies in [unreasonable] restraint of trade. Section 7 of the Clayton Act says:

> No corporation engaged in commerce shall acquire, directly or indirectly, the whole or any part of the stock or other share capital and no corporation subject to the jurisdiction of the Federal Trade Commission shall acquire the

whole or any part of the assets of another corporation engaged also in commerce, where in any line of commerce in any section of the country, the effect of such acquisition may be substantially to lessen competition, or to tend to create a monopoly.

Always before, the Justice Department had been content to let other government agencies worry about the size of banks. It had acted this time apparently because it thought the Comptroller of the Currency was failing to pay due deference to the antitrust laws and because it thought the development of more giant banks was not in the best interest of the country. Within a few months after filing the Philadelphia case, the Justice Department instituted suits to block several other mergers and consolidations approved by the Comptroller.

The two Philadelphia banks argued that the Bank Merger Act had by implication repealed the application of the antitrust laws to bank mergers. In addition, they contended that Section 7 of the Clayton Act did not apply because neither bank was acquiring the stock or share capital of the other and neither bank was subject to the jurisdiction of the FTC. Thus this consolidation fell in neither category covered by Section 7. But, the banks said, if Section 7 did apply, the market in which the effects on competition must be judged was not the four-county Philadelphia area but the Northeastern United States; they wanted to compete with the giant New York banks for loans. After a long trial, Federal Judge Thomas J. Clary in Philadelphia ruled for the banks. He said the Merger Act did not bar application of the antitrust laws to the banking business but that the banks were right in both their Clayton Act arguments. Section 7 did not apply and, even if it did, the consolidation would not substantially lessen competition in the Northeastern United States, which was the appropriate market area, or even, for that matter, in the greater Philadelphia area. Since the consolidation would not substantially lessen competition, he concluded, it could not be an unreasonable restraint of trade that would violate Section 1 of the Sherman Act.

The case forced the Supreme Court to go deeply into the meaning of the antitrust laws. Were banks covered by them? Did Section 7 of the Clayton Act apply to this kind of consolidation in this kind of corporation? What was the relevant market area for judging competition? What percentage of the business in that market area must be involved to violate Section 7? The Court had never given definite answers to these questions, and answers to the last two would have repercussions far beyond the banking industry. If the Justices reached them, they might provide guidelines for all mergers. As a result, when the case was called for argument late on February 20, the courtroom was jammed with lawyers who specialize in antitrust law or who serve as counsel to major corporations.

Assistant Attorney General Lee Loevinger presented the Justice Department's case. He told the Court that the decision of the lower court imperiled the ability of the Justice Department "to cope with the current wave of commercial bank mergers." Then he surprised everyone present by choosing to base his argument only on Section 1 of the Sherman Act, relying entirely on his brief for discussion of the Clayton Act. The crucial factors, he said, were the relevant market area and the extent of control that is barred by the Sherman Act. He fired statistics at the Justices until they almost reeled in their seats. The new bank, he said, would be 50 per cent larger than its nearest rival, three times the size of the third largest bank in the area, and larger than all the smaller banks combined. The only business justifications for the consolidation were the increase in the largest permissible single loan the new bank could make and the gain in prestige its size would bring.

"Wouldn't it also enable the consolidated bank to compete with New York banks for larger loans?" Goldberg asked.

Loevinger admitted that it would, since some Philadelphians

had to go to New York for loans in excess of the maximum Philadelphia's largest bank could handle. But he said only 1/100th of 1
per cent of the customers of these two banks had any need for
loans larger than they could already make, and those customers
constituted such a microscopic submarket as to be irrelevant.

"Weren't there several business executives and a former
Deputy Comptroller who came and testified in the court below
that there was no Philadelphia bank adequate to meet the needs
of the city's industry? What do you make of that?" asked Goldberg.

Loevinger said no witness had testified that the new consolidated bank could acquire any of the large loans that New York
banks now made to Philadelphia businesses. Whether anyone
would take advantage of its increased loan limit was purely con-
jectural.

"The record indicates there are many larger banks in smaller
cities," Goldberg said. "Is it not logical to assume that they resulted from mergers?"

"No, sir. There is no evidence to that effect."

"Are you saying that those banks 'just growed,' like Topsy?"

"I have no recollection and there is no evidence on that point."

Turning to the relevant market, Loevinger emphasized that
the two banks did almost all their business in four counties. A
bank's customers are normally residents of the area where it is
located, and most people deal with local banks. There is outside
competition for only a small fraction of a locality's commercial
banking business. He argued that since preservation of competition is the aim of the Sherman Act, the relevant market area
should be that in which there is effective competition. Banks
have only their services to sell, and they render their services in
the area where they are located. He compared banks with gas
stations. When a motorist stops at a gas station, it's because he
wants service where that station is. By considering the market
area as extending beyond the four counties around Philadelphia,

Loevinger said, the lower court had disregarded the 99.99 per cent of their services that the banks rendered locally.

"Is it your position that any merger in any city giving a bank one third of the banking business is bad *per se*?" Goldberg asked.

This was important. The Court had never specified the percentage of business in any field that a single corporation could control without violating the antitrust laws. Lawyers thus were unable to give their clients any definite answer when they demanded to know whether it was illegal for them to buy another company that would give them 20 or 30 or 40 per cent of the market.

"We are not arguing for a *per se* rule here," Loevinger answered. "We do maintain that where there is no other business reason, such control [35 per cent] violates the Sherman Act. In this case, to rule that the merger is not an antitrust violation would be to rule that the number of banks in the Philadelphia area may be limited to three." He quoted an opinion written by District Judge Edward Weinfeld in another case:

> ". . . the Congress in its efforts to preserve the free enterprise system and the benefits to flow to the Nation and to the consuming public did not, in enacting the antitrust laws, intend to give free play to the balancing power of gigantic enterprises and leave the less powerful purchaser helpless. What the Congress sought to preserve was a social and economic order not dependent on the power of a few to take care of themselves."[1]

This was a classic statement of the American ideal of a free enterprise system composed of many businesses competing vigorously for business and therefore charging the consumer the lowest possible price. Weinfeld had contrasted that system with one in which only a few monster corporations compete, perhaps halfheartedly, among themselves.

Philip Price, the Girard Bank's lawyer, began his argument

by emphasizing that this case really was a dispute between the Justice Department and the Comptroller of the Currency. The Justice Department was particularly unhappy about this consolidation, he implied, because its advice had been ignored by the Comptroller. The fundamental reason for the suit, he said, was that the Justice Department didn't understand the banking business. A bank differs from other enterprises, he asserted, in that it cannot control its deposits, its interest rates are regulated by law, and it is strictly regulated by government agencies; it is impossible for a bank to engage in a price war or to control the money market. A bank merger thus could be properly judged not solely on its competitive aspects but only on its general effect upon the public interest. He said Loevinger's "three-bank" argument was "foolishness" because there were seventeen banks in Philadelphia and forty-one in the four-county area.

Goldberg asked him, "In addition to the capacity to attract larger loans, what other business justification is there for the merger?"

Price replied that Philadelphia needed a bank large enough to handle its needs. He pointed to the testimony of Philadelphia executives that their corporations would prefer to borrow from a local bank but could not because all the Philadelphia banks were too small to give them the large loans they needed.

"Is it your position that no competitive advantage results from the merger?" Goldberg asked.

Price admitted the new bank would have some advantages, but insisted that they would only improve its competitive position against even larger banks; they would not aid it materially in competing with smaller banks.

Turning to the Clayton Act, which Loevinger had chosen not to discuss, Price said it did not apply to this case. This was not an acquisition of stock so the first part of Section 7 didn't apply. Since banks were specifically exempted from Federal Trade Commission jurisdiction, the second part didn't apply either. He noted that the Justice Department had been working for ten years to persuade Congress to amend the law so as to bring banks under Section 7 but Congress had declined to act.

When Price's time expired, Arthur Littleton, counsel for the Philadelphia National Bank, took the lectern. He conceded that the Bank Merger Act of 1960 did not exempt banks from the antitrust laws. Since Mr. Price had shown why Section 7 was out of the case, he proceeded, that left only Section 1 of the Sherman Act. The government, he said, had failed to show that this consolidation restrained trade in any way whatsoever. It was not aimed at monopolizing the banking business in Philadelphia, but at preventing that business from going elsewhere. That city, he said, "fairly swarms" with solicitors from out-of-town banks looking for big loans. Producing a list of the leading banks in 110 cities with populations over 100,000, Littleton pointed out that in seventy-eight other cities a single bank controlled a greater share of the banking assets than the new bank would in Philadelphia. Why, he implied, had the government not shown the anti-competitive effects of concentration in those cities unless, of course, there were none?

Justice Black seized upon the figure of 88.4 per cent of the banking assets in Gary, Indiana, controlled by one bank. "Do you need much proof that there is a lack of competition where one bank controls 88 per cent of the assets?" he asked.

Littleton said that a former Deputy Comptroller had found adequate banking competition in every city in the nation but one with over 50,000 people.

"Those figures," said Black, "might indicate that the Comptroller has not been doing very much controlling."

When Loevinger rose to close the argument, Black got in the first word. Did the Justice Department agree that Section 7 of the Clayton Act did not apply to bank mergers?

It did not. Loevinger pointed out that the Department argued in its brief that the consolidation involved an acquisition of stock, so that it was covered by the first part of Section 7, and was not an acquisition of assets beyond the reach of the second part.

"If Section 7 is applicable, we have an entirely different case, do we not?" Brennan asked.

Under Section 7 the Justice Department could win its case merely by proving that the merger might substantially lessen competition. Under the Sherman Act it could win only if it could prove that the merger was an unreasonable restraint of trade. The difference between "might substantially lessen" and "was unreasonable" is a considerable one.

Loevinger agreed. He said the consolidation clearly led to a lessening of competition.

"Then why didn't you argue it?" Brennan snapped.

Loevinger said he was willing to rely on the discussion in his brief. It depended upon the construction of the documents through which the consolidation had been arranged. Their technicalities had been "drafted by Philadelphia lawyers," and were best left out of the oral argument, he said.

"Are you waiving your Section 7 position?" asked Black.

"No, sir!" replied Loevinger.

When the argument ended, the case seemed much less important than it had at the start. The banks had backed down on their claim that the Bank Merger Act exempted them from the antitrust laws. The Justice Department seemed unenthusiastic about its contention that Section 7 of the Clayton Act applied to this merger. Loevinger had focused the attention of the Justices on the Sherman Act and apparently hoped to win on that ground. During the oral argument the issues in dispute seemed to have been narrowed to include only the relevant market area and the effects on competition under Sherman Act standards. While answers to these questions would be important, the edge had been taken off the case. If the Clayton Act was out of the case, as the banks argued and as the Justice Department seemed close to admitting, no percentage figure would be forthcoming to show what share of a market had to be dominated in order to lessen competition substantially. The Court might deal with a percentage figure in terms of the Sherman Act, but the provisions of that Act are involved far less frequently and thus are far less important in merger cases than are those of the Clayton Act.

chapter 13

RELIGION IN THE SCHOOLS

AT 11:30 A.M. ON FEBRUARY 27, AN UNUSUAL HUSH FELL OVER the courtroom. The lawyers who had been arguing about the rights of two men charged with housebreaking in Spokane, Washington, gathered their papers and left the counsel tables. The Chief Justice announced, "Number 119, William J. Murray et al. versus John Curlett et al." Clerk John Davis stood, glanced around the courtroom, and replied, "Counsel are present." A new set of attorneys took seats at the counsel tables. The Chief Justice looked at the lean, sallow man approaching the lectern and formally recognized him: "Mr. Kerpelman."

"Mr. Chief Justice," said Leonard J. Kerpelman, "may it please the Court. This Bible-reading and Lord's Prayer case that is before the Court today has unique interest for all of us."

With those quiet words the arguments began in the most explosive cases facing the Justices this term. It had been less than a year since the Court's decision in *Engel v. Vitale*, which held unconstitutional the official sponsorship in New York's public schools of a twenty-two-word prayer composed by the State Board of Regents. But the same issue—religion in the public schools—was before the Court again in two cases. In one of them Maryland's highest court had upheld the constitutionality of a Baltimore school board rule requiring that every public school class begin each morning with the reading of a selection from the Bible and the recitation of the Lord's Prayer. In the other a three-judge federal court in Pennsylvania had reached a contrary decision about a state law requiring that ten verses of the Bible be read each day in the public schools.

The courtroom was crowded that Ash Wednesday as the arguments began. Many lawyers who were fascinated with constitutional litigation had abandoned their work for the day to listen. The line of spectators hoping for seats in the courtroom stretched down the marble hall at the entrance to the chamber past the busts of Chief Justices Vinson, Stone, and Hughes to the long flight of stairs that led to the street. The press section was full.

The direction that the argument in these cases would take had been determined the preceding spring when the Court decided the New York prayer case. Attorneys for Maryland and Pennsylvania had only two alternatives: they could attempt to distinguish what was done in their schools from what was done in New York; or they could call upon the Court to reverse its ruling of the previous June. At the time of that ruling much had been made of the fact that the Justices were dealing with a prayer composed by a state board. In these cases the prayer had been adopted, but not composed, by the local school boards. The distinction was tenuous but the attorneys could try it nevertheless.

Kerpelman began his argument in the simplest possible way. The case, he said, was a difficult one. Every human being was concerned about the meaning of life and man had developed complex systems of religious beliefs at the same time he was developing complex systems of government. "I think," he added, "that the most libertarian and noble system of government is the one established by the Constitution. It is so noble that it is hard to live up to. One noble doctrine is the wall of separation between church and state."

Immediately, Justice Stewart broke in. "I've read the First Amendment many times and I've never read that kind of language in it. What does it say?"

Kerpelman flipped through his notes to find the exact words of the First Amendment. " 'Congress shall make no law respecting an establishment of religion, or prohibiting the free exercise thereof; or abridging the freedom of speech, or of the press; or of the right of the people peaceably to assemble, and to petition the Government for a redress of grievances.' " After reading those words, Kerpelman admitted the Amendment said nothing about a wall of separation between church and state, but he argued that the Court had interpreted the Amendment to require such separation.

Stewart's question had laid bare the difference between his approach to the First Amendment and that of the other Justices, particularly Black. Stewart had been the lone dissenter in *Engel v. Vitale* the preceding June. He remarked then that he thought the Court was not helped in reaching a proper judgment by "the uncritical invocation of metaphors like the 'wall of separation,' a phrase nowhere to be found in the Constitution." He had not elaborated his point at that time but had been satisfied to say that he thought New York officials had not established an "official religion" merely "by letting those who wanted to say a prayer say it." The Court's majority had long before adopted Thomas Jefferson's phrase "wall of separation," and it was particularly dear to the heart of Justice Black, who had written the *Engel* opinion. He had used it there just as he had used it in many prior opinions. In 1947 Black had said, "The First Amendment has erected a wall between church and state. That wall must be kept high and impregnable. We could not approve the slightest breach." In *Engel* he had added that the First Amendment "must at least mean that in this country it is no part of the business of government to compose official prayers for any group of the American people to recite as a part of a religious program carried on by government."

As Kerpelman started to go on with his argument after answering Stewart, Justice Brennan interrupted. "Does the Balti-more school system say which version of the Lord's Prayer should be used?"

Kerpelman said it did not. "The rule itself seems to be an in-vitation for a short religious war each day," he added.

Goldberg asked whether Kerpelman's clients had any objec-tion to adding a fourth "R"—Religion—to the three "R's" usually taught in the schools. Kerpelman said they had no objection if religion were presented objectively, as history or literature. But Baltimore was not doing that, he said. "What we have here is a religious ceremony . . . set up by the school, conducted by the school. It is sectarian, as any ceremony must be. A ceremony is a different thing from a study."

Kerpelman's clients were Madalyn J. Murray and her son, six-teen-year-old William J. Murray III. They were atheists who claimed the school board's rule threatened their religious liberty "by placing a premium on belief as against nonbelief and sub-jects their freedom of conscience to the rule of the majority." The Baltimore school board had first promulgated a rule re-quiring Bible-reading and prayer in the schools in 1905, although the practice dated back to 1836. After Mrs. Murray protested, the board amended the rule to let a child be excused from the opening exercises if his parents formally requested it. This did not solve her son's problems, she claimed, because he was abused, both verbally and physically, for not participating in the morn-ing exercises.

As Kerpelman compared the facts in his case with those in *Engel*, Justice Harlan interrupted. One factor in that case was not present this time, he said. "There is no suggestion that the state composed this prayer, is there?"

Kerpelman agreed. In New York the State Board of Regents had written a twenty-two-word prayer that it hoped was ac-ceptable to all denominations. But, Kerpelman argued, the Court was not concerned in *Engel* with who wrote the prayer but with who sanctioned it. And the prayer in his case had the sanction of a state board.

Kerpelman agreed when Stewart suggested that it could be assumed that most Baltimore parents approved of the morning exercises and wanted them continued.

"Then if we strike this provision down, we are interfering with the free exercise of their religion, aren't we?" Stewart asked. This was part of the argument he had made briefly in his dissent the preceding June.

Kerpelman said he didn't think so. "It's a new concept to me that a majority's right to free exercise of religion should overwhelm the minority's right to be safe from the establishment of religion. . . . This exercise is establishing a religion in the schools against the petitioners' right not to have a religion established."

"But your clients can walk away from the ceremony, can't they?" Stewart asked.

Kerpelman said this was an illusion. The child who leaves the room while the others are praying "has no answer to those who think that would be an ungentlemanly or immoral thing to do."

"It seems to me," Stewart said, "there are two provisions affecting religion in the First Amendment. . . . One of them deals with free exercise of religion and the other with the establishment of religion. These two, separate, distinct clauses sometimes run into conflict with each other. . . . If the evidence should show that a vast majority of the children in the Baltimore schools and their parents want to open their day with a religious exercise, we would be interfering with their right to freely exercise religion [if we struck this down]."

Before Kerpelman could comment, Justice Black broke in. "Is that correct?" he asked. "Can one come in and interrupt our proceedings because he wants to pray? Is this what the Free Exercise Clause protects?"

"I'm not talking about a disorder," Stewart answered from his end of the bench. "There are constitutional rights that apply to all of us. . . . I'm only suggesting that the Establishment Clause and the Free Exercise Clause sometimes collide. It's a fallacy to lump them all together and say the Constitution deals with the separation of church and state."

Kerpelman, trapped in this unusual crossfire, looked from one Justice to another.

Justice Goldberg intervened. "The two clauses cannot be read so as to have an established church. Is that not right?" he asked. The question seemed intended to end the exchange between Stewart and Black and return the argument to Kerpelman.

Kerpelman agreed with Goldberg. Schools, he said, should deal with secular subjects. His clients "don't want to have any dogma in religious matters thrust on them. The Lord's Prayer is a Christian prayer, but even among Christians themselves there is disagreement as to the version to use. You always run into problems when the government gives favor to one religion or another or to religion over non-religion. . . . This case, of course, makes everyone uncomfortable. A large majority of this country love this prayer. It is a beautiful prayer. . . . It gives us great discomfort to have to face the fact that this ceremony is an unconstitutional ceremony."

"Would your argument go so far as to say that a period of silent prayer, designated as such, would be unconstitutional?" Goldberg asked.

"It's quite possible that that would be a constitutional procedure," Kerpelman said.

"There is no earthly way you could enforce a ban against a man's thoughts or his prayers," Black mused.

"What if there were no law about it, what if 99 per cent of the students . . . decided to get together two or three minutes early each morning and say the Lord's Prayer?" Stewart asked.

Kerpelman said that would be constitutional, but that was not this case because in Baltimore the state was telling them to do it.

"I couldn't agree with you more if there was any compulsion,"

Stewart said. "But this state has a specific provision that you can walk away from it. . . . Might it not be wise to remand this case to take evidence, to see who wants to have this prayer and what happens to those that don't? Most parents would like to have this prayer for the free exercise of their religion."

Again Black interrupted. "They want to use the taxpayers' money to carry out their religious exercises," he snapped.

There was no use to send the case back for trial, said Kerpelman, because the facts were all known. "It is quite clear that most people want the schools to use the prayer. But if they were in the minority, they wouldn't feel the same way."

Black asked, "If a majority voted to use this prayer, why couldn't it use the whole day for religion if it wanted to?"

The question went unanswered as Kerpelman took his seat, somewhat bewildered by the steady fire of questions and the sharp debate on the bench.

The outline of that debate within the Court was clear. Stewart was squarely challenging the "wall of separation" concept and wanted to get this case into the shape that would best fit his argument. If the facts established that a majority of students wanted to pray, Stewart seemed prepared to argue that they had a constitutional right to conduct that religious activity in the schools. The action of the school board, he seemed to be saying, did not establish a religion but simply enabled them to exercise that right. Black was avidly defending his view that the Constitution demanded a "wall of separation."

Francis B. Burch, Baltimore city solicitor, began his argument by trying to take a position midway between those of Black and Stewart. "Our position is simply that the Establishment Clause of the First Amendment is a matter of degree," he said. "The wall of separation is a matter of degree. It is not an absolute, fixed wall." The question to be answered in this case, Burch said, was whether "religiousness" was the main reason for Bible-reading and prayer in the schools. He recalled that the

Court had upheld the constitutionality of Sunday Blue Laws because they had lost their primary identification with religion and now simply reflected the desire of state legislatures to provide a day of rest and quiet. Morning exercises in the schools of Baltimore were like that, he said. "The practice had in it something other than religiousness itself. . . . It has a significant salutary effect in many respects. . . . It is a way of teaching moral values."

Burch's approach was quite different from that taken by many who had criticized the *Engel* decision. They had claimed that religious exercises in the public schools were perfectly constitutional and the Court had distorted the First Amendment in holding otherwise. For the purpose of his argument, Burch admitted that religion in the schools was unconstitutional. But he contended that Bible-reading and recitation of the Lord's Prayer were not religious exercises. They were used, he argued, to bring discipline and calm to the classroom.

With a wry smile Stewart said, "Just give them tranquilizing pills. It would do the same thing."

When the laughter died down, the Chief Justice asked Burch about schools, such as those in Hawaii, where a majority of the students were of Japanese or Chinese descent. "Do you say that in schools of that kind it would be proper to have a Buddhist ceremony and make all the Christian children participate in it or have their parents request they be excused?"

"If the school authorities should determine that morning exercises would have a salutary effect other than the teaching of religion," Burch said, "then they have the right to make such a selection of materials as will do the best job. If they thought the Buddhist ceremony was the best to set the tone for the day, then it would be all right."

"If it depends on the majority of the parents of a school district, doesn't this mean a different teaching of religion in every school?" Black asked.

Burch said perhaps it did.

"Are you disavowing for the State of Maryland that which I understand to be the genesis for all the commotion we have here?" asked Black. "Are you disavowing that the purpose is to increase the interest in that particular religion?"

Burch said he was not disavowing that but was going beyond it. The school authorities were trying to establish morality and discipline and had chosen Bible-reading and prayer as a way of doing it.

"How can you argue this is not a religious ceremony based on the Christians' Bible and their most beloved prayer?" Black asked.

Burch said, "I do not think it partakes of a religious ceremony. It has other values. . . . I think it's intended to start the children off in the right spirit."

Justice Harlan shook his head and interrupted with a pained expression on his face. "I think it would be helpful if you start with the premise that it is a religious exercise. Would you tell us whether this case can be distinguished from *McCollum, Torcaso,* and *Engel* and, if not, then are you asking the Court to overrule those cases and why?"

In each of these cases the Court had cut back intrusion of religion into public affairs. In 1948 in *McCollum* the Court had held unconstitutional a plan under which the schools in Champaign, Illinois, provided classrooms and allowed ministers of certain religions to conduct religion classes during school hours. The Court had said that arrangement provided the very aid for religion banned by the Establishment Clause. In 1961 in *Torcaso* the Justices had held unconstitutional a Maryland law that no one could hold state office unless he professed to believe in God. This law, the Court said, discriminated against those who believed in a non-Christian God or who did not believe in any God. The *Engel* case was the New York Regents Prayer case.

Burch said the Maryland situation was easily distinguishable from that in New York. New York state officials had composed a prayer while the prayer that was used in Maryland had been composed 2,000 years before by Jesus.

"Is it your basic point that a state may not compose a prayer but may select a prayer?" Goldberg asked.

Yes, said Burch, as long as the material selected did not put the state in the position of sanctioning a new prayer.

Harlan asked what Burch did with the *McCollum* case. "I have no problem with it," Burch said. In Illinois the schools were involved in a program that was teaching particular brands of religion. Bible-reading and prayer were not the teaching of religion.

Burch had divided the hour of argument assigned him with George W. Baker, a deputy solicitor of Baltimore. Baker turned the discussion immediately to the Free Exercise Clause. "If the Establishment Clause is not violated," he began, "we say that the Free Exercise Clause is not violated as long as there is an excuse system and no compulsion." He said the case was much like *Barnette v. West Virginia*, decided almost twenty years earlier. That was the case in which Frankfurter had dissented when the Court held that West Virginia could not require Jehovah's Witnesses to participate in the salute to the American flag, because their religion taught them not to worship a graven image and they believed the flag salute did precisely that. Justice Jackson's opinion for the Court in that case said:

> Struggles to coerce uniformity of sentiment in support of some end thought essential to their time and country have been waged by many good as well as by evil men. Nationalism is a relatively recent phenomenon but at other times and places the ends have been racial or territorial security, support of a dynasty or regime, and particular plans for saving souls. As first and moderate methods to attain unity have failed, those bent on its accomplishment must resort to an ever increasing severity. As governmental pressure toward unity becomes greater, so strife becomes more bitter as to whose unity it shall be. Probably no deeper

division of our people could proceed from any provocation than from finding it necessary to choose what doctrine and whose program public educational officials shall compel youth to unite in embracing. . . .Those who begin coercive elimination of dissent soon find themselves exterminating dissenters. Compulsory unification of opinion achieves only the unanimity of the graveyard.

It seems trite but necessary to say that the First Amendment to our Constitution was designed to avoid these ends by avoiding these beginnings. . . .

The case is made difficult not because the principles of its decision are obscure but because the flag involved is our own. . . . If there is any fixed star in our constitutional constellation, it is that no official, high or petty, can prescribe what shall be orthodox in politics, nationalism, religion, or other matters of opinion or force citizens to confess by word or act their faith therein.[1]

Baker told the Justices that Bible-reading and prayer in Maryland were similar to the flag salute in West Virginia. The Court had not ruled that the schools must abandon the flag salute; it only ruled that children who did not want to participate must be excused. Since Maryland allowed children to be excused from the morning Bible-reading and prayer, he said, the situations were identical.

Stewart broke in. Since the Murrays contended that the excuse system in Maryland was phony, wouldn't it be wise to remand the case to find out what the facts really were?

As Baker began to answer, Goldberg pointed out that the State of Maryland had conceded the truth of all the allegations the Murrays had made. Goldberg read from William Murray's complaint that the system of excuse had caused him "to lose caste . . . to be subjected to reproach and insult." Baker agreed that the facts stood admitted because of the manner in which the case had been considered in the trial court.

Then Baker asked the Justices to consider what would happen

if the Murrays won. "If the Court fails to draw the line in this case," he said, "there's not much left. Those who now clamor in the school cases won't stop if they win in the Supreme Court. The inevitable consequences will be continued litigation leading to the elimination from all public works and institutions of all forms of church-state contact which have the slightest connotation of religiousness. . . . They won't stop until they remove every vestige of religion from public life." The phrase "In God We Trust" would be removed from coins, he asserted, and suits would be brought to stop prayer in the legislatures and courts and to eliminate chaplains in the armed forces and prisons.

"What would happen if you win?" Black asked. "Is there any reason why if you can have three minutes, you can't have forty? If you can have forty, why can't you have six hours?"

Baker said that would be different because that would involve teaching religion while a three-minute opening exercise only sets the tone for the day.

Maryland's attorney general, Thomas B. Finan, spoke briefly on behalf of the state. He had filed a brief, joined by the attorneys general of eighteen other states, asking the Court to uphold the practice of Bible-reading and prayer. According to his survey, thirty-nine states permitted opening devotional exercises, while only seven states—Alaska, California, Illinois, Nebraska, Washington, Wisconsin, and Wyoming—forbade them. Finan agreed with Baker that the Maryland case involved "an exercise within the schools to create a climate of moral teaching." But he attacked the whole line of the Court's decisions which, he said, were allowing "non-theism to override theism."

The Chief Justice broke in. "Why do we have to make it an issue between atheism and Christianity? Are you saying that the only people who should ask to be excused are atheists?"

Finan agreed that he was. He said no one other than atheists should be opposed to Bible-reading and recitation of the Lord's Prayer in the schools. His analysis totally ignored the comments made in connection with these two cases by Jews, Unitarians, and members of some other religious groups.

"Let's suppose that Utah adopted a law saying that they would open schools by reading the Book of Mormon . . . and they excused any child who did not want to hear the Book of Mormon read. Would that be all right?" Goldberg asked.

"Yes, it would, Your Honor, if they were free to walk out."

"Then the contest would be which church could get control of the school board," Douglas said.

"You're suggesting that the Constitution gives a local option as to which particular brand of religion will be read and taught in the schools," Black said.

Finan said, "One can carry any example to extremes. . . . The basic thing that people feel today is that we must not set up a fetish about mentioning religion in the schools."

Black told him that the Murrays weren't complaining about just mentioning religion in the schools. "You have picked out two particular things to mention," he said. "I might agree with your choice but others don't."

The red light on the lectern showed that Finan had used up all his time. As he sat down, Kerpelman returned to the lectern to answer the arguments put forward by Baltimore and Maryland.

Before he could begin, Douglas asked, "Would your argument be the same if the Quaker pattern was used, a period of silence?"

"That would be constitutional," Kerpelman said.

"I suppose an atheist could stand there and think about his disbelief in God," Stewart commented.

"Would it be constitutional if it were denominated a Quaker ceremony?" Goldberg asked.

"No, sir," said Kerpelman. "That would be unconstitutional."

Kerpelman said he opposed reappraisal of *Engel* and the other cases. What was needed was not a re-evaluation of the cases, he said, but a "reawakening of the moral and ethical bases for those cases. There is more of a need for charity and love on the part of the majority who have offended the minority."

"You're getting off the Constitution," Harlan cut in sharply.

Kerpelman apologized. The case, he added, was not just a case brought on behalf of atheists. "William Murray represents Catholics in a Protestant area when Catholics find the King James version objectionable. William Murray represents Protestants in a Catholic area when Protestants find the Douay version objectionable. William Murray represents humanists. He represents many groups."

As Kerpelman's time ran out, Black recalled the verses in Matthew that immediately precede the Lord's Prayer:

> "And when thou prayest, thou shalt not be as the hypocrites are: for they love to pray standing in the synagogues and in the corners of the streets, that they may be seen of men. Verily I say unto you, they have their reward. But thou, when thou prayest, enter into thy closet, and when thou hast shut the door, pray to thy Father which is in secret; and Thy Father which seeth in secret shall reward thee openly."[2]

When he finished repeating them, Black said, "I found out this is a very strong belief throughout the country in the last year." Apparently, the mail that crossed his desk after he wrote the Court's opinion in *Engel* had contained letters from many persons who thought religion belonged primarily in the home and in the church.

As Kerpelman picked up his papers, the Chief Justice called for case number 142, Abington Township School District versus Edward Lewis Schempp, et al. Philip H. Ward III, the clean-cut young lawyer for the Pennsylvania township, moved to the lectern.

His case was different, he said. Although the Lord's Prayer was recited in the Abington schools, the state law required only that ten verses of the Bible be read daily without comment. It was that law he would defend and not the use of the Lord's Prayer. Under that law, anyone who objected could be excused from the exercises, but the Schempps had never asked that any of their children be excused. The exercises were conducted each morning over the public address system, Ward explained, when all students were in their home rooms. "First is the fact for the day," he said. "They pull something out of the *World Almanac*. How tall Mt. Everest is, for example. The ten verses of the Bible are then read without comment."

"The *World Almanac* comes first?" Harlan asked.

"Yes, sir," said Ward. "It's an attention-getter."

"Sort of a loss leader, huh?" Stewart said.

When the laughter died down, Ward continued: "Next the Bible-reading is followed by the Lord's Prayer, the flag salute, and announcements for the day. The broadcast is performed by students in the radio and television class. They take turns conducting the broadcast and each one is encouraged to use his own version of the Bible and to choose the verses he wishes to read."

"There's no evidence in the case, as I understand the posture of it, of what would happen if a child asked to be excused, is there?" Stewart asked.

Ward replied, "Mr. Schempp testified—"

"But that's his subjective belief," Stewart said before Ward got out more than the three words. "There's no evidence of what might happen because it hasn't happened, is there?"

Ward agreed just as the red light flicked on. The Chief Justice nodded to him and said, "We'll recess now, Mr. Ward. You can resume your argument in the morning."

The day had gone about as expected. Maryland had tried to distinguish its practices from those of New York; Pennsylvania had not yet had an opportunity to present its full case. That night the lawyers on both sides huddled to talk about the way the Justices were treating the case and to plan the next day's strategy. The lawyers for Pennsylvania could try to persuade other Justices that Stewart's approach to the problem was the best, but in light of *Engel* this seemed unlikely to succeed. Or they could pursue the argument that voluntary participation made the case similar to the West Virginia flag salute case, though that argument, too, had been weakened by the New York decision. Or they could support Maryland's contention that Bible-reading and prayer in the school program were not religious exercises, even though the Justices had shown little sympathy for that argument.

The courtroom was crowded again the next morning as Ward resumed his argument. The audience was speckled with clerical collars, but they suggested the depth of religious feeling aroused by the case far less forcefully than had the ashes on the foreheads of a great many spectators the day before, Ash Wednesday.

On the signal of the Chief Justice to resume, Ward immediately returned to the idea that Pennsylvania was trying merely to teach morality and had picked the Bible as a source of moral principles. "We're teaching morality, without religion, cut adrift from theology," he said.

"But this is teaching from which students can be excused," Brennan cut in. "Why do you teach it differently? Is it consistent with your argument that you excuse them? The fact that you do excuse them raises a question if, in fact, all you're doing is teaching morality. You don't excuse them from arithmetic, do you?"

"Maybe we should not excuse them," Ward said, "but that is what the people of Pennsylvania decided to do."

"Aren't you pushing us too far?" Goldberg asked. "Aren't you denigrating the Bible?"

Ward denied that. Pennsylvania was teaching morality and was using the Bible to do it.

"That's a very difficult argument to understand," Goldberg said. "The Bible is the greatest religious document the world has ever had, isn't it? Yet you say you read it not for what it is but for something else."

The Bible had values other than religious values, Ward insisted. This case was different from a case involving prayer, he said, because "suggesting the children say a prayer is suggesting a completely religious act. We are suggesting that the children listen to ten verses from a monumental work."

"Are you asking us to overrule [*Engel v.*] *Vitale?*" Warren asked suddenly.

"No," Ward replied. "*Vitale* was suggesting the children perform each morning a purely religious act."

"The Lord's Prayer is a prayer, is it not?" Warren asked.

"This statute requires only Bible-reading," Ward replied.

"Suppose the students agree on reading that part of the Bible which *is* the Lord's Prayer?" Warren asked.

"That is different from asking the children to say the prayer," Ward replied. "That is an announcement of how Jesus taught his followers to pray. Suppose my son went to school in Iraq and they read the Koran in school. . . ."

Douglas interrupted. "I happen to know there is no First Amendment in Iraq."

Ward went on. "If they read the passage from the Koran where Mohammed tells his followers how to pray, I do not think my son would thereby be required to pray."

"If the statute required the children to repeat the Lord's Prayer, is it unconstitutional?" Warren asked.

"Yes, sir."

"Under *Engel?*"

"Yes, sir."

There was a stir in the courtroom. The Maryland attorneys looked at each other aghast. Ward had told the Justices that he thought what Baltimore was doing was unconstitutional. The two groups of state officials had been expected to stay together in their arguments, but Ward, under the sharp questioning, was conceding the unconstitutionality of Maryland's practice in an effort to save Pennsylvania's.

Stewart, who had expressed sympathy for Maryland's argument, promptly stepped in. "Would it be unconstitutional even if you excused them?" he asked.

"Yes, sir," Ward said. "You are asking them to profess a belief in religion."

"What about *Barnette*?" Stewart said, turning to the flag salute analogy Burch had made the preceding day. "Would you say so if there was a statutory provision for excusing a child?"

"I think because of the nature of the prayer, it has no secular meaning. It is a purely religious act," Ward said.

As Stewart continued to press him, Ward backed off and agreed that, without coercion by the state, saying a prayer might be constitutional. But the damage to Maryland's case was done. Here was one public official willing to admit that prayer could not be justified as a way of teaching morality or maintaining discipline.

"Do you think the legislature adopted [the Bible-reading] because of its morality or its religious faith?" Black asked.

Ward said the Bible was adopted to teach morality because Americans are familiar with it and agree with its moral principles. The Koran was not adopted, he said, because it is unfamiliar and some of its teachings are strange.

"Is it not true that the Bible was really chosen because it is a Holy Book?" Black asked.

Ward said he could not agree. "It is that and so much more. It is so much a part of the tradition of this country." The morals taught by the Bible are not those of Christians alone, he said. The people of Pennsylvania chose that particular book because the state needed "to use a book everybody approves of."

"Everybody?" Black asked pointedly.

"A vast majority," Ward answered.

"What if the state said, 'We choose the Bible because it is a religious book. We will let children be excused but we want this read because it is our religion'?" Black said.

"That would be unconstitutional."

"So it gets down to a question of whether we can say the Bible is a religious book?"

"No. The question is whether Pennsylvania can use the Bible as a source of morality."

"Would you agree that the most productive and golden years of Christianity have been those when government let it alone and its worst years have been the years public officials got hold of it and corrupted it? Do you agree with that?" Black asked.

Ward said he agreed with that but that Pennsylvania was not taking hold of religion.

"Suppose there is one hour of moral instruction in which the Bible is read and objecting children are excused? Is this acceptable?" Warren inquired.

Ward said the problem was in determining what is reasonable. If the period were an hour long, men could think the school was teaching religion and not morality.

"Is one hour of morality unconstitutional but ten minutes all right?" Warren asked.

Ward said it was a matter of degree. The question was whether the school was teaching morality or teaching religion.

"Is that not our question today?" Warren asked.

"Yes, sir, it is," Ward said. "Can you use the great values in the Bible to instill morality, despite the fact that no one is coerced? Must the government prohibit this merely because it is a religious book; must the government wipe out this great tradition?"

As Ward sat down, a tall, lanky Philadelphia lawyer, Henry W. Sawyer, took the lectern. He is widely known as an outstanding advocate and several lawyers had come to Court especially to hear him.

Sawyer began by telling the Justices there was nothing voluntary about Bible-reading in Pennsylvania. The law required it. He pointed out that there are things in the Bible that upset his clients, the Edward Schempps. The Schempps were Unitarians and did not believe in the Trinity. Unlike the Murrays in the Maryland case, the Schempps were deeply religious. But they did not want their children exposed in school to things they did not believe, nor did they want to subject their children to social ostracism because of their beliefs.

In addition to containing ideas that differed with the beliefs of some Americans, Sawyer said, the Bible was also a difficult book from which to teach morality. Some parts of it are difficult even for adults to understand unless an explanation is given, and the Pennsylvania law forbade any comment on what was read. Noting the reference in Leviticus about the need for blood sacrifices to God, Sawyer said, "With young children one wonders whether this is good morals." The Bible, Sawyer argued, was not basically a source of morals but a teaching book. "The book teaches from the opening sentence of Genesis to the end of Revelations. . . . The New Testament is a teaching message that was highly controversial teaching then. It is highly controversial teaching now." He cited the part of the New Testament in which Jesus enjoined his followers to turn the other cheek. Not even all Christians agree with that, he said.

Turning to Finan's argument that some teaching of theism was needed in the schools and supported by past practice, Sawyer said this distorted American history. Pennsylvania had picked out only one book from which to teach morality, and had bypassed many valuable books, including the holy scriptures of other religions. "I submit it is not the function of government . . . to blur over religious differences and come out with a single form of morality," he said. Ever since the Middle Ages, when a religion was established by the state, the state said it was not trying to give men religion but was merely trying to make them better. In this case, he said, alluding to the point Stewart had been pressing, "The question is whether it is a constitutional right . . . to be able to pray under the auspices of the state. I think not."

Stewart suggested a hypothetical case. "Assume that there is no statute, that there is a student government, and the students vote to begin each day by reading ten verses from the Bible. What then?"

"If the school authorities let them use the public address system and require the children to listen, it is unconstitutional," Sawyer said. "But if, during recess, all the children who want to, come together and read ten verses, then it is all right. It is the aegis and imprimatur of the state that make it bad. The children have a right to do it, but they have no right to have the state help them."

"But doesn't that violate the free exercise rights of the 99-percent majority?" Stewart asked.

"They have a right to do it, Your Honor, but they haven't got a right to get the state to help them," Sawyer repeated.

"Isn't it true that every state helps religion in a multitude of ways?" Stewart asked. "Fire protection, police protection, tax exemptions?"

Sawyer agreed that was true. There are no absolutes, he said, but only a rule that the courts will ignore minimal cases. As an example, he thought it unconstitutional to use "In God We Trust" on coins, but that this was something about which the courts should not be troubled. It was too minor to matter.

"In other words, that violation is so small that courts would not enjoin it?" Black said.

"Yes, sir."

Harlan suggested, "You would be on stronger ground with Justice Black if you had said the inscription 'In God We Trust' is not a religious exercise."

Then Sawyer turned back to his main argument. He told the Court that the differences in versions of the Bible cannot be glossed over as lightly as the two states had indicated. Dr. Solomon Grayzel, editor of the Jewish Publication Society, had testified at the trial in the lower court about the marked differences between the Jewish Holy Scriptures and the Old Testament of the Christian Bible, and the pronounced anti-Semitism of the New Testament. Grayzel mentioned, for an example, the trial of Jesus as recorded in Matthew, in which Pilate put the final choice of Jesus or Barrabas up to the Jews. The Jews reprieved Barrabas and Pilate washed his hands when the Jews said of Jesus, "His blood be on us and on our children." This one verse, Dr. Grayzel testified, had been the cause of more anti-Jewish riots than anything else in history.

Didn't Dr. Luther A. Weigle, Dean Emeritus of the Yale Divinity School, testify that the Bible was nonsectarian? Justice White asked.

"Dr. Weigle said it was not sectarian among Christians and then he gave a caveat as to Catholics," Sawyer answered. "Also, he admitted that the Revised Standard Version had been publicly burned shortly after its publication. Finally, he admitted that the Bible was nonsectarian only among Protestants." Sawyer added that a dispute over which version should be read in the public schools had resulted in "the most shameful page in Philadelphia history." This was the Nativist riots of 1843 that followed a school board decision allowing Catholic children to substitute the Douay version for the King James version.

Sawyer turned to the history of Virginia and the views of James Madison to strengthen his argument. Madison is always brought into arguments about the First Amendment because he had a major role in drafting it and because vast quantities of his writings have survived the intervening years. In 1785 Madison had opposed the Virginia Assessment Bill which was designed to support religion in general; the assessment was to be imposed on everyone, but each taxpayer would have been allowed to select the church that would receive his share of the tax or, if he preferred, to assign his share to general education rather than to a church. Madison said this would "employ religion as an engine of civil policy," something that should not be permitted. Using religion—Bible-reading and prayer—as a means of getting students into a proper frame of mind for schoolwork was using religion as an engine of government, Sawyer said.

Black brought up Stewart's point, asking Sawyer if he ever saw a conflict between the Establishment Clause and the Free Exercise of Religion Clause.

Sawyer said he did in the case of chaplains in the armed services. Government was establishing religion by providing them, but it would be depriving soldiers of the right to worship freely if it did not. The Free Exercise Clause should win over the Establishment Clause in that instance, he said.

Sawyer then tried to distinguish the *Barnette* case on the ground that a flag salute was a secular act for everyone in West Virginia except Jehovah's Witnesses. No religion was being established when the flag was saluted, he said, so the case was quite different from the two before the Court now. The Jehovah's Witnesses had no right to stop others from doing a secular act. But prayer and Bible-reading were not secular acts. It was disingenuous to say the legislature did not intend the exercises to be a religious exercise.

"What of the argument that the exercises are traditional?" Brennan asked.

"The fact that they are old has nothing to do with it," Sawyer replied. "I think it is the utmost arrogance to talk about our religious heritage in this country and to keep referring to the Holy Bible. It is not a part of the religious heritage of a great many Americans. It seems to be saying that the Pennsylvania schools are Protestant institutions to which all are cordially invited."

John D. Killian III, a deputy attorney general of the State of Pennsylvania, presented a brief rebuttal. "This is not a religious practice, it is an educational practice," he said. "The practice of reading the Bible existed in Colonial days for the purpose of learn-

THE MAKING OF JUSTICE

ing to read and studying religion. . . . If you want to be a good musician, you have to study sacred music and if you want to be a good person, you have to study morality. If you want to be a good citizen and you want your school to help you get that way, you must study morality. What better book is there out of which to study it? . . . We feel that ripping out this practice would express hostility to religion."

There was a great shuffle when Killian concluded. The lawyers moved away from the counsel tables and many spectators rose to leave. The voice of the Chief Justice calling the next case was drowned out by the noise. The argument that everyone had come to hear was over.

It was clear now that the issue facing the Court was of greater emotional than constitutional moment. The outcry about the Court's decision the preceding summer had been a cry that the Justices were taking God out of the schools. Now, the attorneys for the local school boards were only halfheartedly asking the Court to reconsider it. They had decided either that the Court was right or that it was futile to try to get the Justices to change their minds. Instead, they were defending the practices in Maryland and Pennsylvania by playing down the very aspects of Bible-reading and prayer that the Court's critics the preceding summer had played up. They now argued that Bible-reading and prayer were not really religious exercises, and that there was really no religion in the schools for the Justices to take out.

THE BIBLE-READING AND PRAYER CASES FOCUSED PARTICULAR attention on two of the Justices—Brennan and Stewart. Brennan was the only Catholic on the Court, and leaders of his church had strongly condemned the Court's ban on prayer in the New York schools. Since the Roman Catholic Church is sometimes accused of being authoritarian and requiring its members to adopt the views dictated by the hierarchy, Brennan is in a difficult position in any case involving matters on which the Church has taken a stand. If his vote meets with Catholic approval, he may be accused of casting it at the command of the Church rather than on the basis of his own independent judgment. This had happened in 1961, when he concurred in the Court's 5-to-4 avoidance of deciding a case that challenged the constitutionality of the Connecticut anti-birth-control statute. Both Brennan's agreement in *Engel v. Vitale* the preceding term and his questions during oral argument in the Bible-reading and prayer cases suggested that he would vote to hold those practices unconstitutional. But he would probably want to explain his position fully so as, perhaps, to convince other Catholics (as well as Americans generally) that he was right. Stewart, on the other hand, had been the only dissenter in *Engel*, and would have to convince at least four of his colleagues before his view of the First Amendment could prevail.

Stewart's attack on the "wall of separation" language and his efforts to construct a new theory about the First Amendment were in keeping with the independent position he liked to think he held on the Court. A few months after he was appointed, he said, "I suppose it's obvious that some of the senior Justices have very strong views on some subjects. It's only logical that they should. They have thought the questions through in many cases and have come up with answers that satisfy them. I try to approach every case with an open mind." It was clear that he was speaking of Black and Douglas and Frankfurter, who had already been through the major issues facing the Court many times and had developed their own philosophies of the role of the Court and the meaning of the Constitution. Stewart, in 1963, was still in the process of developing his.

As the junior Justice during the late 1950's, Stewart had been the key man on the Court on many cases. Four of the Justices—Warren, Black, Douglas, and Brennan—had placed heavy emphasis on individual rights; the other four—Frankfurter, Harlan, Clark, and Whittaker—were more likely to emphasize the prerogatives of government. Since each group needed Stewart's vote before its views could prevail, his vote was wooed both by counsel during oral argument and by his fellow Justices in the politicking that goes on behind closed doors. One attorney, who was convinced that the other Justices were divided 4 to 4 in his case, jested that he ought to move the lectern down to Stewart's end of the bench and argue the case directly to him. When someone told Stewart about the remark, he said, "Yes, and he would have ended up losing the case by a vote of 8 to 1." Rarely during this period had Stewart committed himself to firm statements of principle. Rather, he based his votes on extremely narrow grounds which left both him and the Court space to shift position without future embarrassment if they wanted to.

Stewart repeatedly and emphatically denied that there are "conservative" or "liberal" blocs on the Court. When he was appointed, newsmen immediately demanded to know whether he was a "liberal" like Black or a "conservative" like Frankfurter. His reply was, "I am a lawyer."

"I have some difficulty understanding what those terms mean even in the field of political life or in the legislative or executive branches," he explained later. "And I find it impossible to know what they mean when they are carried over to judicial work." The differences of opinion among the Justices, he said, did not mean there was a "split" in the Court or "blocs" of Justices. "Many of our cases are on the very frontier of the law," he said, "and I am sometimes surprised how often we are unanimous." (The Court is unanimous in about 40 per cent of its major actions and more than 90 per cent of its minor ones.)

At Thanksgiving, 1962, Stewart made an unusual television appearance, submitting to questions by a panel of students on "Youth Wants to Know." Although the Justices have stepped up their public appearances in recent years, this venture raised a good many eyebrows around the Court. It was considered unwise and somewhat dangerous for a Justice to get himself into a public position where he might be asked questions he could not answer with propriety. The Justices never hold press conferences, although some of them occasionally see newsmen in their chambers, and they are generally reluctant to say anything for public consumption beyond their speeches and written opinions and comments in the courtroom. But the interview with Stewart went off well. He was urbane, suave, and verbally adroit at steering the conversation away from touchy questions, yet he seemed disarmingly frank. His youthful face and his black hair, just beginning to show streaks of gray, belied the popular myth that the Court is composed of nine old men. Stewart charms all his audiences with his candor. He once told a group in Washington, "We don't get together up there every Monday and say, 'What can we do today to foul up the country?' But case after case involves issues that have very definite overtones of the deep conflict between social, economic, and philosophical ideas in our national life. We are an institution that decides those cases."

Stewart's early life contrasted sharply with that of Black or Frankfurter or Goldberg. His father was a Cincinnati lawyer who, when his son was appointed to the Supreme Court, was a member of the supreme court of Ohio. Stewart attended Cincinnati public schools and Hotchkiss before going to Yale College. Upon his graduation in 1937, he went to study for a year at Cambridge University in England and then entered the Yale Law School. After three years in the Navy he went into private law practice and local politics in Cincinnati, serving as Vice Mayor for one year during his two terms on the City Council. President Eisenhower appointed him to the Sixth Circuit Court of Appeals in 1954 and to the Supreme Court four years later. When Stewart took his seat he was only forty-three, the second youngest Justice in 105 years. In that time only Douglas had been appointed at an earlier age.

Soon after Stewart joined the Court, it became clear that at least one trait would distinguish him in the courtroom. He could not resist the opportunity to interpose the witty remark that would bring laughter and break the tension of argument. One crack in 1961, during arguments on the Brown Shoe Company antitrust case, was typical. Brown's attorney argued that all men's shoes don't compete for sales with all other men's shoes, that dress shoes never compete with casual shoes. Solicitor General Cox said they did, too; that Brown's President had come to court to testify wearing casual shoes one day and dress shoes the next. Stewart was obviously about to burst out laughing. He grinned and said, "Maybe it was direct examination one day and cross examination the next."

Stewart and Brennan were the only men on the Court in the 1962–63 term with substantial recent experience on lower courts, but there the similarity ended. Where Stewart is tall, slender, and urbane, Brennan is short, chunky, and bluff. His twinkling eyes and ready handshake seem more like those of a successful Irish politician than a Justice of the Supreme Court. His manner tempts most visitors to his chambers to call him "Bill" within five minutes after they meet him. Almost any morning when the Court is in session, an early riser might see Brennan, dressed in old clothes and a bulky sweater, leaving his house in Georgetown at 6:30 o'clock. He gets his exercise by taking a four-mile hike before the rest of his family is up, and has irritated his law clerks by expecting to discuss every little news story that appeared in the morning newspapers when they pick him up at 9 o'clock to go to work.

Unlike Stewart, Brennan quickly established himself on the Court as a Justice with strong views in certain areas of the law. He, like Black and Douglas, stressed the importance of the guarantees of individual liberties contained in the Bill of Rights. He, like the two senior Justices, thought the Court should follow a vigorous course in protecting those liberties against encroachments from any source for any reason. But Brennan has not subscribed to the sweeping language of the two others about the absolutes in the Bill of Rights or joined in some of their more aggressive defenses of individual rights. Instead, he often relied on slightly narrower grounds to reach the same result.

As the only member of the Court with experience as a state judge, Brennan was particularly attentive to the relationship between federal courts and state courts and to the application of federal constitutional guarantees to trials in state courts. He had been a judge in New Jersey for seven years before Eisenhower appointed him to the Supreme Court in 1956. It was assumed that his views in *Fay v. Noia* would be more than ordinarily persuasive to the other Justices as they debated their decision in that case. While Brennan had shown concern for the concept of federalism, he was much more sensitive to pleas for protection of individual rights. "Far too many cases come from the states to the Supreme Court presenting dismal pictures of official lawlessness, of illegal searches and seizures, of illegal detentions attended by prolonged interrogation and coerced admissions of guilt, of the denial of counsel, and of downright brutality," he once said. "Judicial self-restraint which defers too much to the sovereign powers of the states and reserves judicial intervention for only the most revolting cases will not serve to enhance Madison's priceless gift of 'the great rights of mankind secured under this Constitution.' "[1]

To those who complained that the Court's emphasis on individual rights was destroying the effectiveness of law enforcement officers in the fight against crime, Brennan said, "We are duly mindful of the reliance that society must place for achieving law and order upon the enforcing agencies of the criminal law. But insistence on observance by law officers of traditional fair-procedural requirements is, from the long point of view, best calculated to contribute to that end. However much in a particular case insistence upon such rules may appear as a technicality that inures to the benefit of a guilty person, the history of the criminal law proves that tolerance of short-cut methods in law enforcement impairs its enduring effectiveness."[2]

As a result, Brennan established himself as a member of the libertarian, activist wing of the Court. But that had put him on the spot in cases involving issues like Bible-reading and, particularly, birth control. Libertarians generally regard laws requiring Bible-reading and banning contraceptive devices as infringements on individual freedom, but a great many Catholic leaders approve of Bible-reading, and the Church is directly responsible for anti-birth-control laws which, according to Catholic doctrine, merely outlaw a practice that is a sin. Thus Brennan was in a delicate position. Regardless of the position he took, he would be subject to attack either on the intellectual integrity of his generally libertarian views or on the sincerity of his religious convictions.

chapter 15

A RARE DAY FOR THE COURT

SPRING HAD ALMOST ARRIVED IN WASHINGTON ON MARCH 18. A warm breeze stirred in the trees and the birds were beginning to return from the South. Justice Black and Clay Long, one of his law clerks, rode to work together that Monday from their homes in Alexandria, and Black was smiling and chatting cheerfully. As they crossed the Potomac, Long wondered why his Justice seemed so happy. As the day went on, the answer became clear. Two decisions from which Black had originally dissented were specifically overruled that morning, and two more were overruled in spirit if not in specific terms. Part of the fight he and Douglas had waged for so long was won. No other Justices had ever had such a day as they did that Monday. The Supreme Court had overruled itself many times down through the years but never before had two of its members seen their views in four dissenting opinions become law in one day.

The day began like all other Mondays that winter at the Court. A small group of newsmen gathered to learn what cases the Court had decided. Several Washington lawyers came to listen to the announcement of the decisions. A handful of lawyers were there to be admitted to the bar.

The preliminaries over, the Chief Justice nodded to Goldberg who announced the Court's decision in *Draper v. Washington*,[1] which had been argued just before the Attorney General's appearance in the Georgia county unit case. It was the case of Robert Draper and Raymond Lorentzen, who had been sentenced to forty years in prison for two robberies in Spokane, Washington. It was before the Supreme Court because of the way the State of Washington had handled their appeals. They were too poor to pay the court stenographer to type up the record of their trial. Under Washington's rules the state would pay for the transcript only if the trial judge ruled that the higher court could not make a fair determination of the appeal without it. In this case the trial judge had declined to make that ruling, and their appeal was decided on the basis of the recollections of the trial judge and the attorneys of what happened at the trial. This procedure, Goldberg said, was unconstitutional because it discriminated against the poor. A man who could afford to buy a transcript could have his conviction reviewed by appellate judges who had before them a verbatim record of what had actually happened at his trial; an indigent could get that full review only if the trial judge thought it necessary. Since the appeal was largely based on errors committed by the trial judge, Goldberg said, the trial judge was about the last man who could fairly decide whether or not it was meritorious. Washington must revise its system to provide just as thorough review for the poor man's conviction as the rich man's, Goldberg and the Court ruled.

When Goldberg finished, White leaned forward and said, "I regret that I cannot join the Court's opinion. I have filed a dissent in which Mr. Justice Harlan, Mr. Justice Stewart, and Mr. Justice Clark join." It was another 5-to-4 decision in which Goldberg joined the four members who had so often been in the minority in the past—the Chief Justice, Black, Douglas, and Brennan. To the four dissenters, the system established by the State of Washington did give a poor man an adequate hearing.

The second decision announced that morning was similar.[2] It involved George Robert Brown, who faced a death sentence for murder in Indiana. Brown wanted to appeal the trial judge's denial of his request that his case be reopened. Under Indiana law, he could appeal that denial if he could afford to pay the costs or if the public defender certified the appeal was worth while. Brown couldn't pay the costs, and the public defender had decided that Brown's appeal was frivolous. The Supreme Court, with Stewart writing the opinion, ruled unanimously that this procedure was unconstitutional because it put Brown in a totally different position from men who had money. Here the question was not merely a matter of what happened on appeal; it was the difference between an appeal and no appeal. Those with money could appeal; Brown could not.

These two decisions were the latest in a long series by which the Court had been eliminating inequities between rich and poor criminal defendants in both federal and state courts. For years the country had endured two standards of justice. Some men could hire the best lawyers, could use the services of private investigators to find evidence to disprove their guilt, could appeal their convictions and get full review by at least one court and perhaps more. The man without money had long lacked many of these opportunities to defend himself. The Justices, obviously upset by the difference money could make in the application of criminal law, had gradually narrowed that difference. All of them agreed on the basic principle that the Constitution required all those charged with crime to have at least a fairly equal opportunity to present a defense. Where they disagreed was on how that opportunity should be made available. In the federal courts everyone was now assured of a lawyer. Gideon's case, in which that rule might be extended to cover the state courts, was still to be decided. *Draper* and *Brown* carried forward the process of equalizing the treatment of the rich and the poor on appeal.

It was 10:33 when the Court disposed of the opinions in those two cases and Brennan said, "I have the opinion and judgment of the Court in Number 38, Fay versus Noia."[3] It was becoming clear that this was decision Monday for states' rights; this was the third case dealing with state criminal procedures. Noia, whose conviction for murder had been based on a confession made under duress, was serving a life sentence in New York.

Noia's case, Brennan said, had required the Court to "comprehensively examine the scope of the federal habeas corpus jurisdiction." That examination had not produced a unanimity of opinion. The vote was 6 to 3 and the first words of Harlan's dissent were: "This decision, both in its abrupt break with the past and in its consequences for the future, is one of the most disquieting that the Court has rendered in a long time." Brennan and a majority of the Justices had gone farther than the appellate court and had cut even more deeply into what the attorneys for New York described as that state's sovereignty. In fact, this decision plus those in the two other cases that morning would suggest to many lawyers and judges that the Court was driving the states' diverse systems of criminal justice into a single, comprehensive system, patterned on federal criminal law and procedure. In Noia's case the Court took the step in the name of justice and in the name of the "Great Writ."

The Great Writ, the writ of habeas corpus, had been described a few days earlier by Goldberg as the one thing that "may be the difference between the American system and the Soviet system." The writ is a court order requiring whoever has control of a prisoner to bring him to court and convince the judge of the legality of keeping him a prisoner. An official receiving one of these orders—jailer, mental hospital superintendent, or military commander—has no choice but to explain the situation to the judge. In his opinion, Brennan wrote, "Although in form the Great Writ is simply a mode of procedure, its history is inextricably intertwined with the growth of fundamental rights of personal liberty. . . . Its root principle is that in a civilized society, government must always be accountable to the judiciary for a man's imprisonment; if the imprisonment cannot be shown to conform with the fundamental requirements of law, the individual is entitled to his immediate release."

The writ has been used, as the means of ending illegal imprisonment, in English courts for more than 650 years and in American
courts since they were first established. While the Constitution
says nothing about when or how or why federal courts should
use this power, it does say, "The privilege of the Writ of Habeas
Corpus shall not be suspended, unless when in Cases of Rebellion
or Invasion the public Safety may require it." Down through
the years, the writ has been used by the federal courts to free men
the judges were convinced were illegally confined in state as
well as in federal institutions. In Noia's case it was used once
again. He was being held in prison in violation of his federal constitutional rights, the six Justices said. His conviction was admit-
tedly based on a confession that had been extracted from him in
violation of due process of law. That was not evidence upon
which he could be sent to prison. The writ should be used to free
him.

It was not the circumstances of Noia's confession or his constitutional right to have it excluded from evidence that made
the case so troubling to Harlan. What bothered him was the effect of the decision on the federal system of government and its
two coexisting sets of courts, state and national. A majority of
the Justices were using the writ of habeas corpus to slice through
the insulation that had been laid over one of the places where
the two court systems rubbed against each other, insulation that
had been carefully applied to avoid direct and open conflict between the systems. Now, the Supreme Court was specifically
overruling one of the insulating decisions and was overruling
another without saying so. Those decisions had rested on the
theory that the federal courts, before exercising their tremendous power under habeas corpus to free state prisoners, should
give the state courts every possible opportunity to protect the
constitutional rights of a man like Noia. To assure this, the Supreme Court had ruled that a man convicted in a state court must
appeal his conviction, and must use every other means the state had

provided to attack it, before the federal courts would consider helping him. The Justices had even said that when a man was one day late in filing his appeal, and the appeal was dismissed for that reason, he had forever forfeited his right to federal habeas corpus relief because he had failed to take advantage of the review the state provided. These and similar rules, the Supreme Court had said, were necessary to keep the federal system in balance, to keep state judges from thinking their power was really secondary because a federal judge could override them at any moment.

Noia's case had brought two basic principles into direct conflict. He had failed to appeal his conviction, had failed to exhaust his state remedies. Thus, if the demands of the federal system were to be met, there was no way for his case to be heard in the federal courts. But the demands of justice and of the fundamental reason for the Great Writ were not met. Noia was in prison in violation of his constitutional rights. The solution adopted by Brennan and a majority of the Court was to cut through the insulation that protects the federal system. Since Noia had no present remedy in the state courts for the wrong he was presently suffering, he could turn to the federal courts. The doctrine that a man's failure to appeal or to exhaust his state remedies forfeited forever the protection of federal habeas corpus was abandoned.

When Brennan finished announcing his opinion, Harlan said, "The Court has turned its back on history and struck a heavy blow at the foundation of our federal system." The decision in this case was "a square rejection of long-accepted principles governing the nature and scope of the Great Writ." The basic principle the Court rejected, he said, was that the federal courts lack power to review a judgment of a state court that rests upon an adequate state ground. Since Noia was still in jail only because he had failed to meet the requirements of state law, Harlan said, his detention rested on an adequate state ground. By cutting out the heart of this principle, the Court was saying that federal authority could ignore the adequate-state-ground theory. The effect was that a judgment of a state court would never be final until the federal courts had looked over the record to see that no federal rights had been violated. "I recognize that Noia's predicament may well be thought one that strongly calls for correction," Harlan concluded. "But the proper course to that end lies with the New York Governor's powers of executive clemency, not with the federal courts."

Clark and Stewart joined in Harlan's sharp criticism of Brennan's opinion. Clark wrote a brief opinion in which he called for Congress to restore "the writ of habeas corpus to its proper place in the judicial system." The decision, Clark said, disrupted the "delicate balance of federalism." He added:

> The rights of the States to develop and enforce their own judicial procedures, consistent with the Fourteenth Amendment, have long been recognized as essential to the concept of a healthy federalism. Those rights are today attenuated if not obliterated in the name of a victory for the "struggle for personal liberty." But the Constitution comprehends another struggle of equal importance and places upon our shoulders the burden of maintaining it—the struggle for law and order. I regret that the Court does not often recognize that each defeat in that struggle chips away inexorably at the base of that very personal liberty which it seeks to protect. One is reminded of the exclamation of Pyrrhus: "One more such victory . . . , and we are utterly undone."

There was hardly time to let the words of Clark and Harlan sink in before the Court reversed still another state criminal conviction. This case also involved indigents and the kind of proceeding they were entitled to when they appealed their convictions.[4] Under California law the state appellate judge examined the trial records in cases of indigents and decided whether or not an attorney should be appointed to represent them in their appeals. The Supreme Court, Douglas announced, found this system unconstitutional because California, too, was discriminating against the poor. The California courts always heard full arguments on appeals made by those who could pay the costs of their cases, including counsel fees. The Justice said they must do the same for the poor man, and must provide a lawyer to brief and argue his appeal. As in *Noia*, White joined the majority of Warren, Black, Douglas, Brennan, and Goldberg to make the vote 6 to 3. Douglas breezed through the case so rapidly that the full import of what he was saying escaped most of his audience. After careful reading of his opinion, it became evident that the Court was ruling that there was a constitutional right to counsel on the first appeal from a state criminal conviction, regardless of the defendant's ability to pay his lawyer. No one quite realized it at the time, but this decision clearly predicted the result of Clarence Earl Gideon's case.

Douglas turned quickly to his second opinion. It was in the Georgia county unit case that Robert Kennedy had argued.[5] The Court, however, did not rule, as Kennedy had suggested, that the particular system used in Georgia was unconstitutional while leaving the constitutionality of other county unit systems for another day. Instead, the Justices squarely faced the question of the constitutionality of all county unit systems and ruled, 8 to 1, that they were all unconstitutional. It adopted the reasoning of Morris Abram—"A vote is a vote is a vote."

What Georgia's system did, Douglas said, was to give every qualified voter one vote and then to count them so that the rural votes weighed more heavily than the urban votes. "If a state in a statewide election weighted the male vote more heavily than the female vote or the white vote more heavily than the Negro vote, none could successfully contend that that discrimination was allowable," he wrote. "How then can one person be given twice or ten times the voting power of another person in a statewide election merely because he lives in a rural area or because he lives in the smallest rural county? Once the geographical unit for which a representative is to be chosen is designated, all who participate in the election are to have an equal vote—whatever their race, whatever their sex, whatever their occupation, whatever their income, and wherever their home may be in that geographical unit. This is required by the Equal Protection Clause of the Fourteenth Amendment. The concept of 'we the people' under the Constitution visualizes no preferred class of voters. . . . The conception of political equality from the Declaration of Independence, to Lincoln's Gettysburg Address, to the Fifteenth, Seventeenth and Nineteenth Amendments can mean only one thing—one person, one vote."

The decision was acceptable to all the Justices save Harlan. To him this ruling, like the one in *Noia*, flew in the face of history. The theory of "one person, one vote" had never been accepted political philosophy in England, the American Colonies, or the United States, he wrote. If that basis for the Court's decision was wrong, as he contended it was, Harlan thought the constitutionality of any county unit system turned on whether the particular system was rational. Was it designed to meet a justifiable need of the people of Georgia? Since it might be rational for the state to decide rural interests needed protection in the state capital and in its representation in Washington, he thought the case should be sent back to the trial court for a hearing on whether the system was rational.

Harlan pointed out that Douglas's opinion did not even mention the four prior cases in which the county unit system had been unsuccessfully challenged. This, he said, was "symptomatic of the swift pace of current constitutional adjudication." Normally the Court takes pains to explain why it is overruling prior decisions but Douglas did not even mention *South v. Peters* in which the Court upheld the Georgia system as constitutional. What bothered Harlan was that the Court was ignoring its traditional, careful role in its haste to confront and to sweep away inequities in American life.

When Harlan finished, Black began to read his opinion for the day. *Betts v. Brady* must be overruled, he said. Clarence Earl Gideon, who had scrawled out his appeal in a Florida jail, had established a new constitutional principle.[6] The sound of pleasure was in Black's voice as he spoke. He had vigorously dissented in 1942 when *Betts v. Brady* was decided. That decision, Black said, was out of the stream of the Court's thinking and was an anachronism when handed down. What was wrong with it, he said, was the failure of the Court in 1942 to recognize that the Sixth Amendment's guarantee of counsel was a right essential to a fair trial. In decisions prior to 1942 the Court had strongly indicated that the right to counsel was such a fundamental right, but in *Betts* the Court had broken with its "own well-considered precedents." Now the Court would return to them. He added:

> Not only these precedents but also reason and reflection require us to recognize that in our adversary system of criminal justice, any person hailed into court, who is too poor to hire a lawyer, cannot be assured a fair trial unless counsel is provided for him. This seems to us to be an obvious truth. Governments, both state and federal, quite properly spend vast sums of money to establish machinery to try defendants accused of crime. Lawyers to prosecute are everywhere deemed essential to protect the public's interest in an orderly society. Similarly, there are few defendants charged with crime, few indeed, who fail to hire the best lawyers they can get to prepare and present their defenses. That government hires lawyers to prosecute and defendants who have the money hire lawyers to defend are the strongest indications of the widespread belief that lawyers in criminal courts are necessities, not luxuries. The right of one charged with crime to counsel may not be deemed fundamental and essential to fair trials in some countries, but it is in ours.

Although none of the Justices disagreed with the result of Black's opinions, three of them wrote separate opinions to add a few words of their own. Harlan, again, was unhappy. *Betts v. Brady* should be overruled, he said, but the case and the view of the Court in 1942 were "entitled to a more respectful burial than has been accorded." Harlan was careful to point out that he concurred with the Court's judgment on the understanding that it did not "embrace the concept that the Fourteenth Amendment 'incorporates' the Sixth Amendment as such." Thus Black's opinion for the Court was not as sweeping as Black would have liked it to be; it did not adopt his thesis that the Fourteenth Amendment incorporates the provisions of the Bill of Rights as such. But it did add one more of the protections of the Bill of Rights to the list of those applied to the states. In a brief concurrence Douglas also took note of this point. He said that while ten Justices had apparently accepted Black's fundamental thesis over the years, no five of them had ever been on the Court at the same time. "Yet," he added, "happily, all constitutional questions are always open. And what we do today does not foreclose the matter."

The Chief Justice announced the Court's last opinion of the morning. It was in the case of Charles Townsend, who complained that a federal judge in Chicago had wrongfully refused to give him a full hearing on his claim that the police had taken his confession of murder after giving him a truth serum.[7] The Court, dividing 5 to 4, agreed that the judge should have given Townsend a full hearing. All the Justices agreed that if Townsend's claim were true he should be released or retired because the confession was coerced and could not be used as evidence against him. They also agreed unanimously that if Townsend raised facts which, if true, would entitle him to his release, the federal district court had power to conduct a hearing. They divided, however, on whether they should compel the lower court to hold a hearing in this particular case. The majority, with Black, Douglas, Brennan, and Goldberg again voting with Warren, said they would compel that hearing. They then went on to set standards by which federal district courts were to decide when hearings were required in habeas corpus cases. The four dissenting Justices thought these standards would compel too many hearings and would often force federal courts to track back over issues previously decided in state courts.

It was now clear why Black had been so cheerful that morning and why Harlan looked more and more disgruntled as the morning progressed. Black's dissent in *Betts* had now been largely accepted through the Court's opinion in *Gideon*. His views and those of Douglas in *South v. Peters* had been adopted in the county unit case. Their view in two earlier habeas corpus cases had been written into law in *Fay v. Noia*. Harlan, on the other hand, had been through one of the most unproductive mornings a member of the Court has ever had. In all of the decisions that touched in one way or another on states' rights, he objected to the Court's opinions. In five of the seven he dissented, and in the other two he agreed with the result but wrote concurring opinions that set his views apart from those of the majority. In two of his dissenting votes Harlan was joined by Clark, Stewart, and White, and in two others by Clark and Stewart.

The morning finally gave an indication of the direction the "new" Court, with its two new Justices, might be taking. Both White and Goldberg had voted with the "liberal" wing on the crucial cases—*Noia*, *Gideon*, and the Georgia county unit case. Their votes in those cases, as well as in the ones involving indigents, seemed to show more concern for the rights of individuals than for institutional barriers and traditions. But the two had split on the details of the criminal cases, Goldberg showing the greater concern for establishing an absolute equality for rich and poor and White taking a more pragmatic, less idealistic, approach. But with only this much evidence, it was too early to foretell the direction of the "new" Court. Douglas once said it takes three years for a Justice to go around the track once. Until that time had passed, and he had considered the variety of issues it brought, the philosophical content of a Justice's opinions could rarely be predicted with any assurance.

The impact of the day's decisions on the states was tremendous. Perhaps on no other single day since the Civil War had states' rights taken such a beating. In each of the seven decisions the Court had used the Fourteenth Amendment to strike down state laws and policies. The net result was to confine more narrowly the area in which the states were free to experiment and to adopt laws they thought fitted their particular needs. The decisions nationalized more areas of the law by guaranteeing that all Americans, regardless of where they lived, would have the same rights, which would be respected by their state governments.

Just a few days before this black Monday for states' rights, Senator John A. Stennis of Mississippi said that "a constitutional revolution has taken place in the last thirty years or so" in the United States.[8] The source of this revolution, Stennis said, was the Supreme Court. He was partially right. The American constitutional system had been going through a revolution for thirty years. The powers exercised by the federal government had increased enormously and the proportionate role of state governments had decreased sharply. The Supreme Court had played a major role in this revolution. But, as the *Gideon* case illustrated, it had not played that role alone. For the Court to have said in 1800, or even in 1925, that every state must provide legal counsel to those too poor to pay for it would have been unthinkable. But times change, and now even the American Bar Association, long known as the spokesman for conservative lawyers, praised this decision as a "great advance in the administration of criminal justice." The reason for the change, for this part of the revolution, was that once expressed by Frankfurter: "Not the least significant test of a civilization is its treatment of those charged with crime. . . ."

In the years since 1920 the Court had steadily extended the nationalization process in the criminal law by applying the federal Constitution's guarantee of individual rights to the states. Its standard for doing so was the Fourteenth Amendment's guarantee that no state would deprive an individual of life or liberty without "due process of law." The Court had ruled "due process" required the states to measure up to the nation's sense of justice. The national conscience, as the Court understood it, now required the states to provide higher standards in criminal trials. Thus it had begun to enforce on a national basis the right to counsel in criminal cases, the right to be free from unreasonable searches and seizures, the right not to be punished in a cruel and unusual fashion. There could be no argument but that this process was altering one aspect of the federal system. The states had once been free to establish their own systems of criminal law without regard to the guarantees of individual rights contained in the federal Constitution's Bill of Rights. That freedom, which had allowed the various states to develop systems to meet the needs they thought were created by their various physical, economic, and social situations, was now being sharply limited.

But this was only part of the revolution in the federal system that was under way. The other part dealt with the growing power of the federal government over economic and social problems. The Supreme Court was also involved in that aspect of the revolution. In the late 1930's it stopped imposing the limitations it had previously placed on federal power. Before that time the Court had struck down as unconstitutional Acts of Congress concerning child labor, working hours for women, agricultural production, and industrial regulation generally. It had done this against the will of a great majority in Congress and, presumably, a great majority of the American people. In many instances the Court had acted on the ground that these matters were beyond the scope of the powers given to Congress by the Constitution. But by the late 1930's the Court found that Congress did have power, after all, in its authority to regulate interstate commerce and to provide for the general welfare. As it did, Congress exercised that power and steadily moved in to regulate broad areas of economic activity. It was here that the power of state governments—states' rights—suffered its greatest decline. When the federal government stepped in, the state governments had to step out.

But the basic reason for this revolution in the federal system may have been the inability or unwillingness of state governments to cope with the twentieth century. Cities and problems now flowed across state lines in a way never thought of when the Constitution was written. Modern communication and transportation often made state lines irrelevant. Some states had been alert to the changes in the needs of their citizens and in the way those citizens thought about government. Other states had not been so alert and their governments looked backward rather than forward.

First the President and the Congress and then the Court had moved to fill the void left by the inaction of state governments. The President and Congress were the initiators of the broad expansion of federal power in the economic field. The Court's role had been simply to avoid holding executive and legislative action unconstitutional by finding in the Constitution sources of the powers the other two branches of government were wielding. In other areas the Court was the initiator. It moved to guarantee equal rights for Negroes only after years of inaction by state governments and by Congress. It moved to eliminate discrimination against urban dwellers in their state legislatures only after the state legislatures persistently refused to eliminate it themselves. It moved to raise the standards of criminal justice only after giving the states an opportunity to increase those standards themselves. This particular Monday in March, 1962, was only another step in this long process. It was noteworthy that two of the three major decisions affected only a handful of states. The *Gideon* case would change the rule only in Florida, Alabama, Mississippi, South Carolina, and North Carolina. The unit-vote decision would affect only Georgia, Mississippi, and Maryland.

The Court's rulings in these and in other cases were anticipated by many states that had previously adopted the rules now made national. This suggests that a few states, by refusing to respond to the demands of society in a new era, were responsible for much of the diminution of state power. The source of the constitutional revolution about which Senator Stennis spoke may be as much in the states as in the Supreme Court.

chapter 16

SEGREGATED LUNCHROOMS

Few protest movements have had so quick and so deep an effect on American life as the sit-in demonstrations against racial discrimination. The sit-ins pinpointed the area in which discrimination against Negroes was most openly practiced and most sharply resented. Never, in many parts of the South, could Negroes be served at lunch counters with whites. Never could they be seated in the same restaurant with whites. Never could they drop into the corner drugstore to sit at the soda fountain and drink a milk shake.

The sit-in movement began in a dormitory room at the Agricultural and Technical College of North Carolina at Greensboro on the night of January 31, 1960. Four young Negroes, all freshmen, had been talking for weeks about segregation. On that particular night one of them said, "We've talked about it long enough. Let's do something." The something was a walk to the dime store the next day, a Monday, to get coffee. The manager told them they could not be served because local custom did not allow him to serve Negroes. They sat and waited. Negroes working in the kitchen came out to tell them they were doing a bad thing. But when they returned to the campus twenty other young Negroes volunteered to join them, and together they drew up the ground rules that later governed all sit-ins—no loud voices, no protests, no name-calling. Each day for the rest of the week the group went downtown in Greensboro.

The group grew steadily in size as students from other Greensboro colleges—Negroes from Bennett College and a few whites from the Women's College of the University of North Carolina—joined. By Friday white teen-agers were heckling. By Saturday the store was jammed with Negroes who sat and waited for service and with whites who cursed and chanted. Police cleared the store after a bomb threat, and on Monday the lunch counter did not open. That ended, temporarily, the Greensboro demonstration, but the idea quickly spread.[1]

In cities all over the South, Negroes sat in at lunch counters. They were rebuffed in almost every city, though the tactics of officials and of the stores varied. In some places they were arrested for violating state laws and local ordinances requiring segregation. In others they were arrested for breaking the peace on the theory that their activities were likely to cause riots. In still others they were arrested for trespassing on private property. Almost invariably, the demonstrators were convicted and their appeals slowly worked through the court system toward the Supreme Court. In the first few cases that reached it, the Court reversed the convictions of those charged with violating state and city ordinances requiring segregation. These laws, the Court said, were clearly unconstitutional. No state or city could require a store owner to discriminate, because the Fourteenth Amendment required each state to provide all persons "equal protection" of its laws. That requirement no more allowed a state to require store owners to discriminate against Negroes than to discriminate against them itself. In the second group of cases the Court upset a series of convictions in Louisiana where Negroes were charged with breaching the peace when they sat in at lunch counters. The Negroes had been convicted without any evidence that they had breached the peace, the Court said; they were orderly and polite. Conviction without any evidence of an offense clearly denies due process of the law. The Court did not say so, but it was clear from the trial records that if anyone breached the peace it was the white hecklers. In none of these cases did the Supreme Court reach the fundamental constitutional issue raised by the sit-in demonstrations. It remained undecided when the Court heard arguments in a half-dozen sit-in cases during election week in 1962.

Typical of these new cases was one called *Peterson v. City of Greenville*. James Richard Peterson was one of ten Negro boys and girls who were arrested on August 9, 1960, after they went into the S. H. Kress store in Greenville, South Carolina, and sat down at the lunch counter. When the store manager saw them, he had an employee call the police, turn off the lights, and close the counter. When a police captain and several other officers arrived, the manager announced that the lunch counter was closed and asked everyone to leave. The ten Negroes, who had been sitting at the counter about five minutes, remained seated. They were promptly arrested, searched, and taken to police headquarters. The manager never actually asked the police to arrest them, and he testified at their trial that he asked them to leave because integrated service was "contrary to local custom" and violated a Greenville city ordinance requiring separation of the races in restaurants. The police and the manager conceded that the Negroes were clean, well dressed, and unoffensive in conduct. The manager testified that the patronage of Negroes was solicited in all departments of his store other than the lunch counter.

Some of the other cases argued with *Peterson* introduced different elements. In New Orleans three Negro and one white college students were arrested at the McCrory 5 and 10 Cent Store on September 17, 1960. New Orleans had no city ordinance requiring segregation. In Birmingham two Negro ministers, Reverend Fred L. Shuttlesworth and Reverend Charles Billings, were convicted of inciting two college boys to commit criminal trespass by sitting in at a lunch counter. In another Birmingham case ten young Negroes were convicted of trespass for sitting in at lunch counters. Birmingham, like Greenville, had a city ordinance requiring segregation, but the Negroes' attorney had neglected to mention it during their trial.

The fundamental constitutional issue raised by all the sit-ins was: can a state use its power to help a store owner discriminate against a particular group of citizens? An answer to this question would be a landmark in American constitutional law. Before the cases were argued, Solicitor General Cox asked the Court for permission to intervene on behalf of the United States. He explained the importance of the cases to the federal government:

> This problem involves not only the power of the States but also the constitutional rights of millions of American citizens. On the one hand, millions of Negroes . . . are subjected to racial discrimination in private businesses open to the public . . .[they] claim that the involvement of the States in their convictions violates the equal protection clause of the Fourteenth Amendment. On the other hand, the respondents invoke both the power of the States to preserve order and the freedom and responsibility of individuals to make their own decisions concerning the use of private property and choice of associates. Thus, the basic issue in these cases involves the competing claims of large numbers of citizens, and of the States, and is of grave importance to the country as a whole.[2]

The Fourteenth Amendment claim made by the Negroes was complex. It rested on the provision that each state must provide every person with "equal protection of the laws." It was generally accepted that this provision meant a state could not pass a law that directly discriminated against anyone. The law had to treat all citizens equally. This was the basis for the Court's 1954 decision that a Negro student could not be denied admission to a particular public school solely because of his race. For a state school to turn him away because he was a Negro while it accepted another child who was white, the Supreme Court said, was for an agency of the state to discriminate against the Negro, to deny him equal protection of the laws. The key finding was that separate schools, regardless of their physical attributes or their staffs, were inherently unequal. To separate the Negroes because of their race, the Court said, was to give them a badge of second-class citizenship. But the Court's most far-reaching decision had come seven years before the school cases. In *Shelley v. Kraemer* the Court had ruled that no court could enforce a restrictive covenant based on race. Such covenants had been used to keep neighborhoods all white. Everyone buying a house in a "restricted" development was required to sign a covenant that he would not sell it to persons of certain ancestries, usually Negroes and Jews. If he tried to, his neighbors could get a court order to enforce the covenant and block the sale. In *Shelley v. Kraemer* the Supreme Court ruled that the courts would not enforce these covenants. The Equal Protection Clause prohibited the use of government power, judicial as well as legislative and executive, to enforce discrimination, the Court said.

The attorneys for the sit-in demonstrators relied heavily on the *Shelley v. Kraemer* precedent. They argued that there was no difference between a court using its power to enforce a property owner's covenant to discriminate and a court using its power to enforce a store owner's decision to discriminate.

The attorneys for the Southern cities and states argued that the two situations were unlike. In the restrictive covenant cases, they said, there had been a willing seller and a willing buyer; the courts had stepped in at the request of an outsider to keep the two from doing what they wanted to do. In the sit-in cases the courts were stepping in at the request of the store owner to enable him to do what he wanted to do—to discriminate against Negroes as was his constitutional right.

Attorneys for the demonstrators made still another argument, which turned on whether the store owners actually did have a constitutional right to discriminate. Shortly after the Civil War, Congress passed a law under its power to enforce the Fourteenth

Amendment which forbade inns and places of amusement to discriminate. In the *Civil Rights Cases*, the Supreme Court held that law unconstitutional. It ruled that the Fourteenth Amendment, which says, "No State shall . . . ," barred only discriminatory actions by states or subdivisions of states or their officers, and not those by individuals. Unless a state was involved, the Court said, discrimination was permissible. In the following years many cases arose in which the question was whether a state's connection with particular activities was sufficient to bring them under the Fourteenth Amendment—whether the activities involved "state action." The law of what constituted "state action" developed in cases most of which had nothing to do with racial discrimination. They involved, instead, the Fourteenth Amendment's prohibition against depriving a person of life or liberty without due process of law. When a sheriff beat a prisoner to death, did this violate the guarantee that a state would not deprive anyone of life without due process? That is, was the killing by the sheriff, an officer of a subdivision of the state, "state action"? As the years went by, however, the theory of state action began to be applied in racial discrimination cases. The Court ruled, for example, that a restaurant run by private individuals but located in a building belonging to a state could not constitutionally discriminate; the state's ownership and the lease to the restaurant were sufficient "state action" to bring the Fourteenth Amendment into play. In the sit-in cases the attorneys for the demonstrators made three arguments. One was that the *Civil Rights Cases* should be overruled and the Fourteenth Amendment interpreted to eliminate the right of business establishments to discriminate. The second was that the states' licensing of the stores was sufficient state action to invoke the Fourteenth Amendment. The third was that all businesses that opened their doors to the general public must be assumed to have waived any right to discriminate and to fall under the Fourteenth Amendment's bar.

Each of these arguments presented serious difficulties. If the Court accepted the analogy of *Shelley v. Kraemer* and ruled that courts could not enforce private decisions to discriminate, store owners could discriminate but could not call the police to arrest Negroes who demanded service. This would leave the owners no alternative but physical force to eject those they wanted to discriminate against, and the courts would cease performing one of their most important functions as an alternative to violence in settling private disagreements. If the Court overruled the *Civil Rights Cases*, its decision would have implications far beyond the field of racial discrimination; not only would the restaurant owner be required to desegregate but so might the beauty parlor and the undertaker, the dancing school and the baby-sitter. If the Court said that issuing a license was sufficient "state action" to bar discrimination, its decision would apply to all who held licenses—doctors, lawyers, teachers. In fact, the legal problems raised by the sit-in cases were so complex and the possible results so far-reaching that they made these cases the most difficult and the most important ones on the Court's calendar in the 1962–63 term.

It was almost noon on May 21 when Chief Justice Warren announced that he had the Court's judgment in case number 71, James Richard Peterson, et al. versus the City of Greenville.[3] Up to that point the morning had been fairly uneventful. Goldberg had announced a 7-to-2 decision holding that the New York Stock Exchange was subject to the treble damage provisions of the antitrust laws.[4] Stewart had announced a unanimous decision that the federal government could not appeal an order of a federal judge granting a prisoner's request that he be resentenced.[5] Harlan had announced a 5-to-4 decision upholding the Federal Power Commission in abandoning its old system of rate-making and inaugurating a new one.[6] But there was a stir in the courtroom as the Chief Justice began to read. Everyone jumped to the conclusion that because Warren was announcing the decision, the convictions of the demonstrators had been reversed. But on what grounds? Taking no chances on saying something he did not intend, the Chief Justice read carefully from his opinion:

> The evidence in this case establishes beyond doubt that the Kress management's decision to exclude petitioners from the lunch counter was made because they were Negroes. It cannot be disputed that under our decisions "Private conduct abridging individual rights does no violence to the Equal Protection Clause unless to some significant extent the state in any of its manifestations has been found to have become involved in it." . . .
>
> It cannot be denied that here the City of Greenville, an agency of the State, has provided by its ordinance that the decision as to whether a restaurant facility is to be operated on a desegregated basis is to be reserved to it. When the State has commanded a particular result it has saved to itself the power to determine that result and thereby "to a significant extent" has "become involved" in, and in fact, has removed that decision from the sphere of private choice. It has thus effectively determined that a person owning, managing or controlling an eating place is left with no choice of his own but must segregate his white and Negro patrons. The Kress management, in deciding to exclude Negroes, did precisely what the city law required.
>
> Consequently these convictions cannot stand, even assuming . . . that the manager would have acted as he did independently of the existence of the ordinance. The State will not be heard to make this contention in support of the convictions. For the convictions had the effect, which the State cannot deny, of enforcing the ordinance passed by the City of Greenville, the agency of the State. When a state agency passes a law compelling persons to discriminate against other persons because of race, and the State's criminal processes are employed in a way which enforces the discrimination mandated by that law, such a palpable violation of the Fourteenth Amendment cannot be saved by attempting to separate the mental urges of the discriminators.

The Court had found a way to avoid the difficult issues in that case. Its ruling would mean the reversal of thousands of sit-in convictions still pending in the lower courts. But the fundamental issues—the attack on the *Civil Rights Cases*, the analogy with *Shelley v. Kraemer*, the licensing arguments—had not been reached.

Quickly the Chief Justice turned to the second case. It was from New Orleans where no ordinance required segregation. But the Court found in the evidence statements by the Mayor of New Orleans and top police officials that desegregation of restaurants would not be tolerated.[7] "[We] need not pursue this inquiry further," the Chief Justice said. "A State, or a city, may act as authoritatively through its executive as through its legislative body. . . . As we interpret the New Orleans city officials' statements, they here determined that the city would not permit Negroes to seek desegregated service in restaurants. Consequently, the city must be treated exactly as if it had an ordinance prohibiting such conduct. . . . The official command here was to direct continuance of segregated service in restaurants, and to prohibit any conduct directed toward its discontinuance; it was not restricted solely to preserve the public peace in a nondiscriminatory fashion in a situation where violence was present or imminent by reason of public demonstrations. Therefore here, as in *Peterson*, these convictions, commanded as they were by the voice of the State directing segregated service at the restaurant, cannot stand."

Turning to the two Negro ministers from Birmingham who were convicted of inciting two college students to commit criminal trespass, the Chief Justice said their convictions must be reversed because they had not incited anyone to commit a crime.[8] He noted that the Court was simultaneously reversing the convictions of several demonstrators for sitting in at Birmingham lunch counters.[9] They were not guilty because Birmingham, like Greenville, had an ordinance requiring segregation. If the demonstrators had not committed a crime, the Chief Justice said, those who had incited them to demonstrate were not guilty of any crime.

Two Justices, Douglas and Harlan, were dissatisfied. Douglas wanted the Court to decide now the basic constitutional questions. Harlan, on the other hand, thought the Court's majority had proceeded with too broad a brush. He dug more deeply than had Warren into the details of the cases and argued that those details did not support the Court's broad factual generalizations.

The result was completely satisfactory to no one except the thirty-one demonstrators whose convictions were reversed. The Southern cities and states had again lost in their efforts to retain enforced segregation, but the demonstrators had not gained the statement of a constitutional right—not to be discriminated against by businesses serving the general public—for which they had argued. As the Court recessed for the day, it handed down a written order directing that another sit-in case involving five Negro students who attempted to ride the merry-go-round at Glen Echo, an amusement park in Maryland just outside the District of Columbia, be reargued in the fall.[10] The difficult issues, that order made clear, had been put off another year. In Maryland there were no laws compelling segregation, as in Birmingham and Greenville. There were no official statements indicating that segregation was the state's policy, as in New Orleans. There seemed to be nothing but a decision of the amusement park to discriminate and an effort by the police and the courts to enforce its decision. The stage was set for a major constitutional struggle in the next year over the issues that had first been raised in Greensboro, North Carolina, on February 1, 1960.

The separate opinions of Douglas and Harlan laid out some of the problems and some of their implications. Douglas wrote:

> If this were an intrusion of a man's home or yard or farm or garden, the property owner could seek and obtain the

aid of the State against the intruder. For the Bill of Rights, as applied to the States through the Due Process Clause of the Fourteenth Amendment, casts its weight on the side of the privacy of homes. . . .

But a restaurant, like the other departments of this retail store where Negroes were served, though private property within the protection of the Fifth Amendment, has no aura of constitutionally protected privacy about it. Access by the public is the very reason for its existence.

. . . We live under a constitution that proclaims equal protection of the laws. That standard is our guide. . . . And under that standard business serving the public cannot seek the aid of the state police or the state courts or the state legislatures to foist racial segregation in public places under its ownership and control. The constitutional protection extends only to "state" action, not to personal action. But we have "state" action here, wholly apart from the activity of the Mayor and police, for Louisiana has interceded with its judiciary to put criminal sanctions behind racial discrimination in public places. She may not do so consistently with the Equal Protection Clause of the Fourteenth Amendment.

The criminal penalty (60 days in jail and a $350 fine) was imposed on these petitioners by Louisiana's judiciary. That action of the judiciary was state action. Such are the holdings in *Shelley v. Kraemer* . . . and *Barrows v. Jackson*. . . . Those cases involved restrictive covenants. . . .

. . . In our time the interdependence of people has greatly increased; the days of *laissez faire* have largely disappeared; men are more and more dependent on their neighbors for services as well as for housing and the other necessities of life. By enforcing this criminal mischief statute, invoked in the manner now before us, the Louisiana courts are denying some people access to the mainstream of our highly interdependent life solely because of their race. Yet, "If there is any one purpose of the Fourteenth Amendment that is wholly outside the realm of doubt, it is that the Amendment was designed to bar States from denying to some groups, on account of their race or color, any rights, privileges, and opportunities accorded to other groups. . . ."

Business, such as this restaurant, is still private property.

Yet there is hardly any private enterprise that does not feel the pinch of some public regulation—from price control, to health and fire inspection, to zoning, to safety measures, to minimum wages and working conditions, to unemployment insurance. When the doors of a business are open to the public, they must be open to all regardless of race if *apartheid* is not to become engrained in our public places. It cannot by reason of the Equal Protection Clause become so engrained with the aid of state courts, state legislatures, or state police.[11]

On the other hand, Harlan wrote:

In deciding these cases the Court does not question the long-established rule that the Fourteenth Amendment reaches only state action. . . . And it does not suggest that such action, denying equal protection, may be found in the mere enforcement of trespass laws in relation to private business establishments from which the management, of its own free will, has chosen to exclude persons of the Negro race. Judicial enforcement is of course state action, but this is not the end of the inquiry. The ultimate substantive question is whether there has been "State action of a particular character" (*Civil Rights Cases*, . . .)—whether the character of the State's involvement in an arbitrary discrimination is such that it should be held *responsible* for the discrimination.

This limitation on the scope of the prohibitions of the Fourteenth Amendment serves several vital functions in our system. Underlying the cases involving an alleged denial of equal protection by ostensibly private action is a clash of competing constitutional claims of a high order: liberty and equality. Freedom of the individual to choose his associates or his neighbors, to use and dispose of his property as he sees fit, to be irrational, arbitrary, capricious, even unjust in his personal relations are things all entitled to a large measure of protection from governmental interference. This liberty would be overridden, in the name of equality, if the strictures of the Amendment were applied to governmental and private action without distinction. Also inherent in the concept of state action are values of federalism, a recognition that there are areas of private rights upon which federal power should not lay a heavy hand and which should properly be left to the more precise instruments of local authority.[12]

Thus, the issues were drawn between the Justices in the Court just as they had been drawn months earlier between Negro customers and white owners in stores and restaurants all over the country. The Justices had avoided so far the major constitutional question and, as almost always happens, when they finally decided it, the situation that raised it would be changed. The Negro drive for desegregation was already moving away from the sit-ins. A few days before the Court announced its rulings, large-scale demonstrations had erupted in Birmingham. A few days later, the street demonstrations ended with a pledge from Birmingham businessmen that they would desegregate some lunch counters. New Orleans, too, was already desegregating its restaurants. And even Glen Echo, the source of the case the Justices had postponed still another year, had announced that Negroes were welcome. The demonstrators had in large part won their point at the lunch counters. It remained to be seen whether they would wholly win it in the courts.

chapter 17

A FIGHT OVER WATER

FOR YEARS WILLIAM O. DOUGLAS HAS BEEN THE ENIGMA OF THE Supreme Court. "Brilliant" and "unpredictable" are the adjectives most frequently used to describe him. Many times since President Roosevelt appointed him in 1939, Douglas has anticipated the Court in his ideas and theories about constitutional law. With Justice Black, for example, he had protested since 1942 that a trial could not provide due process of law unless the defendant was assured the assistance of counsel, a principle finally adopted during the 1962–63 term. His opinion in the sit-in cases was one the Court might adopt the next year or ten or twenty years later, but it certainly was not one a majority of the Justices would accept in 1963. Like most of his opinions in recent years, it was short and blunt. Douglas wastes few words although he writes more than any other member of the Court. Year after year he produced more opinions than any other Justice. In addition, he wrote books and pamphlets and magazine articles and speeches by the score. One of his fellow Justices once described Douglas as the only man he knew who could sit on the bench listening to arguments while writing a book about his travels abroad. Douglas could be writing away, he said, and suddenly look up to ask the key question in the case. How a man could follow an argument closely enough to do that and write a book at the same time was beyond him, the other Justice remarked.

Douglas's book writing is only a part of his complex nature. A tough, grizzly man, he flees Washington at the end of every term (sometimes in the past before the end) to seek out the wilderness, in the Far West, in Asia Minor, in Russia. By 1963, much of his enthusiasm for the work of the Court seemed to be gone. More and more frequently, lawyers and scholars criticized his opinions, not so much for the views they expressed or the results they reached as for the sloppy and careless fashion in which they proceeded from one point to another. It was clear that Douglas was a man in a hurry: he kept two secretaries busy all the time while the other Associate Justices used only one, and he relied less on his law clerk for help in research than the other Justices did. Only rarely did passion and deep feelings creep into his work on the Court. He gave the impression of casting his votes and expressing his views without becoming personally involved in the issues before the Court.

Those votes and those views have, over the years, usually coincided with those of Justice Black. The *United States Reports*, the official publication of the Court's opinions, are full of lines reading, "Mr. Justice Black, joined by Mr. Justice Douglas dissents," or vice versa. Douglas was, like Black, a dissenter in the four cases overruled on the states' rights Monday in March. But, unlike Black, Douglas took little detectable satisfaction in that triumph. He was already moving ahead to other areas, his mind roaming far afield from the immediate business of the Court.

Suddenly, and without warning, on the first Monday in June Douglas shattered that façade of disinterest. Dissenting from the Court's decision in the California-Arizona water dispute, Douglas let his passion overflow.[1] In sharp language he denounced the decision and, in words tinged with bitterness, he denounced the author of the Court's opinion—Hugo Black. His words sounded like those often uttered by some of the Court's harshest critics and usually aimed directly at Black and Douglas. "Much is written these days about judicial law-making," Douglas said, "and every scholar knows that judges who construe statutes must of necessity legislate interstitially." But this particular decision, he added, "will, I think, be marked as the baldest attempt by judges in modern times to spin their own philosophy into the fabric of the law, in derogation of the will of the legislature." Black had been accused of this before by other members of the Court, but never by Douglas.

As Douglas read on, his face, always ruddy, flushed and his voice began to bristle. "The decision," he said, ". . . has made the dream of the federal bureaucracy come true by granting it, for the first time, the life-and-death power of dispensation of water rights."

There was a heightening of attention in the courtroom as Douglas read. The sharp words, the tone of voice, were unlike him. His anger was aroused and on public display as it had seldom been in recent years.

Abandoning his written opinion momentarily, Douglas pointed out sarcastically that Black's opinion was fifty-two pages long. "The advantage of a long opinion is that it's very difficult to see how it fails to reach the right result. You get lost in the words," he said. The opinion contained little substance and consisted mainly of "words and colorful writing." It was "a committee report rather than an opinion worthy of this Court."

There was no sound in the courtroom except that of reporters busily scribbling. Black looked straight ahead, his narrow face and deep blue eyes expressionless. Goldberg spun in his chair at the end of the bench so he could see his colleagues. The other Justices listened quietly. The lawyers looked at each other quizzically and shrugged their shoulders. A few minutes earlier, when Black announced the Court's decision in the case, it was clear he took particular pride in this particular opinion. It was a long opinion, as Douglas said, and it did contain colorful writing. But that was part of Black's style.

Nothing seemed to explain why Douglas had so suddenly

turned on Black or why the water case had so infuriated him. The case was complex—the twenty-two hours of argument the Court had devoted to it emphasized that. And the Justices were in sharp disagreement. Four of them—Clark, Brennan, White, and Goldberg—joined in Black's opinion. Harlan and Stewart dissented with Douglas though not nearly so vehemently. The decision itself seemed to show only one possible explanation for Douglas's outburst, which was its departure from the traditional way of apportioning water rights in the West. Since Warren had disqualified himself, Douglas alone on the Court was from the Far West and might have been expected to regard himself as the Western-water-law expert. However, Clark and White were also from Western states with water problems, and they agreed with Black.

The decision concluded more than forty years of dispute over which states were entitled to use how much water from the Colorado River. In 1921 Congress authorized the states claiming that water to reach an agreement among themselves. Although the states did enter into the Colorado River Compact, negotiations failed to settle the disagreement. Eight years later, Congress passed the Boulder Canyon Project Act in an effort to solve some of the problems. In 1962 the Supreme Court was thrust into this morass of traditional water apportionment, an interstate compact, and two Acts of Congress, by Arizona's suit to clear the title to the water so that plans for the giant Central Arizona Reclamation Project could be formulated.

Black's opinion gave Arizona a substantial victory. He said Congress had established, in the Boulder Canyon Act, a comprehensive method of apportioning the water between Colorado, Arizona, and Nevada. The division did not depend on the interstate compact because the Act gave the Secretary of the Interior authority to accomplish the division by making contracts for delivery of the water behind federal dams. As a result, Black said, the first 7.5 million acre-feet of water in the Colorado was to be divided with California getting 4.4 million, Arizona 2.8 million, and Nevada .3 million. That division, he said, applied only to the mainstream water, because Congress had decided each state was entitled to the water from the tributaries of the Colorado in that state. In times of shortage, he added, the statute also gave the Secretary of the Interior power to decide how necessary reductions would be apportioned. The decision meant that Arizona would have the water it wanted for its reclamation project near Phoenix, that California must look elsewhere for the water it desperately needed for the expanding area around Los Angeles, and that the Secretary of the Interior would have to solve the problems the Court had passed over.

The three dissenting Justices were convinced that Congress never intended to delegate to the Secretary so much power, as Harlan put it, "over the fate of a substantial segment of the life and economy of three states." Douglas contended in his bitter comments that the division totally disregarded the traditional rule for apportioning water in the West, which essentially is "first come, first served." California would have been far better off if it had been applied, because California was the first state to make extensive use of Colorado River water.

The Court adjourned a few minutes after Douglas finished his comments. Instead of the ordinary chatter about the decisions of the day that usually buzzes through the halls, all the comments were directed at Douglas's performance. Had something happened to mar his long-standing friendship with Black? No one seemed to know but the two Justices, and they said nothing. Questions put to their old and close friends brought only an amazed "Really?" in response to accounts of the morning's events.

For several weeks, however, Douglas had been under heavy pressure. Early in April, Mercedes Douglas, whom he had married after his first wife divorced him, had announced that she too would seek a divorce. Persistent rumors arose that Douglas would next marry Jean Carol Martin, a young woman recently graduated from Allegheny College with whom he had frequently been seen, and that he would retire from the Court the next fall when he reached sixty-five and became eligible for retirement with full pay.* He promptly denied any plans for imminent retirement and refused to comment on his personal plans. Criticism of his second divorce was widespread. One member of the Court was widely reported, although probably apocryphally, as having told him, "One Justice, one divorce"— a play on his "one man, one vote" language in the Georgia county unit case. It was conjectured that Black had commented unfavorably on his divorce and plans for remarriage, and that those comments accounted for his diatribe against Black in the water case.

Douglas's activities off the bench often brought him as much criticism as those on it. In his early days on the Court he sometimes left Washington before the end of the term because he had made commitments, had completed his work, and saw no reason to sit around and wait for his colleagues. In later years his books on his summer travels became best-sellers and prompted criticism that he neglected the work of the Court for his outside activities. During the 1962–63 term Douglas produced such a remarkable flow of magazine articles and speeches as to inspire gossip that he needed substantially more than his $35,000 salary to meet his expenses—which included, it was pointed out with some malice, alimony for one and now perhaps a second ex-wife. As it turned out, however, no alimony for Mercedes Douglas became necessary, because she, too, remarried as soon as their divorce became final.

Douglas has always been an individualist and perhaps no word describes him better than that. He was the only member of the

* The rumors were accurate in one respect. He married Miss Martin during the summer of 1963.

Court to speak out on issues of public policy far removed from the Court's work. He often talked about foreign affairs, usually in terms critical of American policy. He called for the admission of Red China to the United Nations as a way of curbing its lawlessness and charged that "intrigues" by the Pentagon and the Central Intelligence Agency work against the best interests of the United States. He said that American foreign aid often harms rather than helps underdeveloped nations because of its emphasis on military matters. These comments were frequently condemned on the theory that a Justice of the Supreme Court has no business talking publicly about such matters, but Douglas paid no attention. He kept on saying what he wished on whatever subject he chose, evidently believing that even a Justice has a right of free speech.

One of his favorite subjects was the outdoors and the imperative necessity of taking steps to preserve the nation's wilderness areas. In 1954, after the *Washington Post* editorially supported a scenic highway along the old Chesapeake and Ohio Canal, Douglas challenged the editors to a hike along the 185-mile length of the Canal so he could show them why it should be saved from the bulldozer and the automobiles. Robert Estabrook and Merlo Pusey accepted his challenge and survived the trek from Cumberland, Maryland, back to Washington. While it never agreed totally with Douglas, the *Post* did thereafter modify its position.

Douglas shares his love of the outdoors with most Pacific Northwesterners, and he comes by it honestly. Although he was born in the town of Maine, Minnesota, he grew up in Yakima, Washington. He graduated from Whitman College in Walla Walla, Washington, and set out for New York and the Columbia Law School with a load of sheep destined for the Chicago stockyards. He arrived in New York with six cents in his pocket and was almost turned away as a tramp from his fraternity's Columbia chapter. That foreshadowed the scene at the end of a hike down the C&O Canal a few weeks before his outburst against Black, when Justice Douglas, Secretary of the Interior Stewart Udall, and Senator Paul Douglas of Illinois were refused service at an inn because they looked like tramps. After graduating second in his class at Columbia, Douglas spent two years in a Wall Street law firm and then began a full-time teaching career, first at the Columbia Law School and later at Yale. He went to Washington in 1935 as a Securities and Exchange Commissioner and was its chairman when President Roosevelt appointed him to the Court. He was then forty years old, the youngest Justice in 126 years.

Douglas's casual attitude even appears on the bench, where he often sits with a pencil jammed behind one ear, his glasses pushed down his nose, and his unruly hair sticking up in all directions. He has the stature and the rough appearance of a mountaineer. More than once he has been the only Justice to show up at a White House reception without the traditional formal silk hat. He might have been a successful politician; he was talked about as the Democratic vice-presidential candidate both in 1944 and in 1948, but that was not what he wanted. Once he lapsed into his Western drawl when newsmen queried him about it. "I never was a-runnin'," he said. "I ain't a-runnin' and I ain't a-goin' tuh."

chapter 18
THE FINAL MONDAY

JUNE AT THE SUPREME COURT IS ALWAYS HECTIC. THE JUSTICES are eager to leave for vacation. Their staffs are tired after the long winter and spring. The amount of work that must be done before the term can end is overwhelming.

Before Memorial Day in 1963 the Justices let the word be passed quietly that they hoped to finish on June 17. This date seemed possible, but unlikely. There were twenty-seven decisions yet to be announced and more than 500 petitions that ought to be disposed of. Yet those around the Court were fairly sure the Justices would not stay beyond June 24. Chief Justice Warren had plans to leave for Europe late that week, and the Court staff had learned that his plans were a reliable indicator of the end of the term. As the days in June went past, rumors about adjournment flew around the Court building. On June 4 ten cases were decided and thirty-eight petitions were disposed of. From the chambers of one Justice during that week came word that adjournment would be the 24th; too much work remained to be done. On June 11 only six decisions were announced but 137 petitions were cleared away. In addition, the Court formally announced its intention to adjourn on the 17th. Skepticism nevertheless persisted among some employees of the Court. They had learned from long experience that it was not really safe to make vacation plans until formal adjournment actually occurred.

On June 17 the press room of the Court was crowded. For

weeks now, the handful of reporters who write about the Court regularly had been joined by reporters and editors of religious publications. Each Monday since the two Bible-reading cases were argued, the religious press had expected the decision. If the Court were to adjourn today, as it had said it would, the Bible-reading and prayer decisions would have to be announced. Many Washington correspondents of newspapers and press services, large and small, were also there that morning. The Court frequently dominates the news on the day it adjourns, and everyone wanted to be where the news was breaking.

A few minutes before 10 o'clock Bert Whittington pulled his cart into his office. Piled on it were a dozen stacks of opinions, all carefully laid face down. As Whittington and his secretary stacked them in his locked file cabinet one newsman after another poked his head into their office to see if this day was really the last. Whittington's only comment was, "Lots of them."

Upstairs, the courtroom was filling rapidly. When the Justices filed in at 10 o'clock, the chamber was jammed. More than sixty lawyers were there to be admitted to the bar. In addition, the beautiful summer day had brought thousands of tourists to Washington and many of them were there to see the Court in action. There, too, were retired Justices Burton and Reed. In the box reserved for special guests were the wives of Justices Black, Clark, Harlan, Brennan, and White. Among the lawyers there to listen to the announcements were several high-ranking federal officials. All the seats assigned to the press corps were full, and reporters overflowed into the narrow corridor separated from the north side of the courtroom by bronze screens.

As the Chief Justice welcomed one lawyer after another to the bar of the Court, the other Justices chatted quietly among themselves. Douglas, as usual, was busy with paper work at the bench before him—perhaps a draft of another book. On the north end of the bench White and Brennan kept a stream of conversation going. Every few minutes one of the Justices snapped his fingers. A page boy in knickers ran to his side and carried a note to someone in the audience. Finally, at 10:25 the last of the lawyers took the oath. The Chief Justice nodded at Goldberg, who began to read. The last day of the term had begun.

Goldberg had the Court's judgment in a case which involved the meaning of one sentence of the 1952 immigration laws.[1] The sentence defined what an "entry" into the United States was. The sentence was, like many of those in Acts of Congress, a bit ponderous:

> The term "entry" means any coming of an alien into the United States, from a foreign port or place or from an out-lying possession, whether voluntarily or otherwise, except that an alien having a lawful permanent residence in the United States shall not be regarded as making an entry into the United States for the purposes of the immigration laws if the alien proves to the satisfaction of the Attorney General that his departure to a foreign port or place or to an outlying possession was not intended or reasonably to be expected by him or his presence in a foreign port or place or in an outlying possession was not voluntary: *Provided*, That no person whose departure from the United States was occasioned by deportation proceedings, extradition, or other legal process shall be held to be entitled to such exception.

The question before the Justices was whether this meant an alien who lived in Los Angeles had "entered" the country when he returned from a visit of an hour or two in Ensenada, Mexico, a few miles down the coast from San Diego. The point, hardly of any great moment, was critical to George Fleuti. It made the difference between his continued residence in the United States and his deportation to Switzerland. Fleuti had come to the United States as a resident alien in 1952. He had made the brief visit to Mexico in 1956. In 1959 the Immigration and Naturalization Service began action to deport him on the grounds that prior to his "entry" into the country from Mexico he had committed a crime involving moral turpitude. The immigration laws bar all persons with such convictions from "entering" the country. The deportation effort failed when it was discovered that the crime Fleuti had committed was only a misdemeanor, which by definition did not involve moral turpitude. Then a new deportation proceeding was instituted on the ground Fleuti should have not been allowed to "enter" the country in 1956 because at that time he was "afflicted with a psychopathic personality," namely, that he was a homosexual. The Ninth Circuit Court of Appeals barred the deportation effort because it thought the term "psychopathic personality" was too vague to warn a homosexual that he was included in the term. By holding that the phrase was too vague, the appellate court said it was unconstitutional for any statute using only that term to be applied to homosexuals. A majority of the Justices, Goldberg announced, had concluded that this constitutional question need not be reached. In accordance with its practice of deciding a constitutional question only when there was no other way of disposing of the case, the Court had decided to dispose of this one upon the definition of "entry." It said Fleuti had really not "entered" the country when he returned from that Mexican trip. Congress surely did not mean such casual trips to endanger the status of a resident alien, Goldberg said. The Court would therefore read the statute to mean that only trips outside the country which were "meaningfully interruptive of an alien's permanent residence" resulted in new "entries" upon return. Four members of the Court, however, thought the majority was straining too hard to avoid deciding the constitutional issue. Justice Clark, speaking also for Harlan, Stewart, and White, said the majority were constructing rather than construing the statute. The law certainly didn't say what the Court said it said, Clark argued, and if Congress had intended it to mean that it would have said so.

Goldberg's opinion was not overly persuasive and it did give an unusual meaning to the word "entry." It seemed as if the Court had decided that the application of the law to Fleuti was unjust and that the best solution was to stop that application in the easiest possible manner. Congress could countermand the Court's new interpretation of the statutory definition by passing a new law. But if the Court had chosen instead to rule on whether the phrase "psychopathic personality" was unconstitutionally vague as applied to homosexuals, it would have gotten into problems that are continually troublesome to the psychiatric as well as the legal profession.

After Clark concluded his brief dissent, Goldberg quickly announced the decision in another deportation case, and Clark, with the same three Justices joining him, again dissented.[2] White then read an opinion by Stewart announcing the Court's decision that the State of New Mexico had power to forbid a local newspaper and radio station to carry the advertisements of optometrists mentioning the price of eyeglasses, even though the optometrists lived and did business in another state, and the paper and the station served parts of both states.[3]

None of the decisions so far seemed to evoke much interest from the audience. Spectators kept coming and going as the guards kept the seats full almost all the time. Members of the press corps were stirring restlessly and wondering when and if the Justices would get to the Bible-reading and prayer cases. Speculation had been that either the Chief Justice or Justice Black would have those opinions. Black was the obvious choice because he had written the *Engel* decision the preceding spring and had often been the Court's spokesman on cases involving religion. The Chief Justice, however, had often chosen to write opinions himself in cases which were of great national interest or threatened widespread criticism. In addition, his case load this term had been fairly light. But if either Black or Warren had the prayer case, the decision would be a long time coming.

The rotation from junior to senior Justices was just getting started.

The ears of the lawyers perked up when Brennan said he had the Court's judgment in Number 83, the United States versus the Philadelphia National Bank.[4] This was the Court's big business case for the term and the decision had been eagerly awaited by the financial and legal communities. Its outcome would decide the fates of several bank consolidations besides that of the PNB and the Girard Trust Corn Exchange Bank. Brennan quickly made it clear that the Department of Justice had won and that the merger of Philadelphia's second and third biggest banks was barred by the antitrust laws. But the Court's reasoning came as a surprise. It took as the ground for decision Section 7 of the Clayton Act, the argument for which Assistant Attorney General Loevinger had chosen to rely solely on his brief. Brennan said a majority of the Justices agreed with the lower court judge that the Bank Merger Act of 1960 did not exempt banks from the antitrust laws. But that was the extent of their agreement. The language of Section 7 of the Clayton Act left no loophole for consolidations of this type, he said. Congress intended that Section to bar the "entire range of corporate amalgamations, from pure stock acquisitions to pure asset acquisitions." If the Court interpreted the Act as the banks did it would create a large new loophole in a law that was designed to close loopholes. It was irrelevant that the Justice Department thought for the past ten years that such a loophole existed. "If mergers in industries outside the FTC's jurisdiction were deemed beyond the reach of Section 7, the result would be precisely that difference in treatment which Congress rejected," Brennan said.

Turning to the definition of the relevant market in bank merger cases, Brennan said the four-county area in which all the branches of the two Philadelphia banks were located was the appropriate one. That was where the actual competition existed, and the desire of the banks to compete with New York banks in other markets was irrelevant. Anticompetitive effects in one market could not be justified by procompetitive effects in another. In attempting to give new meaning to the antitrust laws, Brennan said that a firm controlling at least 30 per cent of its market threatened the undue concentration that the Clayton Act forbade. The new bank would have controlled 34 per cent of the banking business. In an effort to simplify for lawyers and lower courts the meaning of Section 7, the Court said:

> Specifically, we think that a merger which produces a firm controlling an undue percentage share of the relevant market, and results in a significant increase in the concentration of firms in that market, is so inherently likely to lessen competition substantially that it must be enjoined in the absence of evidence clearly showing that the merger is not likely to have such anticompetitive effects.

When Brennan finished his announcement, Harlan said, "I suspect that no one will be more surprised than the Government to find that the Clayton Act has carried the day for its case in this Court." He and Stewart thought the decision was totally wrong. It "almost completely nullified" the Bank Merger Act of 1960. That Act had been designed to let the Comptroller of the Currency judge bank mergers on broad public policy grounds, but henceforth they would be judged solely on competitive grounds. "The only vestige of the Bank Merger Act which remains is that the banking agency will have the initial veto," Harlan concluded.

In a short memorandum Goldberg agreed with Harlan and Stewart that Section 7 of the Clayton Act did not apply in this case. But he said he did not necessarily dissent from the Court's ruling because he thought there was a substantial Sherman Act question.

Strangely, both the Justice Department and the banks had judged their cases wrongly. The Justice Department had won the votes of Brennan, Warren, Black, Douglas, and Clark—White did not participate—on the ground it had seemed to think was the weakest. The banks had won the votes of Harlan and Stewart on a point they conceded during oral argument. It was clear the decision would slow down the wave of bank mergers that had been sweeping the country and would put the Department of Justice in the key position with reference to bank mergers that it already held in other industries. The anticompetitive effect of any bank merger would now be more important in determining its permissibility than would the other aspects which the Comptroller of the Currency had weighed heavily in the past. In addition, those arguing for an economy composed of small, competitive businesses had won again. The Court was now as ready to give the antitrust laws an interpretation that would be effective against big business as it had been reluctant to do so in the early years of the century.

It was 11:15 when Harlan finished explaining his dissent and Clark took the floor. He had the Court's opinions in a complicated patent case involving the new zigzag sewing machine of the Singer Manufacturing Company and in a minor dispute over the meaning of an arbitration clause in government construction contracts.[5] Neither case seemed either to fascinate the large audience or to excite much interest among the Justices. White and Brennan frequently exchanged whispers, as did Black and Warren. Goldberg, sitting on the far left end of the bench, had no one to talk to because of Stewart's absence, so he spent his time watching his colleagues. Stewart had an out-of-town engagement that day.

The casual tone of Clark's voice seemed to change a bit as he began to announce his third opinion of the morning. "I also have Numbers 142 and 119," he said. "Abington Township School District versus Schempp and Murray v. Curlett."[6] A deep quiet settled on the courtroom. The only sounds were the pages moving quickly to distribute copies of the opinions.

chapter 19

THE GOVERNMENT IS NEUTRAL

AT 11:34 A.M., EASTERN DAYLIGHT TIME, THE TELEPRINTERS in newspaper offices and radio stations all over the country fell silent. Then, as their bells began to ring for attention, the United Press International machines typed out:

> BULLETIN
>> 1ST LEAD COURT (A19)
>> WASHINGTON, JUNE 17 (UPI)—THE SUPREME
> COURT RULED TODAY THAT USE OF THE LORD'S PRAYER
> AND BIBLE READING AS DEVOTIONAL OPENING EXERCISES
> IN PUBLIC SCHOOLS IS UNCONSTITUTIONAL.
>> MORE-1135AED
> UPI A108 WA
>> URGENT
>> 1ST ADD 1ST LEAD COURT WASHINGTON (A107)
> XXX IS UNCONSTITUTIONAL.
>> THE COURT'S OPINION WAS DELIVERED BY JUSTICE
> TOM C. CLARK.
>> MORE-JD1136AED. . . .

The machines of the Associated Press said much the same thing in different words.

Clark had begun to read his opinion four minutes before the teletypewriters began to carry their bulletins. The wire service reporters in the courtroom were handed copies of all the opinions seconds after Clark began to read. They stuffed them into pneumatic tubes and sent them down to Charlotte Moulton of UPI and Paul Yost of AP, who were waiting in small rooms directly below the courtroom. They thumbed through the opinions and handed their bulletins, prepared previously in alternatives, to the teletype operators sitting beside them.

In the press room 200 feet away Bert Whittington was putting copies of the opinions in dozens of outstretched hands. In the courtroom itself only the handful of persons who had been given the opinions knew the outcome by the time the bulletin flashed into the newsrooms. Most of the spectators would not know the result until Clark reached that point in his opinion, and they would not know the vote until all the dissents and concurrences were read.

But Clark did not keep the audience in suspense long. He began his announcement by reading from his opinion:

> Once again we are called upon to consider the scope of the provision of the First Amendment to the United States Constitution which declares that "Congress shall make no law respecting an establishment of religion or prohibiting the free exercise thereof. . . ." These companion cases present the issues in the context of state action requiring that schools begin each day with readings from the Bible. While raising the basic questions under slightly different factual situations, the cases permit of joint treatment. In light of the history of the First Amendment and of our cases interpreting and applying its requirements, we hold that the practices at issue and the laws requiring them are unconstitutional under the Establishment Clause, as applied to the states through the Fourteenth Amendment.

As he continued to speak, Clark began to lay emphasis on particular words and add additional comments that would not appear in the Court's public record. From the text, he read:

> It is true that religion has been closely identified with our history and government. As we said in *Engel v. Vitale* . . . , "The history of man is inseparable from the history of religion. And . . . since the beginning of that history many people have devoutly believed that 'More things are

wrought by prayer than this world dreams of.' " In *Zorach v. Clauson* ..., we gave specific recognition to the proposition that "[w]e are a religious people whose institutions presuppose a Supreme Being." ... This background is evidenced today in our public life through the continuance in our oaths of office from the Presidency to the Alderman of the final supplication, "So help me God."

Then he said, in an aside, "So do all the oaths I have taken." Clark noted that each House of Congress opens each morning with a prayer. "In this Court," he added, "you heard, if you were here this morning, that sessions are opened by the Crier who invokes the grace of God." He mentioned the chaplains in the military services and a report by the Bureau of the Census that 64 per cent of all Americans are church members while only 3 per cent profess no religion.

It can be truly said, therefore, that today, as in the beginning, our national life reflects a religious people who, in the words of Madison, are "earnestly praying, as ... in duty bound, that the Supreme Lawgiver of the Universe ... guide them into every measure which may be worthy of his ... blessing...."

This is not to say, however, that religion has been so identified with our history and government that religious freedom is not likewise as strongly imbedded in our public and private life.

Here Clark interrupted his prepared opinion to insert the fact that forty-nine of the fifty states have such guarantees in their constitutions. Americans, he added, have come from all over the world and eighty-three—he repeated the number—eighty-three religious bodies, each with more than 50,000 members, now exist in the United States.

It was 11:45 when Clark reached into judicial history for an unknown quotation to forward the Court's view. It came from an unpublished opinion of Judge Alphonzo Taft, father of President and Chief Justice William Howard Taft and grandfather of the late Senator Robert A. Taft and of prominent churchman Charles A. Taft. Taft had written in 1870 that the Constitution required "absolute equality before the law of all religious opinions and sects. . . . The government is neutral, and, while protecting all, it prefers none, and it disparages none."

By this time the wire services had spread the word that the decision was by an 8-to-1 vote with only Stewart dissenting. In the courtroom only a small handful of people knew of either the vote or the dissent.

Clark began to skim over large parts of his written opinion. He took note of the criticism of Black's opinion in the *Engel* case a year before, and he touched briefly on the religion cases the Court had decided in the past—*Everson, McCollum, Zorach, Torcaso*. As he reached the last five pages of his twenty-three-page opinion, Clark began to follow his written words carefully and to stress what seemed to him important. His dry Texas accent made it seem that he was conversing with his audience rather than announcing a major Supreme Court decision.

> The wholesome "neutrality" of which this Court's cases speak thus stems from a recognition of the teachings of history that powerful sects or groups might bring about a fusion of governmental and religious functions or a concert or dependency of one upon the other to the end that official support of the State or Federal Government would be placed behind the tenets of one or of all orthodoxies. This the Establishment Clause prohibits.

Clark paused a moment and added, "This is beyond the power of Congress and of the state legislatures."

Returning to his prepared text, Clark explained that a further reason for neutrality was the Free Exercise Clause, "which recognizes the value of religious training, teaching, and observance, and more particularly, the right of every person to freely choose his own course." Clark began to peck on the bench with his index finger as he departed from his text again to add, "and to choose his own religion without any compulsion from the state."

From the written opinion Clark read:

> As we have indicated, the Establishment Clause has been directly considered by this Court eight times in the past score of years and, with only one Justice dissenting on the point, it has consistently held that the clause withdrew all legislative power respecting religious belief or the expression thereof. The test may be stated as follows: what are the purpose and the primary effect of the enactment? If either is the advancement or inhibition of religion then the enactment exceeds the scope of legislative power as circumscribed by the Constitution. That is to say that to withstand the strictures of the Establishment Clause there must be a secular legislative purpose and a primary effect that neither advances nor inhibits religion. . . . The Free Exercise Clause, likewise considered many times here, withdraws from legislative power, state and federal, the exertion of any restraint on the free exercise of religion. Its purpose is to secure religious liberty in the individual by prohibiting any invasions thereof by civil authority. Hence it is necessary in a free exercise case for one to show the coercive effect of the enactment as it operates against him in the practice of his religion. The distinction between the two clauses is apparent—a violation of the Free Exercise Clause is predicated on coercion while the Establishment Clause violation need not be so attended.

The argument of Pennsylvania that Bible-reading was not a religious act and of Maryland that prayer was said only to quiet the students down were dismissed by Clark briefly. "Surely the place of the Bible as an instrument of religion cannot be gainsaid, and the State's recognition of the pervading religious character of the ceremony is evident from the rule's specific permission of the alternative use of the Catholic Douay version as well as the recent amendment permitting nonattendance at the exercises," he said. "None of these factors is consistent with the contention that the Bible is here used either as an instrument for nonreligious moral inspiration or as a reference for the teaching of secular subjects."

It was no defense for the states to claim that these exercises were only minor encroachments on the First Amendment. "The State says this is just a small breach in the wall of separation, just a trickle," Clark said, "but as Madison says a trickling stream today may all too soon become a raging torrent."

That, it seemed, was the one sentence that explained the Court's attitude toward the First Amendment. When the case was argued, Black asked again and again, "If they can have two minutes, why can't they have five? If they can have five, why not all day?" In constitutional terms the Court thought there was no difference between permitting a school to hold brief religious exercises and to devote all its efforts to teaching religion.

Clark tried to make it clear that the Justices were not saying the Court objected to classes about religion or to historical comments that indicated the role religion had played in American life:

> We take it, as do all Americans, that one's education is not complete without a study of comparative religion. . . . It certainly may be said that the Bible is worthy of study for its literary and historic qualities. Nothing we have said here indicates that such study of the Bible or of religion, when presented objectively as part of a secular program of education, may not be effected consistent with the First Amendment. But the exercises here do not fall into those categories. They are religious exercises, required by the States in violation of the command of the First Amendment that the Government maintain strict neutrality, neither aiding nor opposing religion.

The tension in the courtroom persisted as Clark reached the last two paragraphs of his opinion. He was speaking slowly and carefully now, sticking close to his prepared opinion.

Finally, we cannot accept that the concept of neutrality, which does not permit a State to require a religious exercise even with the consent of the majority of those affected, collides with the majority's right to free exercise of religion. While the Free Exercise Clause clearly prohibits the use of state action to deny the right of free exercise to *anyone*, it has never meant that a majority could use the machinery of the State to practice its beliefs. Such a contention was effectively answered by Mr. Justice Jackson for the Court in *West Virginia Board of Education v. Barnette*. . . .

As he mentioned Jackson, Clark looked up and added, with a gesture to his right, "He sat in the next chair to where I'm sitting." Then he quoted from Jackson's brilliant opinion in the *Second Flag Salute Case*:

"The very purpose of a Bill of Rights was to withdraw certain subjects from the vicissitudes of political controversy, to place them beyond the reach of majorities and officials and to establish them as legal principles to be applied by the courts. One's right to . . . freedom of worship . . . and other fundamental rights may not be submitted to vote; they depend on the outcome of no elections."

After pausing to let the quotation sink in, Clark went on:

The place of religion in our society is an exalted one, achieved through a long tradition of reliance on the home, the church and the inviolable citadel of the individual heart and mind. We have come to recognize through bitter experience that it is not within the power of government to invade that citadel, whether its purpose or effect be to aid or oppose, to advance or retard. In the relationship between man and religion, the State is firmly committed to a position of neutrality. Though the application of that rule requires interpretation of a delicate sort, the rule itself is clearly and concisely stated in the words of the First Amendment.

He departed one last time from his text to add, "Government is committed to a rule of strict neutrality. Here we believe that rule had been violated."

The tension in the courtroom broke. Spectators stirred in their seats. Newspaper reporters hurried quietly to the door. Lawyers whispered to each other.

Before Clark settled back in his big chair, he added that he had been asked to announce that Douglas had filed a concurring opinion and that Stewart had filed a dissent. As Clark relaxed, Brennan began to read from his concurring opinion. It was seventy-seven pages long—three times that of Clark.

Brennan read the first fourteen pages of his opinion and skimmed through the remainder, but the essence of what he had to say was in his first few sentences:

> Almost a century and a half ago, John Marshall, in *M'Culloch v. Maryland*, enjoined: ". . . we must never forget, that it is *a constitution* we are expounding.". . . The Court's historic duty to expound the meaning of the Constitution has encountered few issues more intricate or more demanding than that of the relationship between religion and the public schools. . . .
>
> . . . Nevertheless it is this Court's inescapable duty to declare whether exercises in the public schools of the States, such as those of Pennsylvania and Maryland questioned here, are involvements of religion in public institutions of a kind which offends the First and Fourteenth Amendments.
>
> . . . The fact is that the line which separates the secular from the sectarian in American life is elusive. The difficulty of defining the boundary with precision inheres in a paradox central to our scheme of liberty. While our institutions reflect a firm conviction that we are a religious people, those institutions by solemn constitutional injunction may not officially involve religion in such a way as to prefer, discriminate against, or oppress, a particular sect or religion. Equally the Constitution enjoins those involvements of religious with secular institutions which (a) serve the essentially religious activities of religious institutions; (b) employ the organs of government for essentially religious purposes; or (c) use essentially religious means to serve governmental ends where secular means would suffice.

Farther along in his opinion, Brennan tried to deal with some of the criticism the Court had already received. He recalled the arguments made months before that if Bible-reading and prayer were unconstitutional, all vestiges of religion in public life were unconstitutional. That, Brennan asserted, was not at all true. Using the three tests he had spelled out, Brennan indicated his view that provisions for chaplains in the armed forces or in prisons were constitutional. The saying of prayers in legislative chambers "might well represent no involvements of the kind prohibited by the Establishment Clause." This decision did not touch tax exemptions given to religious groups or practices like Sunday Blue Laws that had lost their religious meaning. The Court was not foreclosing teaching about the Bible or about the differences in the beliefs of religious groups. He concluded:

> The principles which we affirm and apply today can hardly be thought novel or radical. They are, in truth, as old as the Republic itself, and have always been as integral a part of the First Amendment as the very words of that charter of religious liberty. No less applicable today than they were when first pronounced a century ago, one year after the very first court decision involving religious exercises in the public schools, are the words of a distinguished Chief Justice of the Commonwealth of Pennsylvania, Jeremiah S. Black:
>> "The manifest object of the men who framed the institutions of this country, was to have a *State without religion*, and a *Church without politics*—that is to say, they meant that one should never be used as an engine for any purpose of the other, and that no man's rights in one should be tested by his opinions about the other. . . ."

By 12:38, when Brennan finished, the Associated Press and United Press International were already carrying stories about public reaction to the decision. At 12:05, UPI reported:

URGENT

    REACTION—WITH COURT (A107)

    WASHINGTON, JUNE 17 (UPI)—THE TWO TOP
OFFICIALS OF THE UNITED PRESBYTERIAN CHURCH IN
THE U.S.A. SAID TODAY THE SUPREME COURT DECISION
ON PRAYER AND BIBLE READING IN PUBLIC SCHOOLS
"UNDERSCORES OUR FIRM BELIEF THAT RELIGIOUS IN-
STRUCTION IS THE SACRED RESPONSIBILITY OF THE
FAMILY AND THE CHURCHES."

    THE REV. SILAS G. KESSLER, HASTINGS, NEB.,
MODERATOR, AND THE REV. EUGENE CARSON BLAKE,
PHILADELPHIA, STATED CLERK OF THE 3.5 MILLION
MEMBER PROTESTANT DENOMINATION, SAID IN A JOINT
STATEMENT:

    "NOW THAT THE COURT HAS SPOKEN, RESPONSIBLE
AMERICANS WILL ABIDE BY ITS DECISIONS IN GOOD
GRACE."

The two ministers had prepared the statement several days in advance. They had been sure, as had most observers of the Court's work, what the outcome would be, and they wanted to head off aggravated comments like those that had come from the ministry a year earlier about the *Engel* case. Over the preceding weekend every major news organization in Washington had received a packet of materials from the Council of Churches of Greater Washington and the Jewish Community Council of Greater Washington. The materials were clearly designed to provide a source of balance to the criticism of the decision holding Bible-reading and prayer unconstitutional. Some religious leaders were more cautious. A young minister was in the courtroom that morning to get a copy of the opinion and fly with it to New York so that the Right Reverend Arthur Carl Lichtenberger, Presiding Bishop of the Protestant Episcopal Church, could read it before making a public comment.

At 12:52, UPI carried its first story about congressional reaction:

URGENT

CONGRESS—WITH COURT (A118)

WASHINGTON, JUNE 17 (UPI)—CONGRESS REACTED
SHARPLY TODAY TO THE SUPREME COURT RULING OUTLAWING
BIBLE READING AND USE OF THE LORD'S PRAYER IN PUBLIC
SCHOOLS. THERE WAS SOME TALK OF A POSSIBLE CONSTITU-
TIONAL AMENDMENT TO PRESERVE THE PRACTICE.

SEN. GEORGE D. AIKEN, R-VT., SAID THAT "IF IT
IS ILLEGAL TO QUOTE THE BIBLE OR READ THE LORD'S
PRAYER IN PUBLIC SCHOOLS IT'S ILLEGAL IN CONGRESS,
TOO." AIKEN SAID THE DECISION CAN BE CHANGED ONLY
BY A CONSTITUTIONAL AMENDMENT.

SENATE DEMOCRATIC LEADER MIKE MANSFIELD, MONT.
SAID ONLY "THE SUPREME COURT HAS ITS FUNCTION—
WE HAVE OURS." ASKED IF THE SENATE WOULD DROP ITS
OPENING PRAYER, HE REPLIED QUICKLY: "NO, SIR!"

SEN. FRANK CARLSON, R-KAN., WHO HEADS THE
INTERNATIONAL CHRISTIAN LEADERSHIP MOVEMENT,
SAID:

"PRAYER AND RELIGIOUS SERVICE IS FUNDAMENTAL
IN THE NATION'S HISTORY AND I REGRET TO SEE A DE-
CISION THAT IN ANY WAY LESSENS THE NEED FOR SOUND
PRINCIPLES THAT ARE SO BASIC."

Aiken's comments, in particular, were ill-informed, particularly in the light of Brennan's opinion and of the footnote that
Justice Black wrote a year before. But by 12:52 Brennan's
comments had not been moved on the news tickers. All the
Congressmen had were the hastily written news stories that
quoted only four paragraphs from Clark's opinion and a few
paragraphs from the dissent and the concurrences. At that point
it was likely that even the authors of the news stories had not
had time to read any of the opinions carefully.

In a brief concurrence Goldberg re-emphasized what Justice
Brennan had said:

. . . today's decision does not mean that all incidents of
government which import of the religious are therefore and

without more banned by the strictures of the Establishment Clause. As the Court declared only last Term in *Engel v. Vitale* . . . :

> "There is of course nothing in the decision reached here that is inconsistent with the fact that school children and others are officially encouraged to express love for our country by reciting historical documents such as the Declaration of Independence which contain references to the Deity or by singing officially espoused anthems which include the composer's professions of faith in a Supreme Being, or with the fact that there are many manifestations in our public life of belief in God. Such patriotic or ceremonial occasions bear no true resemblance to the unquestioned religious exercise that the State . . . has sponsored in this instance."

The language he quoted from the *Engel* case was the footnote in Black's opinion that had been generally disregarded during the preceding year.

Douglas, however, took a very different approach. His view, critics of the Court had suggested, would be the ultimate result. The Establishment Clause, he said, is not limited to precluding the state from conducting religious exercises. It also forbade the state "to employ its facilities or funds in a way that gives any church, or all churches, greater strength in our society than it would have by relying on its members alone." In these cases the mechanism of the state was being used to finance a religious exercise that only some of the people wanted and that violated the sensibilities of others. "Such contributions," he said, "may not be made by the State even in a minor degree without violating the Establishment Clause."

All the Justices except Stewart joined in Clark's opinion, just as all except Stewart had joined a year earlier in Black's. Goldberg's concurrence was joined by Harlan. That meant that at least Brennan, Goldberg, Harlan, and Stewart, and probably others, had rejected the position Douglas expressed.

Stewart, of course, disagreed with all his colleagues. But even he did not vote to uphold the practices in Maryland and Pennsylvania. His vote was simply to remand the cases for the taking of more evidence. In his dissent he elaborated the point he had made during the oral arguments. In his view the Court was applying "mechanistic definitions" in finding that the Bible-reading and prayer violated the Establishment Clause. What bothered him was a feeling that the Court was ignoring the right of Christian students to exercise their religion freely by listening to the Bible and praying. He said:

> It might also be argued that parents who want their children exposed to religious influences can adequately fulfill that wish off school property and outside school time. With all its surface persuasiveness, however, this argument seriously misconceives the basic constitutional justification for permitting the exercises at issue in these cases. For a compulsory state educational system so structures a child's life that if religious exercises are held to be an impermissible activity in schools, religion is placed at an artificial and state-created disadvantage. Viewed in this light, permission of such exercises for those who want them is necessary if the schools are truly to be neutral in the matter of religion. And a refusal to permit religious exercises thus is seen, not as the realization of state neutrality, but rather as the establishment of a religion of secularism, or at the least, as government support of the beliefs of those who think that religious exercises should be conducted only in private.

The state laws and regulations in question, Stewart said, should be regarded as "measures making possible the free exercise of religion." If there was no coercion by the school officials on dissenting students, he explained, the regulations would be valid. He said the cases should be sent back for more evidence on whether, in fact, coercion did exist:

> What our Constitution indispensably protects is the freedom of each of us, be he Jew or Agnostic, Christian or

THE GOVERNMENT IS NEUTRAL

Atheist, Buddhist or Freethinker, to believe or disbelieve, to worship or not worship, to pray or keep silent, according to his own conscience, uncoerced and unrestrained by government. It is conceivable that these school boards, or even all school boards, might eventually find it impossible to administer a system of religious exercises during school hours in such a way as to meet this constitutional standard—in such a way as completely to free from any kind of official coercion those who do not affirmatively want to participate. But I think we must not assume that school boards so lack the qualities of inventiveness and good will as to make impossible the achievement of that goal.

Compared with the reaction a year earlier, the nation received the Court's decision with calmness. Here and there a public official or a minister denounced the decision of the Court. Senator Allen J. Ellender of Louisiana said, "I think it is silly—eight silly old men." (Ellender was seventy-two; the average age of the Justices was sixty-two, and only two were as old as Ellender.) Reverend William H. Dickenson, Jr., of Dallas, pastor of the largest Methodist church in the city, said, "I do not agree with the Justices' opinion that government remains neutral in religious matters." (He made the statement in Dallas while Brennan was still reading his opinion.) In general, however, Jewish leaders and some Protestant leaders supported the Court, while some Protestants and most Catholics said that the Justices were wrong. The newspapers divided about the same way they had a year earlier, and most political leaders were cautious, apparently afraid they would be caught off base as some of them had been before.[1]

The divisions among the Justices reflected no sectarian positions. Clark, a Methodist, had written the majority opinion. Brennan, the one Catholic Justice, had concurred. So had Goldberg, the one Jewish member. Stewart, the dissenter, was an Episcopalian. What their differences reflected was not a difference in religious belief or in conviction about the need for religion, but a difference about what those general words in the Constitution meant: "Congress shall make no law respecting an establishment of religion, or prohibiting the free exercise thereof. . . ."

chapter 20

FREEDOM TO WORSHIP

As GOLDBERG FINISHED ANNOUNCING HIS CONCURRENCE IN THE Bible-reading cases, dozens of spectators rose to leave the courtroom. But three more cases remained to be decided before the Justices could recess for the summer and one of these also involved the meaning of the Free Exercise of Religion Clause of the First Amendment. It was a case that had drawn little attention; it seemed anticlimactic after the Bible-reading cases. But it further demonstrated the persistent difficulties the Court faces in interpreting the First Amendment.[1]

The case began when Adell H. Sherbert of Spartanburg, South Carolina, sued the State Employment Security Division for unemployment compensation. Mrs. Sherbert worked in a textile mill there for many years prior to 1959. She became a Seventh-Day Adventist in 1957 and, in 1959, when the mill shifted from a five-day to a six-day week, she told her employer that her religious beliefs forbade her to work on Saturday. When she failed to appear for Saturday work, she was fired. She then applied for unemployment compensation but was rejected on the ground that she had refused to accept available employment. The Board said there were jobs open for her in several mills if only she would work on Saturdays. She claimed that by denying her benefits because she refused to work on Saturdays, the Board was abridging her right freely to exercise her religion.

In an opinion by Brennan, a majority of the Supreme Court said she was right. What South Carolina was doing, Brennan wrote, was forcing Mrs. Sherbert to choose between her religion and her right to unemployment compensation.

> Our holding today is only that South Carolina may not constitutionally apply the eligibility provisions so as to constrain a worker to abandon his religious convictions respecting the day of rest. This holding but reaffirms a principle that we announced a decade and a half ago, namely that no State may "exclude individual Catholics, Lutherans, Mohammedans, Baptists, Jews, Methodists, Non-believers, Presbyterians, or the members of any other faith, *because of their faith, or lack of it*, from receiving the benefits of public welfare legislation." *Everson v. Board of Education*.

The case was not disposed of that easily, however, because Brennan's view was not acceptable to four members of the Court. Douglas and Stewart agreed with his result but for quite different reasons. White and Harlan dissented. It now seemed remarkable that eight of the nine Justices joined in Clark's Bible-reading opinion. While Brennan and four of his colleagues saw no problem in reconciling their decision with the Sunday Blue Law cases, the other four Justices did. In those cases the Court had rejected claims that a Jew's right to free exercise of religion was infringed by laws requiring him to close his store on Sunday. The law meant, the Jewish merchants asserted, that if they obeyed the teachings of their religion, they could open their stores only five days a week and could not compete with stores that were open six days a week. A majority of the Justices ruled that the law had a strong basic purpose unconnected with religion, that the state legislatures had reasonably decided that the health and welfare of the people demanded a uniform day of rest. The Blue Laws did not require the Jewish store owner to do anything his religion forbade, though it did make his faith a business liability.

Douglas, Harlan, Stewart, and White all thought the Court's decision in *Sherbert* in effect overruled the Blue Laws decisions. Stewart and Douglas said if the Court was really overruling them, they approved. They had dissented from the Blue Law decisions and thought they should not stand. Harlan and White thought the Blue Law cases were correctly decided, and dissented because they believed the Court's result in *Sherbert* was inconsistent. But Brennan, who had also dissented in the Blue Law cases, vigorously denied the interpretation the four placed on his opinion. His efforts to distinguish Mrs. Sherbert's situation from that of the Jewish merchants was, however, far from convincing. He said the Blue Law states had a "strong state interest in providing one uniform day of rest for all workers." Their valid objective, he added, could not be accomplished if exemptions were made for Seventh-Day Adventists or Jews because that would create practically insurmountable administrative problems. There was no such overriding objection in this case, he said. He did not say so, but the implication was that the South Carolina board could have worked out an accommodation between Mrs. Sherbert's claim of religious freedom and its administration of unemployment compensation without much effort, and should therefore have done so. The administrative difficulties in the Blue Law cases, on the other hand, were so great that a state could not honor the religious claim without completely abandoning the "strong state interest" underlying the laws.

In the day's three cases on government and religion—*Sherbert* and the two Bible-reading cases—six members of the Court wrote nine opinions totaling about 45,000 words. Only Warren, Black, and White were not heard from, and Black had written the earlier prayer opinion while Warren had written the Blue Laws opinion.[2] Those opinions, though only a small fraction of the work of the Court in the 1962–63 term, provided some insights into the difficulties the Justices face. The applicable words of the Constitution, the clauses of the First Amendment, are certainly not indisputable in meaning. "A word is not a crystal, transparent and unchanged," Justice Holmes once said, "it is the skin of a living thought and may vary greatly in color and con-

THE MAKING OF JUSTICE

284

tent according to the circumstances and the time in which it is used."[3] Yet to the Justices falls the task of deciding cases, which requires them to decide what the words of the Constitution mean, or at least what they believe they mean, and how they should be applied in each case.

The difference between Brennan's two opinions, the one for the Court in *Sherbert* and his concurrence in the Bible-reading cases, illustrates one of the problems a Justice always faces in presenting his views. When he is writing only for himself, concurring or dissenting, he is free to express his position as strongly and as persuasively as he is able. But when he is writing for the Court, his opinion must reflect a view acceptable to a majority of the Justices rather than the one he may prefer. Brennan's two opinions were markedly different. In his concurrence in the Bible-reading case he was specific and outspoken. In the *Sherbert* case his opinion for the Court was much more general and left conspicuous holes. It gave the impression that much had been left out in order to get five Justices to support it. The nine opinions also showed that the past year's criticism had its effect upon the Justices. Again and again in these opinions they carefully distinguished the practices they were holding unconstitutional from those upon which they were not ruling. And Warren's choice of Clark to write the Court's opinion in the Bible-reading cases reflected, perhaps, a sense of public relations. Clark is generally thought of as a "conservative," while Black, who has usually been the Court's spokesman on problems of religion, is often accused of being radical. A decision announced by Clark might be attacked less fiercely than the same decision by Black. In addition, Clark's opinions tend to be short and sometimes almost folksy in tone, in direct contrast with Black's highly literate but often long and scholarly opinions. The choice of Clark to speak for the Court may have been designed to communicate the Bible-reading decision, inevitably a controversial one, to the nation as quickly, as simply, and as tactfully as possible.

chapter 21

THE LAST DECISIONS

WITH THE OPINIONS ON CHURCH AND STATE, THE COURT HAD disposed of the most explosive cases before it, but the term's work was still not done. To the Chief Justice fell the task of disposing of the last two decisions and hundreds of cert petitions and appeals that remained.

In one of those cases the Court again confronted one of its most troubling problems over recent years. The case involved Edward Yellin and his appearance before the House Un-American Activities Committee in 1958.[1] Yellin refused to answer four questions the Committee asked: where he lived prior to 1957, whether he was a member of the Communist Party in 1949, whether he had known any workers of the Communist Party in labor unions in Gary, Indiana, and whether he knew anything about Communist activity in the Indiana steel mills. He told the Committee that his refusal was not based on the usual ground that his answers might incriminate him. Instead, he was alleging that the questions had no pertinency to a legitimate legislative investigation and that they invaded his First Amendment right of privacy. The Committee rejected his objection, and he was convicted of contempt, fined $250, and sentenced to a year in prison.

Yellin's case, like many contempt-of-Congress cases the Court had faced, brought a witness's claim of individual rights into direct conflict with the Committee's claim that it needed information in order to recommend legislation that would protect the nation against the international Communist conspiracy. But as the Chief Justice read his opinion, it became clear that the Court was steering away from the fundamental issues in the case. The Court was reversing Yellin's conviction but it was doing so on narrow, technical grounds. The conviction, Warren said, could not stand because the Un-American Activities Committee had violated its own rules when it questioned Yellin. He had asked the Committee to hear his testimony in executive session and the Committee's rules provided that it would consider such requests and grant or deny them as it saw fit. As a matter of fact, however, Yellin's request never reached the Committee because the Committee's counsel denied it on his own authority. This, said Warren, was sufficient reason for the courts to refuse to hold Yellin in contempt. "The Committee prepared the groundwork for prosecution in Yellin's case meticulously," he said. "It is not too exacting to require that the Committee be equally meticulous in obeying its own rules."

Black, Douglas, Brennan, and Goldberg concurred in the Chief Justice's opinion, but it was too much for the other four to take. White wrote a long dissent stating the view that due regard for the legislative branch did not permit the courts to place such a narrow construction on the rules of a congressional committee. The Committee, White said, had voted against holding an executive session, and that was enough to satisfy its own rules even though the vote was not taken with specific reference to Yellin's request.

Cases like Yellin's have plagued the Court ever since 1957. Few if any of the Justices approve of the tactics and techniques of the Un-American Activities Committee and the Senate Internal Security Subcommittee, but they have been sorely divided on how they should deal with cases attacking these committees. Warren, Black, Douglas, and Brennan consistently took the position that the two investigating committees, particularly the House Un-American Activities Committee, invaded the constitutional rights of witnesses. They said the committees lacked authority to require a witness to answer questions about his political associations and beliefs, even associations with Communists and beliefs in communism. However, they were never able to muster a fifth vote for that view, which was flatly repudiated when Frankfurter, Harlan, Clark, Whittaker, and Stewart ruled that the committees had power to ask the questions and to require answers so long as they went about it properly. But because those five, particularly Stewart, were sensitive to unfairness in procedures sometimes used by the committees, the Court's decisions formed no clear pattern.

In 1957, before this split between the Justices became so evident, the Chief Justice administered to the House Un-American Activities Committee one of the harshest tongue-lashings the Court has ever directed at another part of the government. In *Watkins v. United States* the Court reversed a contempt conviction by a vote of 7 to 1 on the narrow ground that the Committee's questions lacked pertinency to the subject it had been authorized to investigate.[2] But Warren's majority opinion had gone beyond that narrow holding to question the basic authority of the Committee and to criticize roundly the pattern of its operations. That opinion had set off in Congress and around the country a blistering attack on the Court and on Warren; in many respects it marked the beginning of the superpatriots' campaign to impeach the Chief Justice. Two years later, the Court retreated from Warren's broad language, upholding the contempt conviction of a witness over the bitter dissents of Warren, Black, Douglas, and Brennan.[3] In subsequent cases the Court avoided the fundamental issues raised by those who said their constitutional rights were more important than the function of the Un-American Activities Committee. Other contempt cases were decided, but on narrow, technical grounds similar to that adopted by the majority in *Yellin*.

In late March, however, the Court had again considered the

more fundamental question when it reversed the contempt conviction of the Reverend Theodore R. Gibson.[4] Gibson, then
president of the NAACP's Miami branch, had refused to bring
a list of NAACP members to a 1959 hearing of the Florida
Legislative Investigating Committee. The committee said it
wanted him to refer to the list when it asked him if certain
suspected Communists were members. Gibson refused to do so,
claiming that it would interfere with the right of members
and prospective members to associate freely with whomever
they pleased. The committee had unsuccessfully attempted
three years earlier to get a list of all NAACP members in
Miami, but the NAACP thought then, as it still thought in
1959, that the real purpose of the Committee's action was to
make public the names of NAACP members so that other
organizations, like the White Citizens Councils, could harass
them. The committee insisted, however, that all it wanted to do
was to be sure the NAACP was not being infiltrated by Communists. The Supreme Court split the same way in *Gibson* as it
did in *Yellin*. Goldberg wrote the majority opinion reversing
the conviction; Harlan, joined by Clark, Stewart, and White,
dissented. Goldberg tried hard in that opinion to keep the decision within the framework of the Court's rulings that legislative committees have a right to ask an organization about the
membership of subversives if they have established a "sufficient
connection" between the organization and subversive activity.
The Florida committee, he said, had failed to establish such a
connection in this case.

This summary of the evidence discloses the utter failure
to demonstrate the existence of any substantial relationship
between the N.A.A.C.P. and subversive or Communist activities. In essence, there is here merely indirect, less than
unequivocal, and mostly hearsay testimony that in years
past some fourteen people who were asserted to be, or to
have been, Communists or members of Communist-front or

"affiliated organizations" attended occasional meetings of the Miami branch of the N.A.A.C.P. "and/or" were members of that branch, which had a total membership of about 1,000.

To permit legislative inquiry to proceed on less than an adequate foundation would be to sanction unjustified and unwarranted intrusions into the very heart of the constitutional privilege to be secure in associations in legitimate organizations engaged in the exercise of First and Fourteenth Amendment rights; to impose a lesser standard than we here do would be inconsistent with the maintenance of those essential conditions basic to the preservation of our democracy.

The four dissenters thought the Court was departing from the principles of past cases in which three of them, with Frankfurter and Whittaker, had formed the majority. Harlan wrote, "There can be no doubt that the judging of challenges respecting legislative or executive investigations in this sensitive area demands the utmost circumspection on the part of the courts. . . . But this also surely carries with it the reciprocal responsibility of respecting legitimate state and local authority in this field. With all respect, I think that in deciding this case as it has the Court has failed fully to keep in mind that responsibility." Black and Douglas used that occasion to spell out once more their view that a legislative committee never has the right to inquire into the political beliefs or associations of individuals or organizations. "In my view," wrote Black, "the constitutional right of association includes the privilege of any person to associate with Communists or anti-Communists, Socialists or anti-Socialists, or for that matter, with people of all kinds of beliefs, popular or unpopular. Since, as I believe, the National Association for the Advancement of Colored People have a constitutional right to choose their own associates, I cannot understand by what constitutional authority Florida can compel answers to questions which abridge that right."

The outcome of these two contempt cases made it appear that the new Justices had changed the balance on the Court in this area. Almost certainly, Frankfurter and Whittaker would have voted to uphold both convictions. Goldberg's opinion in *Gibson* seemed to require a higher standard of what was the "sufficient connection" a committee must show before it could compel answers. Warren's opinion in *Yellin* left the distinct impression that the majority was stretching to find a way to reverse the conviction without dealing with the substantive issues. Fortunately for the Court, perhaps, the flow of contempt cases has abated as has the activity of the two congressional committees.

The final decision of the term drew all the Justices together, even though it changed what had appeared to be settled law. The case was that of two federal prison inmates who wanted to sue the government for injuries they claimed were caused by the negligence of prison officials.[5] Henry Winston, once a leader of the American Communist Party, went blind at the federal penitentiary at Terre Haute, Indiana, while serving an eight-year sentence, five years for subversive activities and three for contempt of court. He claimed his blindness was due to medical malpractice by a prison doctor. He had complained of dizziness and loss of balance, which the doctor attributed to hypertension. Months later, it was discovered that Winston had a brain tumor. Carlos Muniz was suing for injuries he received during a fight at the federal correctional institution at Danbury, Connecticut. He said the guards had simply locked the dormitory doors when several other prisoners started attacking him, making no effort to break up the fight. Muniz suffered a fractured skull and lost the use of one eye.

In a dozen or more cases lower federal courts had said there was no remedy for such injuries because the prisoners' suits would be directed at the government, which cannot be sued without its consent. In 1946 Congress had passed the Federal Tort Claims Act to authorize suits against the United States for personal injuries inflicted by government employees. But the lower courts said the Act was not intended to apply to prison inmates. The Supreme Court did not agree, the Chief Justice announced. It thought Congress had intended to allow men with claims like these to have an opportunity to prove them. Although it was not crystal clear that Congress meant the Tort Claims Act to permit suits by prisoners, Warren added, the Court thought it probably did. If it didn't, it could now pass a law to restore the government's immunity to such suits. The Chief Justice observed that the doctrine of sovereign immunity has been gradually relaxed over the years by both federal and state governments to give citizens redress for their government-inflicted injuries and that the decision was in keeping with that pattern.

When he finished that brief announcement the Chief Justice said:

> The other opinions and orders of the Court have been filed with the Clerk and will not be orally announced.
>
> All cases submitted and all business before the Court at this term in readiness for disposition having been disposed of, it is ordered by this Court that all cases on the docket be, and they are hereby, continued to the next term.

With that, Warren nodded to the Court Crier, whose voice rang out as the Justices stood and turned to leave the bench: "This Honorable Court is adjourned until the time and place appointed by Law."

The 1962–63 term was over.

chapter 22

THE TERM IS OVER

THE TERM OF COURT BEGAN IN OCTOBER AS A YEAR FOR SIT-INS, Bible-reading, and prayer, but by June the emphasis had changed. The Court had avoided the constitutional questions raised by the sit-ins. The Bible-reading and prayer decisions, despite the clamor they inspired in Congress and elsewhere, were only an affirmation of the preceding year's interpretation of the First Amendment. If, in the long run of history, this particular term is remembered, it will be for other cases and other decisions. Four of these stand out: *Noia* and the writ of habeas corpus; *Gideon* and the right to counsel; Georgia and its county unit system; and Philadelphia with its two banks. But there are dozens of other cases in which the Court made an imprint on American law during the term. Altogether, the Justices heard arguments in and decided 148 cases. They disposed of another 2,202 without arguments.[1] Many of these were important, certainly to the parties involved, and also to students of law, to businessmen, to defendants in criminal cases, to organized labor. In fact, the term's most important case may lie unnoticed somewhere in the four volumes of opinions the Court produced. Many times in the Court's history, key turning points in the law and major precedents for future decisions have slipped past, totally unnoticed by the public or, occasionally, even by the legal profession.

Throughout this term, however, there seemed to be one principal theme. A majority of the Justices made clear their conviction that the Court's proper role in American government is an active one in regard to the protection of individual rights. This thesis ran through one decision after another, and the views of the two new Justices, though in somewhat differing degree, seemed to fit into it. In the county unit case, in *Noia* and *Gideon*, in the sit-in cases, in the case of poor bug-bitten Gallick, a majority continued on the path marked out by a lesser number of Justices in preceding years. They were willing to use their power to strike down encroachments on individual liberties, regardless of source, whether this meant finding new ways to meet new problems or changing old ways that no longer produced just results.

The voice of Justice Harlan, calling for restraint in the use of the Court's power, was now heard in a symbolic wilderness without the assured support of Frankfurter and Whittaker. From time to time Harlan persuaded Clark and Stewart and White with his views, but the balance of power on the Court had shifted.

The 5-to-4 decisions told the story. There were twelve cases decided by that narrow margin. Ten of these involved the rights of individuals, either in criminal trials, citizenship or deportation proceedings, or civil rights matters. In each of these ten cases, the Court's majority was composed of Warren, Black, Douglas, Brennan, and Goldberg. Two years earlier, before Goldberg and White joined the Court, many of the 5-to-4 decisions involving individual rights had gone the other way with Warren, Black, Douglas, and Brennan the dissenters.

But it was not just the 5-to-4 decisions that made it clear that Black and Douglas had won, at least for the time being, the battle they had waged so long for a sweeping interpretation of the Bill of Rights. The Court was unanimous on one big issue, the right to counsel, and almost unanimous in another, the county unit case, with only Harlan dissenting. On the crucial vote in *Noia*, both White and Goldberg cast their votes with the four activists on the Court in favor of granting Noia a federal writ of habeas corpus, leaving only Stewart and Clark to join Harlan in dissent.

The statistical summary of the term bore out the isolated position Harlan occupied. In the 108 decisions in which the Justices were not unanimous, Harlan was among the dissenters sixty-six times.[2] Clark and Stewart, who agreed with Harlan more often than did any of the other Justices, dissented forty-three and thirty-four times respectively. In earlier years Clark and Stewart and Brennan composed the ideological center of the Court. Now, the center had shifted to Brennan and Warren and Goldberg. A comparison with the term ending just two years earlier was striking. In that term, Harlan dissented twenty-six times (now it was sixty-six), Clark twenty-one times (now forty-three), Douglas seventy (now twenty-eight), Brennan twenty (now six).

Justices' voting statistics can be misleading, but these figures were consistent with the thesis suggested by the votes in the 5-to-4 decisions and the results in other crucial cases—that the Court now had a clear majority for the general propositions that Black and Douglas have long espoused.

Two months after the term ended, Harlan used a speaking engagement in Chicago to express his view of what the Court was doing and what was wrong with it.

> One of the current notions that holds subtle capacity for serious mischief is a view of the judicial function that seems increasingly coming into vogue. This is that all deficiencies in our society which have failed of correction by other means should find a cure in the courts. . . . I venture to say . . . that this view of the cosmic place of the judiciary is not only inconsistent with the principles of American democratic society but ultimately threatens the integrity of the judicial system itself.
>
> A federal system is of course difficult to operate, demanding political genius of the highest order. It requires accom-

modations being made that may often seem irksome or inefficient. But out of that very necessity usually come pragmatic solutions of more lasting value than those emanating from the pens of the best of theoretical planners. Unless we are prepared to consider the diversified development of the United States as having run its course and to envisage the future of the country largely as that of a welfare society we will do well to keep what has been called "the delicate balance of federal-state relations" in good working order.

Apart from what they regard as the shortcomings of the federal system some well-meaning people apparently believe that the judicial rather than the political process is more likely to breed better solutions of pressing or thorny problems. This is a compliment to the judiciary but untrue to democratic principle. That point of view is sometimes difficult for judges to resist for it carries ostensibly authentic judicial hallmarks—the function of statutory construction and the power of judicial review. If the Congress or a state legislature has passed an inadequate statute why should it not be revised by judicial constructions? If the statute is one that is manifestly unwise, harsh, or out-of-date, why should it not be abrogated by the exercise of the power of judicial review? It is said that there can be nothing wrong with the courts so acting because whatever they may do can always be undone by legislative enactment or constitutional amendment.

The objections to such alluring but deceptive plausibilities are more deep-seated than might appear at first blush. For in the end what would eventuate would be a substantial transfer of legislative power to the courts. . . .

The late Speaker of the House Sam Rayburn once observed that "one of the greatest statements that was ever made by anybody was: 'Just a minute.'" He was referring to the catalytic effect of time as a factor in the legislative process. The same factor is important in the judicial process. A judicial decision which is founded simply on the impulse that "something should be done" or which looks no further than to the "justice" or "injustice" of a particular case is not likely to have lasting influence.

Harlan's complaints about this particular term and about the general trend of the Court can be clearly tied to particular decisions and particular issues. The Court, he thought, was being asked to do too much to solve the problems of American society, and it was agreeing to do too much, too readily. Reapportionment and the county unit system were matters better left to the political process than to the courts. The weakness of the Federal Employers Liability Act was one for Congress to cure, not the Court. The injustices of state criminal processes, as illustrated by Noia's case and others, would be better solved if left to the states. His thesis recalled the words Justice Frankfurter had written to Chief Justice Stone years before, that he was writing an opinion to preach "the true democratic faith of not relying on the Court for the impossible task of assuring a vigorous, mature, self-protecting and tolerant democracy by bringing the responsibility for a combination of firmness and toleration directly home where it belongs—to the people and their representatives themselves." [3]

Harlan's position was not the one taken by the Court's most vocal critics. He was neither a states' righter nor a segregationist, and he would never dream of questioning the motives of those who disagreed with him. Instead, his position was that of a cautious, conservative lawyer who was concerned, as he had put it during the term, with "the swift pace of current constitutional adjudication."

There was considerable irony in Harlan's isolation. Two generations earlier, his grandfather had been the outspoken dissenter as the Court used its power to block economic and social change. The first Justice Harlan dissented when the Court announced the separate-but-equal doctrine on racial matters, when it narrowly confined the scope of the Fourteenth Amendment, when it held the income tax unconstitutional, when it read the "rule of reason" into the Sherman Act, and when it denied the power of states to set maximum hours and days of work for bakery employees. His dissents were aimed at the predilection of the Court of his day to read the economic beliefs of its Justices into the Constitution. The second Justice Harlan was not disputing the present Court's acceptance of many of the views for which his grandfather had fought. His objection was that the Court was moving into other fields too quickly and with the same great vigor that had characterized his grandfather.

In many ways Harlan's cautious approach to judicial intervention in public affairs reflected his background. Educated at Princeton, Oxford, and the New York Law School, Harlan had a long career as a successful corporation lawyer on Wall Street before President Eisenhower appointed him to the Second Circuit Court of Appeals in 1954 and moved him up to the Supreme Court a year later. His judicial philosophy was sound rather than brilliant, his opinions sturdy rather than flashy. In terms of technical ability he was clearly one of the best lawyers on the Court. He looked like a Justice—tall, sparse white hair, dignified, serious, quiet, a gold watch chain across his vest under his robe.

Some observers of the Court who admire the trend of its decisions occasionally join with Harlan in his concern about the speed of decision. There was criticism of the civil libertarian groups that forced the Bible-reading and prayer cases upon the Court, not on the ground that the Court was wrong but because the critics thought the cases were poorly timed. Given the problem as it was presented in the cases from New York, Maryland, and Pennsylvania, the Court's answer was predictable with a good measure of certainty. But equally predictable was the reaction against the Court for those decisions. A few of the civil libertarians themselves were asking whether the Court was being pushed into so many new issues as to undermine its fundamental prestige.

That question revealed, of course, concern similar to that Justice Harlan expressed in Chicago. Professor Alexander Bickel of the Yale Law School has suggested that the Supreme Court has often floated a new constitutional principle and then waited a

298298298

few years for its acceptance before trying another. During the
1950's and 1960's the Court floated several major principles without waiting for the nation as a whole to accept any of them. One
can argue that the Court in those years had no choice. The new
principles appeared in cases that came to it for decision, and the
Justices' duty was to decide them, as their views of the Constitution directed, however unpopular the decisions might be.

One decision announced late in April illustrated the dramatic
shift that had come to the Court in the last fifty years. The issue
was whether the Kansas legislature had power to outlaw the
business of "debt adjusting." It had passed a statute making it a
crime for anyone to make a contract with a debtor requiring him
to make periodic payments to a person who would then, for a
fee, distribute the money among the debtor's creditors. The
only exception was a contract of this type made by a lawyer
incident to practicing law. The statute was enacted because the
legislature believed the business of debt adjusting lent itself to
grave abuses of distressed debtors, particularly those with low
incomes.

Frank C. Skrupa, who ran a debt adjusting business in Kansas,
protested to a three-judge federal court that the law deprived
him of his constitutional rights. The business was "legitimate,"
he said; therefore the law violated the guarantee of the Fourteenth Amendment against deprivation of property without due
process of law. The court upheld Skrupa's claim on the basis of
a 1917 Supreme Court decision, *Adams v. Tanner*, which held
that the Due Process Clause permitted state regulation of businesses but did not permit a state to outlaw a business which is
"useful" and not "inherently immoral or dangerous to the public welfare."[4]

The Supreme Court unanimously reversed the lower court's
decision. It said Kansas was free to outlaw the business of debt
adjusting if the Kansas legislature wanted to outlaw it. Justice
Black, in an opinion accepted by all the Justices except Harlan,

spoke disdainfully of the philosophy behind *Adams v. Tanner* "and cases like it." That philosophy was, Black said, "that it is the province of courts to draw on their own views as to the morality, legitimacy, and usefulness of a particular business in order to decide whether a statute bears too heavily upon that business and by so doing violates due process." Then Black added:

> Under the system of government created by our Constitution, it is up to legislatures, not courts, to decide on the wisdom and utility of legislation. There was a time when the Due Process Clause was used by this Court to strike down laws which were thought unreasonable, that is, unwise or incompatible with some particular economic or social philosophy. In this manner the Due Process Clause was used, for example, to nullify laws prescribing maximum hours for work in bakeries, *Lochner v. New York* . . . (1905), outlawing "yellow dog" contracts, *Coppage v. Kansas* . . . (1915), setting minimum wages for women, *Adkins v. Children's Hospital* . . . (1923), and fixing the weight of loaves of bread, *Jay Burns Baking Co. v. Bryan* . . . (1924). . . .
>
> The doctrine that prevailed in *Lochner, Coppage, Adkins, Burns,* and like cases—that due process authorizes courts to hold laws unconstitutional when they believe the legislature has acted unwisely—has long since been discarded. We have returned to the original constitutional proposition that courts do not substitute their social and economic beliefs for the judgment of legislative bodies, who are elected to pass laws. As this Court stated in a unanimous opinion in 1941, "We are not concerned . . . with the wisdom, need, or appropriateness of the legislation." Legislative bodies have broad scope to experiment with economic problems, and this Court does not sit to "subject the State to an intolerable supervision hostile to the basic principles of our Government and wholly beyond the protection which the general clause of the Fourteenth Amendment was intended to secure." It is now settled that States "have power to legislate against what are found to be injurious practices in their internal commercial and business affairs, so long as their laws do not run afoul of some specific federal constitutional prohibition, or some valid federal law."

... Unquestionably, there are arguments showing that the business of debt adjusting has social utility, but such arguments are properly addressed to the legislature, not to us. We refuse to sit as a "superlegislature to weigh the wisdom of legislation," and we emphatically refuse to go back to the time when courts used the Due Process Clause "to strike down state laws, regulatory of business and industrial conditions, because they may be unwise, improvident, or out of harmony with a particular school of thought." Nor are we able or willing to draw lines by calling a law "prohibitory" or "regulatory." Whether the legislature takes for its textbook Adam Smith, Herbert Spencer, Lord Keynes, or some other is no concern of ours. The Kansas debt adjusting statute may be wise or unwise. But relief, if any be needed, lies not with us but with the body constituted to pass laws for the State of Kansas.[5]

Black's opinion clearly illustrated one aspect of the revolution that had occurred on the Court in the last fifty years. The Justices had removed the bonds with which they had previously shackled state legislatures that were attempting new solutions to both old and new social and economic problems.

This entire term of Court, however, even more clearly illustrated the other aspect of that revolution. The Justices had accepted the call, which had been heard with increasing frequency since the early 1940's, to protect individuals' rights of liberty and privacy against the infringements of a growing government, and to eliminate governmental activities which differed in their impact on different classes of citizens if the classes were based upon race, religion, economic standing, or place of residence. The Court had responded to that call, slowly at first but with increasing speed in the most recent decade. Its decisions in cases dealing with racial discrimination, criminal procedures, congressional investigating committees, reapportionment, and Bible-reading and prayer were a part of that response. And it was evident from this term that the present Court had no intention of slowing down or backing away from such challenges. It was prepared to defend the rights of individuals and to reinforce the guarantees of the Bill of Rights, as it interpreted those guarantees, despite the criticism it well knew would come.

As the years go by, the 1962–63 term of Court will tend to merge with those preceding and following it, to lose its distinctiveness, to be tucked away in four tidy volumes of the *United States Reports*. But in those four volumes will be recorded another chapter in the Supreme Court's effort to interpret the words of the Constitution so as to meet the needs of twentieth-century Americans in a way that comports with the determination of eighteenth-century Americans to establish a government that would ensure recognition of the "self-evident" truths that "all men are created equal" and that they are endowed with certain "inalienable rights." The correctness of any interpretation of the words of the Constitution is a matter on which men will always disagree. But during these few months the Court had presented to the nation its interpretation of some of those words and its view of how they should be applied to keep alive the phrase carved over the entrance of its building—"Equal Justice Under Law."

NOTES

Chapter 1   A COURT IN TROUBLE (pages 15–27)

1. Baker v. Carr, 369 U.S. 186 (1962).
2. Engel v. Vitale, 370 U.S. 421 (1962).
3. See *The New York Times*, p. 1, col. 6 (June 26, 1962); p. 1, cols. 3, 8 (June 27, 1962); pp. E9, E11 (July 2, 1962). *The Washington Post*, p. A8, col. 5 (June 26, 1962); p. A1, col. 8 (June 27, 1962); p. A9, col. 1 (July 27, 1962). Paul Blanshard, *Religion and the Schools* (Boston: Beacon Press, 1963), pp. 50–74. *The Supreme Court Review* (Chicago: University of Chicago Press, 1963), p. 2, n. 4 and n. 5, p. 3.
4. Engel v. Vitale, supra, 370 U.S. at 435, n. 21.
5. *The Washington Post*, p. A4, col. 1 (August 4, 1962).
6. Ibid., p. A9, col. 1 (July 7, 1962).
7. *Congressional Record* 7599–7606 (87th Congress, 2nd Session, 1962).
8. Plessy v. Ferguson, 136 U.S. 537 (1896). The Civil Rights Cases, 109 U.S. 3 (1883).
9. *Connecticut Courant* (February 9 and 16, 1801), quoted by Charles Warren in *The Supreme Court in United States History*, Vol. 1 (rev. ed.; Boston: Little Brown and Co., 1922, 1926), p. 20.

Chapter 2   THE TERM BEGINS (pages 28–55)

1. The most thorough account is George B. Leonard, T. George Harris, and Christopher S. Wren, "How a Secret Deal Prevented a Massacre at Ole Miss," *Look* magazine, pp. 18–24 (December 31, 1962). See also *The Washington Post*, p. A1, cols. 5–8 (October 1, 1962); p. A1, cols. 6–8 and p. A4, col. 1 (October 2, 1962). *The New York Times*, p. 1, cols. 4–5, 8 (October 1, 1962); p. 1, cols. 5–8 and pp. 24–28 (October 2, 1962).
2. No stenographic record is kept of the actual occurrences in the courtroom. A partial, official account is kept in the *Journal, Supreme Court, U.S.* Four publications occasionally print report-

ers' versions of Court proceedings. These are *The United States Law Week, The New York Times, The Washington Post*, and *The* (Washington) *Evening Star*.
3. *The New York Times*, p. 8, col. 1 (August 31, 1962).
4. Ibid., p. 20, col. 4.
5. Felix Frankfurter, "Some Observations on the Nature of the Judicial Process of Supreme Court Litigation" (paper given before the American Philosophical Society, April 22, 1954); reprinted in Alan F. Westin, *The Supreme Court: Views from Inside* (New York: W. W. Norton, 1961), pp. 34, 42.
6. Trop v. Dulles, 356 U.S. 86, 119–20 (1958). Dissenting opinion.
7. Quoted in full in A. T. Mason, *Security Through Freedom* (Ithaca, N. Y.: Cornell University Press, 1955), pp. 217 ff.
8. West Virginia State Bd. of Educ. v. Barnette, 319 U.S. 624, 641–42 (1943).
9. Ibid. at 646. Dissenting opinion.
10. Quoted in Occasional Pamphlet No. 3 (Harvard Law School, April, 1959).
11. 76 Harv. L. Rev. 14 (1962).
12. Harlan B. Phillips, *Felix Frankfurter Reminisces* (New York: Reynal & Co., 1960), p. 283.
13. See Noel T. Dowling, *Cases on Constitutional Law* (5th ed.; Brooklyn: Foundation Press, 1954), p. 1295.
14. Learned Hand, "Sources of Tolerance," 79 U. of Pa. L. Rev. 1, 12 (1930), quoted in *The Spirit of Liberty*, edited by Irving Dilliard (New York: Alfred A. Knopf, 1959), pp. 51, 63.
15. Despite rumors that President Kennedy would appoint Abraham Ribicoff of Connecticut to the Court at his first opportunity, Ribicoff was never under serious consideration.
16. Hearings on the Nomination of Charles E. Whittaker (Senate Judiciary Committee, March 18, 1957).

Chapter 3   THE TERM AHEAD (pages 56–70)

1. See Fay v. Noia, 372 U.S. 391, 406 (1963).
2. John P. Frank, *Marble Palace* (New York: Alfred A. Knopf, 1958), p. 116.
3. The best source on the clerks is Chester A. Newland, "Personal Assistants to Supreme Court Justices: The Law Clerks," 40 Ore. L. Rev. 299 (1961).
4. Phillips, *Frankfurter Reminisces*, p. 249.
5. Tom C. Clark, "Internal Operation of the United States Supreme Court," *Journal of the American Judicature Society*, Vol. XLIII No. 2 (August, 1959), pp. 45, 49.

Chapter 4   THE FIRST ARGUMENTS (pages 71–81)

1. William O. Douglas, "Vagrancy and Arrests on Suspicion" (speech at New Mexico Law School, 1960). Excerpts, *The Washington Post*, p. E4, col. 6 (March 23, 1960).
2. United States v. Rabinowitz, 339 U.S. 56, 69 (1950). Dissenting opinion.

Chapter 5   GOLDBERG'S FIRST OPINION (pages 82–94)

1. United States v. Loew's Inc., 371 U.S. 38 (1962).
2. Jungersen v. Ostby & Barton Co., 335 U.S. 560, 572 (1949). Dissenting opinion.
3. Tom C. Clark, "Internal Operation of the United States Supreme Court," *Journal of the American Judicature Society*, Vol. XLIII, No. 2 (August, 1959), p. 51.
4. Frank, *Marble Palace*, pp. 295ff.
5. St. Louis & S.F. Ry. v. Gill, 156 U.S. 649, 657 (1895).
6. Ribnick v. McBride, 277 U.S. 350, 374 (1928).
7. Jordan v. De George, 341 U.S. 223, 226–29 (1951).
8. Buck v. Bell, 274 U.S. 200, 207 (1927).
9. United States v. Schwimmer, 279 U.S. 644, 654, 655 (1929). Dissenting opinion.
10. Everson v. Board of Educ., 330 U.S. 1, 19 (1947).
11. Braunfeld v. Brown, 366 U.S. 599, 616 (1961). Dissenting opinion.
12. Erwin Griswold, "The Supreme Court 1959 Term," 74 Harv. L. Rev. 81, 85 (1960).
13. Oliver Wendell Holmes, Jr., *Collected Legal Papers* (Gloucester, Mass.: Peter Smith, 1952), p. 295.

Chapter 6   ETHICS AND LAW (pages 95–104)

1. *The New York Times*, p. 1, col. 3 (November 12, 1962).
2. *The Washington Post*, p. A1, col. 5 (April 25, 1961).

Chapter 7   THE FIRST SHARP DISAGREEMENTS
(pages 105–22)

1. Federal Trade Commission v. Sun Oil Co., 371 U.S. 505 (1963).
2. N.A.A.C.P. v. Button, 371 U.S. 415 (1963).
3. Wong Sun v. United States, 371 U.S. 471 (1963).
4. Shotwell Mfg. Co. v. United States, 371 U.S. 415 (1963).
5. Quoted by Paul A. Freund on CBS Reports, "Storm over the Supreme Court" (CBS Television, February 20, 1963). Published by CBS as *Oyez, Oyez, Oyez* (1963).

6. Charles L. Black, Jr., *The People and the Court* (New York: The Macmillan Co., 1960), p. 89.
7. Frank, *Marble Palace*, p. 132.
8. Hugo L. Black, "Bill of Rights and the Federal Government," in *The Great Rights*, edited by Edmond Cahn (New York: The Macmillan Co., 1963), p. 54.
9. Dennis v. United States, 341 U.S. 494, 581 (1951). Dissenting opinion.
10. Barenblatt v. United States, 360 U.S. 109, 145–46 (1959), Dissenting opinion.
11. Adamson v. California, 332 U.S. 46, 89 (1947). Dissenting opinion.
12. Chambers v. Florida, 309 U.S. 227, 241 (1939).

Chapter 8 JUSTICE AND THE STATE COURTS
(pages123-40)

1. Letter to Dr. John H. Wu, 1929. Reprinted in *The Mind and Faith of Justice Holmes*, edited by Max Lerner (New York: Modern Library, 1943), p. 435.
2. United States *ex rel.* Caminito v. Murphy, 222 F. 2d 698, 701 (2d Cir. 1955).
3. United States *ex rel.* Noia v. Fay, 300 F.2d 345 (2d Cir. 1962).
4. Betts v. Brady, 316 U.S. 455 (1942).
5. See *The Washington Post*, p. A8, col. 5 (January 13, 1963); p. E3, col. 3 (March 31, 1963). *The New York Times*, p. 1, col. 6 (April 14, 1963). Charles L. Black, Jr., "The Proposed Amendment of Article V: A Threatened Disaster," 72 Yale L.J. 957 (1963).

Chapter 10 THE MIDWINTER RECESS (pages 156–62)

1. Partial Text, *The Washington Post*, p. A18, col. 6 (August 15, 1963).
2. Jencks v. United States, 353 U.S. 657, 681–82 (1957). Dissenting opinion.

Chapter 11 THE LAW IS NEVER STILL (pages 163–77)

1. Roscoe Pound, *Interpretations of Legal History* (New York: The Macmillan Co., 1935), p. 1.
2. Merlo Pusey, *Charles Evans Hughes*, Vol. I (New York: The Macmillan Co., 1951), p. 204.
3. Kennedy v. Mendoza-Martinez, 372 U.S. 144 (1963).
4. Schneider v. Rusk, 372 U.S. 224 (1963).
5. Gallick v. Baltimore & O.R.R., 372 U.S. 108 (1963).

6. McCulloch v. Sociedad Nacional de Marineros de Honduras, 372 U.S. 10 (1963).
7. Guiseppi v. Walling, 144 F.2d 608, 624 (2d Cir. 1944).

Chapter 12 BANKS AND THE LAW (pages 178–90)

1. United States v. Bethlehem Steel Corp., 168 F. Supp. 576, 610 (S.D.N.Y. 1958).

Chapter 13 RELIGION IN THE SCHOOLS (pages 191–214)

1. West Virginia State Bd. of Educ. v. Barnette, 319 U.S. 624, 640 (1943).
2. Matthew 6: 5–6, King James Version.

Chapter 14 TWO YOUNG JUSTICES (pages 215–20)

1. William J. Brennan, Jr., "The Bill of Rights and the States" (lecture at New York University Law Center, February 15, 1961); reprinted in *The Great Rights*, pp. 85–86.
2. Miller v. United States, 357 U.S. 301, 313 (1958).

Chapter 15 A RARE DAY FOR THE COURT (pages 221–36)

1. Draper v. Washington, 372 U.S. 487 (1963).
2. Lane v. Brown, 372 U.S. 477 (1963).
3. Fay v. Noia, 372 U.S. 391 (1963).
4. Douglas v. California, 372 U.S. 353 (1963).
5. Gray v. Sanders, 372 U.S. 368 (1963).
6. Gideon v. Wainwright, 372 U.S. 335 (1963).
7. Townsend v. Sain, 372 U.S. 293 (1963).
8. *The Washington Post*, p. E1, col. 1 (March 24, 1963).

Chapter 16 SEGREGATED LUNCHROOMS (pages 237–49)

1. Daniel H. Pollitt, "Dime Store Demonstrations: Events and Legal Problems of First Sixty Days," 1960 Duke L. Rev. 315.
2. Brief, United States as Amicus Curiae, No. 71, Peterson v. City of Greenville, 1962 Term, p. 3.
3. Peterson v. City of Greenville, 373 U.S. 244 (1963).
4. Silver v. New York Stock Exchange, 373 U.S. 341 (1963).
5. Andrews v. United States, 373 U.S. 334 (1963).
6. Wisconsin v. Federal Power Commission, 373 U.S. 294 (1963).
7. Lombard v. Louisiana, 373 U.S. 267 (1963).
8. Shuttlesworth v. City of Birmingham, 373 U.S. 262 (1963).
9. Gober v. City of Birmingham, 373 U.S. 374 (1963).

10. Griffin v. Maryland, 373 U.S. 920 (1963).
11. Lombard v. Louisiana, supra, 373 U.S. at 274.
12. Peterson v. City of Greenville, supra, 373 U.S. at 248.

Chapter 17 A FIGHT OVER WATER (pages 250–57)

1. Arizona v. California, 373 U.S. 546 (1963).

Chapter 18 THE FINAL MONDAY (pages 258–65)

1. Rosenberg v. Fleuti, 374 U.S. 449 (1963).
2. Gastelum-Quinones v. Kennedy, 374 U.S. 469 (1963).
3. Head v. New Mexico Board of Examiners in Optometry, 374 U.S. 424 (1963).
4. United States v. Pennsylvania National Bank, 374 U.S. 321 (1963).
5. United States v. Singer Mfg. Co., 374 U.S. 174 (1963).
6. School District of Abington Township v. Schempp, 374 U.S. 203 (1963).

Chapter 19 THE GOVERNMENT IS NEUTRAL
(pages 266–80)

1. *The New York Times*, p. 1, col. 7 (June 18, 1963); p. 18, col. 1 (June 19, 1963); sec. IV, p. 4, col. 5 and p. 9, col. 5 (June 23, 1963). *The Washington Post*, p. 1, col. 8 (June 18, 1963); p. 6, col. 1 (June 19, 1963). See also Blanshard, *Religion and the Schools*.

Chapter 20 FREEDOM TO WORSHIP (pages 281–84)

1. Sherbert v. Verner, 374 U.S. 398 (1963).
2. McGowan v. Maryland, 366 U.S. 420 (1961).
3. Towne v. Eisner, 245 U.S. 418, 425 (1918).

Chapter 21 THE LAST DECISIONS (pages 285–91)

1. Yellin v. United States, 374 U.S. 109 (1963).
2. Watkins v. United States, 354 U.S. 178 (1957).
3. Barenblatt v. United States, 360 U.S. 109 (1959).
4. Gibson v. Florida Legislative Investigation Committee, 372 U.S. 539 (1963).
5. United States v. Muniz, 374 U.S. 150 (1963).

Chapter 22   THE TERM IS OVER (pages 292–301)

1. Statistics are compiled by the Court's Clerk. Somewhat differing versions are in 77 Harv. L. Rev. 81–92 (November, 1963) and 32 Law Week 3037–8 (July 16, 1963).
2. 77 Harv. L. Rev. 92 (November, 1963).
3. Mason, *Security Through Freedom*, p. 220.
4. Skrupa v. Ferguson, 210 F. Supp. 200 (D. Kan. 1961); Adams v. Tanner, 244 U.S. 590 (1917).
5. Ferguson v. Skrupa, 372 U.S. 726 (1963).

INDEX

Abram, Morris, 141-42, 148-50, 228
Acheson, Dean, 42
Adams v. Tanner, 298-99
admission to the bar, 72, 259
advisory opinions, 169
Aiken, Senator George D., 276
antitrust laws, 82-84, 97, 178-90, 263-65, 296
appointments to the Court, 45-53; *see* names of individual Justices
Arizona v. California, 57-59, 70, 251-54
Assembly of the States, 138-39

Baker, George W., 200-202
Baker v. Carr, 15-16; *see also* reapportionment; voting
Becker, Representative Frank J., 17
Betts v. Brady, 131-39, 230, 232; *see* right to counsel
Bickel, Alexander, 297
Black, Charles, 114; quoted, 115
Black, Elizabeth (Mrs. Hugo L.), 108, 259
Black, Justice Hugo L., 23, 47-48, 62, 66, 68, 158-60, 188, 216-22, 228, 232, 251-52, 256-57, 262, 265, 277, 286; on establishment of religion, 20-21, 117-18, 119, 193-213 passim, 289; described, 30, 64-65, 108, 115-16, 156, 158; philosophy of, 37, 40-41, 54, 110, 114-15, 123-24, 293-94; on 14th Amendment, 41, 119-21, 122, 231; on Bill of Rights, 41, 114, 117-19; style of opinions, 89, 284; on Fifth Amendment, 113-14; appointment of, 116, 121-22; on First Amendment 117-19, 193-97, 202-203; on right to counsel, 121, 230, 231; on self-restraint, 122; on citizenship, 166-67; on congressional investigations, 286-87, 289-90; on economic due process, 299-300
Black, Jeremiah S., 274
Brandeis, Justice Louis D., 41, 46-47, 50, 64, 110
Brennan, Marjorie (Mrs. Wm. J.), 107, 259

Brennan, Justice William J., 23,
    48, 62, 71, 145, 158, 189, 194,
    206, 213, 216, 222, 228, 231,
    232, 265; description of, 30,
    157, 218-19; appointment of,
    46; philosophy described,
    54, 112, 121, 215, 219-20, 293-
    94; style of opinions, 84, 284;
    on barratry, 107-108; on
    search and seizure, 109-12;
    on habeas corpus, 131, 224,
    226-27; on First Amend-
    ment, 206, 273-74, 281-82; on
    antitrust, 263-65
Brownell, Herbert, 154
Brown v. Board of Education,
    79, 101, 240-41; see also
    school desegregation
Brown v. Lane, 222-23
Brown Shoe Co. v. U.S., 181, 219
Buck v. Bell, 88
Burch, Francis B., 197
Burton, Justice Harold H., 41,
    46-47, 50, 64, 110, 257
Butler, Justice Pierce, 110
Byrd, Senator Robert C., 18

Cahn, Edmond, 117
Caldwell, Millard, 20
Cameron, Judge Ben F., 77
Cardozo, Justice Benjamin N.,
    34, 41, 50; quoted, 41
Celler, Representative Emanuel,
    19
Chayes, Abram, 64
Chicago Daily News, 43
Chicago Tribune, 36
Chief Justice, role of, 68-69, 102;
    see Warren, Chief Justice
    Earl

citizenship cases, 59-60, 88-89,
    164-69
Civil Rights Cases, 241-45, 248
Clark, Mary (Mrs. Tom C.),
    113, 259
Clark, Justice Tom C., 161, 222,
    228, 232, 261, 262, 265; on
    establishment of religion,
    21-22, 266-73; description of,
    30, 162; philosophy of, 54,
    161-62, 294; on conferences,
    66-68; on opinion writing,
    86; on search and seizure,
    111; on foreign flag cases,
    175; on federalism, 227; on
    habeas corpus, 227; on sit-
    ins, 247-48; style of opinions,
    284
Clary, Judge Thomas J., 183
Cleveland, President Grover, 46
coerced confessions, see Fay v.
    Noia; Townsend v. Sain
commerce power, 49, 175-76,
    178-90 passim, 234
common law, 163
congressional investigations, 55,
    60-61, 76-77, 286-90
constitutional interpretation, 49-
    50, 93, 122, 163-70, 284;
    Learned Hand on, 48-49
contempt of Congress, 25, 35, 55,
    60-61, 70, 90-91, 285-87, 290
county unit systems, see Gray
    v. Sanders
Cox, Archibald, 72, 109, 141, 175;
    role as Solicitor General,
    152-55; on sit-ins, 240
criticism of the Supreme Court,
    15, 101-102, 138-40, 177; for
    reapportionment   decision,

16, 26, 35, 138, 139; for school prayer decision, 17-22, 26, 276-79, 297; for civil rights decisions, 23, 25-26, 35; for desegregation decisions, 24-26, 35
cruel and unusual punishment, 166, 168

Davis, James C., 143
Davis, John F., 32
debt adjusting, 298-99
defiance of Court decisions, 85-86; in Mississippi, 28-29
Detroit News, 20
Dickenson, William H., Jr., 279
Doolittle, J. William, 72, 75
Douglas, Mercedes, 254-55
Douglas, Justice William O., 23, 48, 62, 64, 75, 216, 222, 231-32, 265, 286; description of, 30, 65, 250-51, 255-57; philosophy of, 40-41, 54, 110, 121, 123, 250-51, 293-94; on citizenship, 166-67; on First Amendment, 203, 206, 282-83; on voting, 228-29; on right to counsel, 228; on sit-ins, 246-49; on Fourteenth Amendment, 246-49; criticism of Black by, 251-54; on *Arizona v. Calif.*, 253-54; divorce of, 254-55; on congressional investigations, 286-87, 289
Douglas v. California, 227-28
Draper v. Washington, 220-21, 223

Eastland, Senator James O., 23

economic due process, 178, 234-35, 299-300
Edelman, Peter, 62
Eisenhower, President, 46, 53
elections, *see Baker v. Carr; Gray v. Sanders*
Ellender, Senator Allen J., 279
Elman, Philip, 64
Engel v. Vitale, 15-23, 191-95, 198, 203-207, 215, 262, 267-69, 279
equal protection, 24, 79, 238-43; *see also Gray v. Sanders; pauper rights*
Ervin, Senator Sam J., Jr., 17
ethics and law, 95-99
Everson v. Board of Education, 89, 269; *see* religion, establishment of

Fair v. Meredith, 77-79
Faulkner, William, 28
Fay v. Noia 124-31, 140, 219-29, 231-32, 292-93
Federal Employees Liability Act, 170-73
federalism, 127-39, 219-20, 225-28, 232-36, 294-95; *see also* states' rights
Ferguson v. Skrupa, 298-99
Fifth Amendment, *see* self-incrimination
Filvaroff, David, 62
Finan, Thomas B., 106, 202-203, 210
First Amendment, 38-39, 88-89, 107, 117-19, 192-213, 272-74, 281-85
foreign affairs power, 165, 167, 173-76

foreign flag cases, 69, 164, 173-75
Fortas, Abe, 132-37
Fourteenth Amendment, 40-41,
    54, 119-22, 231, 246-49; see
    due process; economic due
    process; equal protection;
    state action
Fourth Amendment, 54, 72-75,
    107-108, 111
Frank, John P., quoted, 63, 116
Frankfurter, Justice Felix, 23, 62,
    115, 216, 223, 289; on reap-
    portionment, 16; retirement
    of, 31, 33-34, 57; description
    of, 33, 42; philosophy of, 36-
    41, 54, 116, 123; on judicial
    self-restraint, 37, 39; appoint-
    ment to Court, 43; on pro-
    cedure, 75; opinions of, 84;
    exchange with Warren, 103-
    104; on FELA, 173; on role
    of Court, 296
freedom of speech, 38-39, 41, 89,
    107, 117-19
Freund, Paul A., 50-51, 64, 93
Fuller, Chief Justice Melville
    W., 67

Gallick v. Baltimore & Ohio RR,
    164, 171-73, 293
Gibson v. Florida Legislative In-
    vestigation Committee, 61,
    69, 288-90
Gideon v. Wainright, 66, 131-38,
    140, 228-35, 292-93
Girard Trust Corn Exchange
    Bank, see United States v.
    Pennsylvania National Bank
Gober v. City of Birmingham,
    239, 245

Goldberg, Justice Arthur J., 56,
    146-47, 151, 158-60, 184-87,
    194, 196, 200, 201, 203, 206,
    228, 231, 232, 262, 286;
    swearing in of, 31-32; ap-
    pointment of, 34-35, 43-45,
    50-52; description of, 43-44,
    156-57, 160; on antitrust,
    82-86; style of opinions, 86;
    on price cutting, 106-107;
    philosophy of, 112, 232, 293;
    on citizenship, 164-68; on
    First Amendment, 203, 206;
    on pauper rights, 222; on
    habeas corpus, 224, 229; on
    immigration, 260-61; on es-
    tablishment of religion, 277;
    on congressional investiga-
    tions, 286, 290
Goldberg, Dorothy (Mrs. Ar-
    thur J.), 32, 82, 107, 157
Goodwin, Richard, 64
Graham, Rev. Billy, 18
Grant, Representative George
    M., 17
Gray, Justice Horace, 64
Gray v. Sanders, 69, 141-52, 228-
    29, 232, 235, 292-93
Grayzel, Solomon, 211-12
Griswold, Erwin N., 92-93;
    quoted, 92

habeas corpus, 81-82, 124-31, 223-
    27, 231-32; see Fay v. Noia;
    Townsend v. Sain
Haight, George I., 59
Hand, Judge Learned, 41, 48-49;
    on constitutional interpreta-
    tion, 49; on statutory inter-
    pretation, 176

Harlan, Justice John Marshall (deceased), 67, 296

Harlan, Justice John M., 62, 107, 134-35, 151, 216, 222, 228, 232, 243, 265; description of, 30, 65, 115, 297; philosophy of, 54, 115, 293-94, 297; style of opinions, 84; on Fifth Amendment, 112-13; on First Amendment, 117, 119, 199, 200, 205, 211, 252-53; on unconstitutionality, 122; on citizenship, 168; on FELA, 172; on habeas corpus, 224-27; on federalism, 226-27, 294-95; on role of court, 229, 294-96; on voting, 229; on right to counsel, 230-31; on sit-ins, 246-49; on antitrust, 264; on congressional investigations, 287-90

Hart, Henry, 131

Hastie, Judge William Henry, 50-51

Head v. New Mexico, 262

Holmes, Justice Oliver Wendell, 34, 40-41, 50, 67, 80, 110, 123, 167, 283; appointment of, 47; on citizenship, 88-89; on constitutionality, 93

Hoover, President Herbert, 18, 46

Hughes, Chief Justice Charles Evans, 50, 81, 87, 164

Hutchinson, George, 71

Illinois ex rel. McCollum v. Bd. of Education, 199-200, 269

immigration laws, 259-62; see Rosenberg v. Fleuti

Irwin v. Dowd, 131; see also Fay v. Noia

Jackson, President Andrew, 47

Jackson, Justice Robert H., 50, 86, 89, 160, 161, 172; on First Amendment, 38-39, 200-201, 272

Jackson, Justice William, 47

Jacobs, Bruce R., 136-37

Jefferson, President Thomas, 47

judicial activism, 40-41, 48, 114-15, 122, 220

judicial self-restraint, 36-40, 54, 122, 252-53, 294-96

jurisdiction of Supreme Court, 58, 169

Justices, concern about criticism, 26-27, 101; religion of, 46-47, 279; work load, 55-57, 61, 69, 76-77, 91-94, 105, 258, 292; manner of decision, 56; staff, 62, 100; chamber, 62, 156-57; role of Chief Justice, 67-68; secrecy, 67; opinion writing, 68, 85-90, 262-63, 284; oral statements, 85; social life, 158-59; see also names of individual Justices

Katzenbach, Nicholas deB., 51

Keating, Senator Kenneth B., 19

Kennedy, Senator Edward, 149

Kennedy, Ethel, 145

Kennedy, Jacqueline, 149

Kennedy, President John F., 28-32, 153; on prayer decision, 19; appointment of Goldberg, 34-36, 43-45, 50-52; appointment of White, 50-52

Kennedy, Mrs. Joseph P. (Rose), 145

Kennedy, Robert F., 28-29, 50-52, 156, 160, 221, 228; on appointments, 52; on apportionment, 141-52

Kennedy v. Mendozo-Martinez, 59-60, 164-70

Kerpelman, Leonard J., 191-200, 203-204

Killian, John D., 213-14

Krock, Arthur, 34-35, 60; quoted, 34

law clerks, 63-65

Leverett, E. Freeman, 146-47

Lichtenberg, Carl, 275

Lippitt, T. Perry, 29-30, 35, 71, 159

Littleton, Arthur, 188

Loevinger, Lee, 184-86, 189, 263

Loew's Inc. v. United States, 82-84

Lombard v. Louisiana, 239, 245

Long, Clay, 221

Los Angeles Times, 20

Madison, President James, 212, 220, 271

Marshall, Burke, 22-23

Marshall, Chief Justice John, 48, 66, 68

Martin, Jean Carol, 255

massive resistance, 108

McCarthy, Senator Joseph, 25

McMurrin, Stanley M., 19

McReynolds, Justice James C., 47, 86-87

Mentz, George D., 137

Meredith, James, 28, 77-79

Minow, Newton, 64

Moulton, Charlotte, 266

Murphy, B. D., 144-45

Murphy, Justice Frank, 161

Murray v. Curlett, 77-78, 191-205, 262, 265-80

NAACP, *see Gibson v. Florida Legislative Investigation Committee; NAACP v. Button;* sit-ins

NAACP v. Button, 107-109

New York Herald Tribune, 121

New York Journal-American, 20

New York Times, The, 20, 34

Nixon, Richard M., 52

Noia, Charles, *see Fay v. Noia*

Oberdorfer, Louis, 64

Parker, Judge John J., 46

pauper rights, 222-24, 228-30, 232, 233

Pennsylvania National Bank, *see United States v. Pennsylvania National Bank*

Peterson v. City of Greenville, 239, 243-44

Pound, Roscoe, 123, 163

Presser v. United States, 60, 69, 76, 90-91; *see* congressional investigations; contempt of Congress

Price, Philip, 186-88

prior experience of Justices, 48-
    50

qualifications for a Justice, 45-50

Raleigh News and Observer, 20
Rankin, J. Lee, 136
reapportionment, 15-16, 35, 54-
    55, 141-52
Reed, Justice Stanley F., 62, 161,
    259
religion: in public schools, 17-23,
    78-79, 191-214, 220, 259, 266,
    292; establishment of reli-
    gion, 20-22, 117-19, 193-
    213, 266-73, 277, 289; free-
    dom of religion, 90, 281-84
Ribicoff, Abraham, 304
Rifkind, Simon H., 59, 95
right to counsel, 66, 112-13, 131-
    38, 221, 228, 230-33
Rivers, Representative L. Men-
    del, 17
Roberts, Justice Owen J., 46
role of Supreme Court, 229, 294-
    97, 300-301
Roosevelt, President Franklin D.,
    27, 43, 45, 47, 116, 121-22,
    257
Roosevelt, President Theodore,
    quoted, 47
Rosenberg v. Fleuti, 260-62
Rusk v. Cort, 59-60, 164-69

Sacks, Albert M., 62
Satterfield, John C., 20
Sawyer, Henry W., 209-13

Schaefer, Walter V., 50-51
Schneider v. Rusk, 169
school desegregation, 24-25, 28-
    29, 77-79
*School District of Abington
    Township v. Schempp*, 77-
    78, 191-97, 204-14, 262, 265-
    80
search and seizure, 73-75, 107-12,
    132-33
Seigel, William J., 124
self-incrimination, 112-13
Shelley v. Kraemer, 241, 245, 247
Sherbert v. North Carolina, 281-
    84
Shiras, Justice George, 87
*Shotwell Mfg. Co. v. United
    States*, 112-13
Shriver, Eunice Kennedy, 145
*Shuttlesworth v. City of Bir-
    mingham*, 239, 245
*Silver v. New York Stock Ex-
    change*, 79, 243
sit-ins, 69, 237-49, 292-93
Sixth Amendment, *see* right to
    counsel
Smith, Representative Howard
    W., 17
Smith, Jean Kennedy, 145
Sobeloff, Judge Simon, 154
Solicitor General, office of, 152-
    55
South v. Peters, 143, 152, 229,
    232
Spellman, Francis Cardinal, 18
state action, 24, 238-49 passim
states' rights, 24-26, 35, 55, 124-
    52, 223, 234-36; *see also* fed-
    eralism

statutory interpretation, 93, 163-64, 176
Stennis, Senator John A., 230, 235
Stewart, Mary Ann (Mrs. Potter), 113
Stewart, Justice Potter, 32, 56, 71, 135-38, 145-49, 227-28, 232, 243, 273; description of, 30, 217-18; philosophy of, 54, 214-16; on work load, 56; style of opinions, 89-90; on freedom of religion, 90, 192-213, 278-79; on citizenship, 166-68; on First Amendment, 192-213 passim, 278-79; appointment, 218; on pauper rights, 223; on congressional investigations, 286-87
Stone, Chief Justice Harlan F., 37, 50, 63, 110; quoted, 87-88
Summerfield, Arthur, 158
Sun Oil Co. v. FTC, 106-107, 180
supremacy clause, 176-77
Sutherland, Justice George, 50
Suttice, Robert D., 62

Taft, Judge Alphonzo, 268
Taney, Chief Justice Roger B., 47
taxation: of gifts, 91-92; Tax Court, 92
Thayer, Ezra Ripley, 64
Thurmond, Senator Strom, 24
Time Magazine, 35
Torcaso v. Watkins, 199-200, 269
Townsend v. Sain, 80; see habeas corpus
Traynor, Judge Roger J., 50-51

Trexler, Jeanne, 62
Truman, President Harry S., 45

U. S. News & World Report, 35
United States v. E. I. du Pont de Nemours & Co., 181
United States v. Muniz, 291
United States v. Pennsylvania National Bank, 182-89, 263-65, 292
United States v. Singer Mfg. Co., 265

Van Devanter, Justice Willis, 50
Vinson, Chief Justice Fred M., 52; quoted, 88
Virginia Assessment Bill, 212
voting, see Gray v. Sanders

Ward, Philip, H., III, 204-209
war power, 165, 167, 175
Warren, Chief Justice Earl, 31-33, 48, 51, 62, 68, 71-72, 216, 222, 228, 231-32, 253, 262, 265, 284-86; description of, 30, 64, 99-101; philosophy of, 54, 95-99, 101-102, 110, 121; on law and ethics, 95-99; appointment of, 99; style of opinions, 103; influence of, 103; exchange with Frankfurter, 103-104; on citizenship, 166; on First Amendment, 198, 202, 206, 209; on habeas corpus, 231; on sit-ins, 243-45; on congressional investigations, 286-87; on contempt of Congress, 290
Washington Post, The, 256
Weigle, Luther A., 212

Weinfeld, Judge Edward,
    quoted, 186
*West Virginia State Board of
    Education v. Barnette*, 38-
    39, 200-201, 209-14, 272
White, Justice Byron R., 56, 107,
    147, 158, 222, 228, 232, 259;
    description of, 30, 52-53, 156,
    158-60; appointment of, 34,
    50-52; on FELA, 171-72; on
    pauper rights, 222; philoso-
    phy of, 232, 295; on First
    Amendment, 282-83; on
    congressional investigations,
    286, 290
White, Marion (Mrs. Byron
    R.), 113, 145, 149, 259
Whittaker, Justice Charles E.,
    retirement of, 50, 53-54, 57,
    216, 289; description of, 53;
    philosophy of, 54; style of

opinions, 84; on citizenship,
    167; on congressional inves-
    tigations, 287, 290
Whittington, Banning E. (Bert),
    105, 259, 267
Williams, Edward Bennett, 72-
    75, 109
Williston, Samuel, 64
Wilson, President Woodrow,
    46-47
Winston, Henry, 290-91
Wong Sun v. United States, 72-
    76, 109-12
Wyatt, Walter, 72

Yarmolinsky, Adam, 64
Yellin v. United States, 77-78,
    285-90
Yost, Paul, 266

Zorach v. Clausen, 268-69